AN ILLUSTRATED GUIDE TO CIVIL PROCEDURE

AN ILLUSTRATED GUIDE TO CIVIL PROCEDURE

MICHAEL ALLEN
STETSON UNIVERSITY COLLEGE OF LAW

MICHAEL FINCH
STETSON UNIVERSITY COLLEGE OF LAW

PUBLISHERS

111 Eighth Avenue, New York, NY 10011
http://lawschool.aspenpublishers.com

© 2006 Aspen Publishers, Inc.
a Wolters Kluwer business
http://lawschool.aspenpublishers.com

Aspen Publishers
Attn: Permissions Department
111 Eighth Avenue, 7th Floor
New York, NY   10011-5201

Printed in the United States of America.

1 2 3 4 5 6 7 8 9 0

ISBN 0-7355-5673-3

Library of Congress Cataloging-in-Publication Data

Allen, Michael, 1967-
   An illustrated guide to civil procedure / Michael Allen, Michael Finch.
      p. cm.
   Includes index.
   ISBN 0-7355-5673-3 (alk. paper)
   1. Civil procedure--United States.   I. Finch, Michael, 1952- .
   II. Title.
   KF8840.A74 2006
   347.73'5--dc22
   2005034773

About Aspen Publishers

Aspen Publishers, headquartered in New York City, is a leading information provider for attorneys, business professionals, and law students. Written by preeminent authorities, our products consist of analytical and practical information covering both U.S. and international topics. We publish in the full range of formats, including updated manuals, books, periodicals, CDs, and online products.

Our proprietary content is complemented by 2,500 legal databases, containing over 11 million documents, available through our Loislaw division. Aspen Publishers also offers a wide range of topical legal and business databases linked to Loislaw's primary material. Our mission is to provide accurate, timely, and authoritative content in easily accessible formats, supported by unmatched customer care.

To order any Aspen Publishers title, go to *http://lawschool.aspenpublishers.com* or call 1-800-638-8437.

To reinstate your manual update service, call 1-800-638-8437.

For more information on Loislaw products, go to *www.loislaw.com* or call 1-800-364-2512.

For Customer Care issues, e-mail *CustomerCare@aspenpublishers.com*; call 1-800-234-1660; or fax 1-800-901-9075.

Aspen Publishers
a Wolters Kluwer business

Dedication and Acknowledgments

Several people made this book possible. First, the visual layout of the *Guide* is due in large part to the efforts of Shannon Mullins, Sharon Gisclair, and Connie Evans of the Faculty Support Services at Stetson. We thank them, and everyone in that office, for their work on this project. We also are both grateful to Stetson University College of Law for its support of this project.

We also want to acknowledge the artistic efforts of our student Tracey Sticco, Stetson College of Law Class of 2007. Tracey drew a number of cartoons that appear in the *Guide* and put up with our (numerous) requests for revisions. We deeply appreciate her efforts.

We also thank the staff at Aspen Publishers. We especially appreciate Rick Mixter, for his inspired belief that legal texts can be practical and occasionally humorous, and Eric Holt, who brought our vision to life.

We should also mention the students we have had the pleasure to teach over the years. Some of these students actually used precursors to the *Guide* and provided valuable comments on it. Others helped shape our own understanding of civil procedure. To them we offer thanks for letting us say the very special phrase "I am a teacher."

Finally, permit us a few more personal thanks. Professor Allen thanks, and dedicates the *Guide* to, his wife Debbie and his two sons, Ben and Noah. They stood (or crawled) by him throughout this effort. It would not have been possible to complete this project without their love and support.

Professor Finch thanks his wife, Lora, an exceptional legal mind, mate, and mother; his daughter Chloe (please go to med school, we have enough lawyers in the family); and his parents and brother.

We hope you learn from and enjoy our work.

Michael Allen & Michael Finch

December, 2005
Gulfport, Florida

TABLE OF CONTENTS

Introduction 1

Chapter One: Origins of the Lawsuit 5

   A.   The Clients Tell Their Story 5

        1.   The Olmans' Employment History 6

        2.   New Management at Full Moon 7

        3.   Bad News 9

        4.   The Olmans Respond 10

        5.   Otis Is Fired 11

        6.   The Olmans Take Legal Action 12

   B.   Lane's First Steps 13

   A Note Concerning: Remedies 13

   A Note Concerning: Lawyers' Ethical Responsibilities to Clients 16

   C.   Preparing to File Suit 19

        1.   Investigating the Facts 19

        2.   Determining the Applicable Law 20

            a.   Sources and Types of Law 20

            b.   Federal Law Applicable to the Olmans' Dispute 22

                (1)   The Olmans' Claims for Discriminatory Treatment 22

   Tactical Tip: List the Elements of Each Potential Claim 23

Task 1.1 24

(2)   Otis' Claim for Retaliation 24

Task 1.2 25

(3)   Federal Law Remedies 25

c.   State Law Applicable to the Olmans' Claims 26

(1)   Statutory Claims for Age Discrimination
and Retaliation 26

(2)   State Common Law Claims 27

Question 1.1 29

Task 1.3 30

D.   Final Considerations Before Drafting the Complaint 31

1.   Determining Jurisdiction and Venue 31

2.   Determining the Time to File Suit 32

A Concluding Note Concerning: Sources of Procedural Law 33

Chapter Two: Commencing the Lawsuit 35

A.   The Complaint 35

Document: Complaint and Demand for Jury Trial 37

B.   Pleading Beyond the Notice Requirement of Rule 8 45

Tactical Tip: Relying on Form Books or "Model" Complaints 46

1.   Preparing for the Defendants' Anticipated Responses 47

Tactical Tip: Alleging the Elements of a Cause of Action 48

2. Preserving the Opportunity to Fully Litigate the Case, with a Minimum of Procedural Cost 48

3. Preserving a Client's Legal Rights 50

4. Pinning Down the Defendants 50

5. Telling a Good Story to the Court, the Defendants, and (Perhaps) the Public 51

6. Complying with a Lawyer's Ethical Obligations 52

    Question 2.1 53

C. Specificity in Pleading 53

D. Filing and Serving the Complaint 54

Chapter Three: The Opening Defense 57

A. Full Moon Responds to the Complaint 57

1. Pre-Answer Motions 61

    a. Power Motions 63

        Question 3.1 64

    b. Pleading Motions 64

        Question 3.2 65

Document: *Defendant Full Moon Sports, Inc.'s Motion to Dismiss for Failure to State a Claim* 68

Document: *Defendant Full Moon Sports, Inc.'s Memorandum in Support of Its Motion to Dismiss for Failure to State a Claim* 69

    c. Other Possible Motions 72

Question 3.3 73

    2.   Full Moon's Answer 73

Question 3.4 74

Question 3.5 76

Document: *Answer and Counterclaim of Defendant Full Moon Sports, Inc.* 78

B.   Belcher's Belated Response to the Suit 84

Question 3.6 84

Chapter Four: Prelude to Discovery 87

A.   Lane Responds to the Defendants 87

Question 4.1 89

Question 4.2 90

B.   The Pleadings Are Closed . . . Or Are They? 90

Question 4.3 91

C.   Case Management 92

A Note Concerning: Appeals 95

Document: *Case Management and Scheduling Order* 97

Chapter Five: Gathering Evidence and Refining Strategy: The Discovery Process 99

A.   Preparing for the Discovery Process 99

Tactical Tip: Party Autonomy in Discovery 101

Task 5.1 102

B.   The Parties Make Their Required Disclosures 102

Tactical Tip: Read the Rules 103

Question 5.1 105

Document: *Required Disclosure Statement of Plaintiffs Otis and
Fiona Olman* 106

Question 5.2 109

C.   Discovery Devices: Uses and Disputes 110

      1.   General Considerations 110

          a.   Relevance and Privilege 110

A Note Concerning: *Common Privileges* 112

          b.   Tools of Discovery 114

A Guide to Gathering Information Under the Rules 114

      2.   Initial Paper Discovery 118

          a.   Lane Begins the Discovery Process 118

               Task 5.2 119

Document: *Plaintiffs' First Request for Production of Documents* 121

Tactical Tip: Subpoenaing Non-Parties 124

               Task 5.3 127

Document: *Plaintiffs' First Set of Interrogatories to Defendant* 128

          b.   Full Moon Responds 130

Document: _Defendant's Responses and Objections to Plaintiffs'_
               First Request for Production of Documents 132

Document: _Defendant's Answers and Objections to Plaintiffs'_
               First Set of Interrogatories 136

               c.   Lane Reacts 140

Tactical Tip: Courts and Discovery Disputes 143

                        Question 5.3 145

               d.   The Discovery Dispute Is Resolved 146

                        Question 5.4 147

       3.   Depositions 150

               a.   Lane Prepares for Depositions 150

A Note Concerning: Corporate Testimony 153

               b.   A Discovery Controversy 154

               c.   Preparing Witnesses 156

               d.   Taking a Deposition 157

Tactical Tip: Taking Effective Depositions 157

Document: _Excerpts of Shockley Deposition_ 159

                        Question 5.5 164

       4.   The Second Wave of Paper Discovery: Admissions 165

D.   Expert Discovery 166

                        Question 5.6 168

Chapter Six: Joinder & Amendment 171

    A.   Structuring a Lawsuit 171

        1.   Otis' Claims Against Full Moon and Belcher 172

                Question 6.1 173

                Question 6.2 174

        2.   Fiona's Claims Against Full Moon 175

                Question 6.3 176

        3.   Full Moon's Counterclaim Against Otis 176

                Question 6.4 177

                Question 6.5 178

    B.   Lane Considers Whether to Amend the Complaint 178

        1.   Joining a New Defendant 178

                Question 6.6 180

        2.   Joining an Additional Plaintiff 181

                Question 6.7 182

        3.   Amending the Pleadings: The Importance of Timing 184

            a.   The Potential Impact of Rules 15 *and* 16 184

            b.   Beating the Statute of Limitations and Rule 15(c) 186

                Question 6.8 187

    C.   Some Concluding Joinder Issues: What Might Have Been 187

1.   Impleader 187

2.   Necessary and Indispensable Parties 189

        Question 6.9 191

3.   Intervention 191

        Question 6.10 192

Chapter Seven: Summary Judgment 193

A.   Tweedy Moves for Summary Judgment 193

1.   The Standard for Summary Judgment 193

        Question 7.1 195

2.   Full Moon's Grounds for Summary Judgment 195

        a.   Proving the Affirmative Defense of Waiver 195

                Question 7.2 196

        b.   Challenging Otis' Claims that Full Moon Acted
                with Ageist Motive 196

                A Note to Students 197

        c.   Challenging Otis' Claim that Full Moon
                Terminated Otis in Retaliation 198

                Question 7.3 199

3.   Preparing and Supporting the Summary Judgment
        Motion 199

Document: *Defendant's Motion for Summary Judgment* 200

Document: *Memorandum in Support of Defendant's Motion for*

Summary Judgment 204

Document: *Affidavit of Chloé Michaela* 211

Question 7.4 213

B.   The Olmans' Response to Summary Judgment 213

1.   Responding to the Liability Release 214

2.   Responding to Full Moon's Contention that It Acted
with Legitimate, Non-discriminatory Motive in
Replacing Otis 215

3.   Raising Doubt About Full Moon's Motive in Terminating
Otis 215

Document: *Memorandum in Opposition to Defendant's Motion
for Summary Judgment* 217

Question 7.5 222

C.   Judge Goodenough's Ruling 223

Document: *Order and Memorandum* 225

Question 7.6 229

Chapter Eight: Trial 231

A.   Preparing for Trial 231

Tactical Tip: The Importance of Preparation 234

B.   The Trial 235

1.   Structure of a Trial and the Role of Procedure 235

The Structure of a Civil Jury Trial 236

2. Selecting a Jury and the Beginning of Trial 237

    Task 8.1 240

3. Otis' Case-in-Chief 241

    Question 8.1 244

Notes Concerning: The Jury 246

4. Full Moon's Case-in-Chief 247

    Question 8.2 248

5. The Jury Deliberates and Reaches Its Verdict 249

Document: *Verdict Form* 251

C. Post-Trial Matters Before Judge Goodenough 254

Document: *Judgment on Jury Verdict* 255

    Question 8.3 256

    Question 8.4 258

Chapter Nine: Final Resolution 259

A. Considering Appeal 259

1. The Olmans' Perspective 259

2. Full Moon's Perspective 260

Document: *Notice of Appeal* 264

B. Settlement Negotiations Continue 265

Document: *Joint Stipulation to Dismiss with Prejudice* 268

Postscript 269

    Otis and Fiona Olman 269
    Bertie Lurch 269
    Sid Shockley 270
    Bruce Belcher 270
    Eleanor Lane 270
    Bart Tweedy 270

Appendix A A-1

  Characters A-1

  Key Events A-3

  Summary of Legal Claims (with Elements) A-5

Appendix B: Selecting a Court to Hear the Suit B-1

    A.   Personal Jurisdiction and Venue B-1

              Question B.1 .... B-3

              Question B.2 .... B-4

  Map of the United States Showing Circuit and District Courts B-5

              Question B.3 .... B-6

    B.   Formally Initiating the Lawsuit B-6

              Question B.4 .... B-7

              Question B.5 .... B-8

    C.   Subject Matter Jurisdiction B-10

              Question B.6 .... B-11

    D.   The Impact of Choice of Forum on the Law Governing the Suit B-14

1.   Choosing Between Different States' Laws B-14

2.   Choosing Between State Law and Federal Procedural
Law B-15

Question B.7 .... B-17

Index I-1

INTRODUCTION

The traditional hallmark of lawyers is their ability to navigate clients through the unfamiliar world of the court system. This special skill rests on a sound knowledge of the rules of civil procedure. You begin developing this skill during your first-year course in Civil Procedure and continue refining it as long as you are a member of the legal profession.

Many of our former students remark that they *really* learned civil procedure when they had to use it in practice. In the context of an actual case, procedural concepts like "notice pleading" and "work product" crystallize into meaning. Practicing lawyers are often surprised to discover the logic and interrelationship of rules that eluded them in law school.

In this Guide, we hope to place you in an authentic litigation setting and assist your learning of civil procedure. We have created a hypothetical employment discrimination suit that illustrates how the rules of procedure can operate in practice. You will be privy to the procedural strategies of lawyers for both plaintiffs and defendants. You will see how these strategies take form in illustrative pleadings, motions, discovery documents, and other materials generated in a suit.

We hope you will do more than watch the case unfold. As the action develops we have formulated questions and "tasks" that allow you to test your working knowledge of procedural rules. You will also begin developing your legal judgment by considering tactical and strategic issues that arise in our hypothetical lawsuit. Along the way we provide a number of "tactical tips" to help you appreciate how the rules can be used pragmatically to advance a client's goals. Even if you never litigate a civil suit, we believe these tips move you closer to the law school goal of "thinking like a lawyer."

A Note on the Hypothetical Case

The hypothetical case is realistic. At the same time, we have condensed our presentation of the case to emphasize the procedural rules of greatest importance to first-year law students. You will have the opportunity to study the litigation process in even greater depth in upper-level courses like Pretrial Practice, Trial Advocacy, and Complex Litigation. We urge you to take these courses if you are interested in being a litigator.

On the scale of real case difficulty, the hypothetical case is relatively simple. But it may not seem simple to you in the beginning. An unavoidable fact of contemporary litigation is that even a "simple" case requires that lawyers negotiate their way through a complex array of facts, substantive law, and procedural rules.

To help you keep a handle on the facts and law involved in our case, we urge you to refer periodically to Appendix A. In this appendix you will find a brief summary of (1) the parties, lawyers, and witnesses; (2) the key facts alleged in the complaint and their chronology; and (3) the legal claims asserted by the parties. As we explain later, practicing lawyers often rely on such summaries to help them keep a case in perspective.

A Note on Organization and Coverage

Civil Procedure teachers and texts organize the subject in different ways. For example, Professor Allen begins his course with the study of subject matter jurisdiction, personal jurisdiction, and the *Erie* doctrine before examining the particular rules governing the litigation process. Professor Finch begins his course with the study of these rules and defers topics like jurisdiction and *Erie* until later in the course.

Both approaches have advantages, and the Guide is suited to either approach. After introducing the dispute that underlies our hypothetical suit, we first examine the procedural rules a lawyer uses in formulating the pleadings and motions that predominate at the outset of litigation. Those of you who have already studied jurisdiction, *Erie,* and related topics can integrate them with the first chapters by using the materials found in Appendix B. Those of you who have not yet studied these topics can defer consideration of Appendix B until later in your course.

The Guide is *not* meant to replace your text or the many treatises on civil procedure. Even a hypothetical case cannot begin to illustrate all the issues that arise under the rules of civil procedure. For that reason, several subjects (like jurisdiction and joinder) will not be covered as comprehensively as your Civil Procedure professor will cover them. So, consider the Guide a companion piece to your course materials.

You should also be aware that Civil Procedure scholars have divergent views of their subject. Your professor's view of the meaning and operation of procedural law will inevitably differ from ours at times. We hope you view this divergence of opinion not as a sign that someone is "wrong," but rather as an introduction to the richness and wonderful ambiguity inherent in the subject.

A Note on Drafting

Procedural rules give lawyers considerable discretion in drafting litigation documents. Lawyers have different approaches to drafting, and usually have sound reasons for their differences.

The hypothetical documents in the Guide represent the authors' best thinking on legal drafting. Other lawyers would no doubt draft these litigation documents differently. But we hope our illustrations come close to demonstrating the values that most thoughtful lawyers and judges share. These are utility, brevity, and simplicity.

By utility we mean accomplishing all that the rules permit a document to accomplish with a minimum of procedural objection. For example, a complaint should adequately state the facts and legal claims supporting the client's suit. It should also lay a comprehensive foundation for the discovery process. At the same time, a document should not invite an excessive number of objections by one's opponent (assuming an ethical opponent). Responding to objections that could have been avoided by more careful drafting interferes with expeditious prosecution of the case and costs the plaintiff needless expense.

By brevity we mean as short as possible. Judges incessantly complain that lawyers waste their time with wordy drafting. It takes less time to draft a verbose document than a brief one. Lawyers sometimes flatter themselves that a longer document is more comprehensive and insightful. Occasionally this is true, but usually it is not.

By simplicity we mean, in addition to brevity, simple language. Law students understandably seek to use the specialized vocabulary they have struggled so hard to learn. Yet this is usually a mistake. Most litigation documents can be drafted without Latin or French phrases. The abundant formalisms found in so-called form books—"Now comes the Plaintiff by and through his counsel and petitions this honorable Court . . ."—serve no purpose and impress no one. The best drafting is typically done by lawyers who have mastered the complexities of the law and yet state their position in a manner comprehensible to a layperson.

References to the Federal Rules and Relevant Law

Each chapter begins with "Rule References," in which we list all rules used in the chapter. Rules discussed in greater depth are bolded and set forth in italics. You will notice that the litigation process does not travel chronologically from Rule 1 to Rule 86. Although there is some chronological ordering to the rules, lawyers often use a particular rule with their eye on a "distant" rule that will be important at a later stage of the suit. We have highlighted some of these interrelationships in each chapter.

There are numerous statutes and cases used in the Guide. Many consist of the *substantive* law that governs this case based on age discrimination and tort law. We have provided you citations for this material, but do not expect you to look it up or master it. On the other hand, an appreciable number of statutes and cases are *procedural* law. You will study most of this material in Civil Procedure.

We have also referred to the "Model Rules of Professional Conduct" from time to time. These are the ethical rules that govern a lawyer's practice of law. You will study these model rules in your upper-level course in Professional Responsibility. But we believe it best to develop a casual acquaintance with rules of professionalism early in your study of Civil Procedure, since these rules can affect the litigation process as much as the rules of procedure.

Finally, we have tried to inject some levity into the Guide. It has been said that studying law is like eating sawdust without butter. From time to time we have attempted to improve your digestion with legal humor—which is not always the same thing as humor. We hope you find these attempts to be a welcome distraction. Some may even help you learn Civil Procedure.

"Say something to me in legalese."

CHAPTER ONE:
ORIGINS OF THE LAWSUIT

Rule References:[1] *5, 11*

A.   The Clients Tell Their Story[2]

Eleanor Lane practices law in Jacksonville, Florida, with her partner, Ramona Quincy. Each spent several years working as a highly-paid associate in a large firm before deciding that "no bosses is better than money." The partnership of Lane and Quincy now specializes in employment discrimination litigation.

In August of 2003, Lane met with *Otis and Fiona Olman*. The Olmans claimed they were victims of age discrimination during a recent corporate downsizing. Here is the Olmans' story.

---

[1]Rules listed in *italics and bold* are discussed in greater detail than other rules. Throughout the Guide, Federal Rules of Civil Procedure are often referred to as "Rules" or "Federal Rules."

[2]As you read the Olmans' story, do *not* be overly concerned with remembering the factual detail. To the extent that detail becomes important later, you will have the opportunity to refresh your memory. Your goal in this chapter should be to understand the gist of the Olmans' story.

1.   The Olmans' Employment History

Otis Olman is 53 years old. Fiona is 49 years old. Both have been avid outdoor recreationists all their lives. Otis has a bachelor's degree in earth sciences from Montana State University, and Fiona has a bachelor's degree in exercise physiology from Slippery Rock State University. The couple met shortly after graduating from college in the 1970s and were married in 1980. They have two grown children.

Otis was first employed by *Full Moon Sports, Inc.* in 1982. Full Moon owns and operates a national chain of retail sporting goods stores. Otis began work as an assistant manager at Full Moon's store in Burlington, Vermont. Otis soon showed an exceptional knack for identifying and marketing quality sporting goods. In 1985, Otis was made manager of the Burlington store.

In 1990, Full Moon asked Otis to become manager of its store in Jacksonville, Florida. Otis was reluctant to make the transfer at first, since he and his wife loved Vermont. But when Otis visited the Jacksonville store, he saw a great opportunity to transform a mediocre business into a premier operation. Besides, his children fell in love with the ocean.

Fiona reluctantly agreed and the Olmans moved to Jacksonville, Florida. Within a few years, Otis transformed the store into the highly successful "Full Moon Sports Outdoor Center." At the center, customers could find top-of-the-line camping gear, outdoor clothing, and sporting equipment used in popular Florida activities like sea kayaking and scuba diving. Otis trained his sales personnel to give expert advice about the equipment they sold. In addition, the store offered instruction in sea kayaking and scuba diving, and sponsored guided outdoor adventures.

In 1995, Fiona began working at the Jacksonville store. By this time, Fiona was an accomplished sea kayaker who had guided many of the store's tours. She became manager of the store's kayak department in 1998, when the existing department manager moved to another state.

2.   New Management at Full Moon

In 2000, Full Moon was acquired by **Mizar, Inc.**, a Delaware corporation with headquarters in St. Louis, Missouri. Mizar owns several subsidiary companies engaged in a broad range of manufacturing activities. One of its subsidiaries is Edge Performance, Inc., which manufactures equipment for "extreme" sports like skateboarding, snowboarding, in-line skating, surfing, and white-water kayaking. Full Moon was Mizar's first attempt to expand into retail sales.

When Mizar acquired Full Moon in 2000, it immediately replaced Full Moon's president. The new president, **Bertie Lurch**, implemented several changes in the company. First, Full Moon introduced extreme sporting goods into its stores. Prominently featured in its extreme line were goods produced by Edge Performance. Second, Full Moon increased television and radio advertising, with a special emphasis on extreme sports. Third, Full Moon made changes in local and regional management.

Full Moon's executive headquarters are in Atlanta, Georgia, and it is incorporated in Delaware. Because Full Moon oversees so many stores throughout the country, it has divided them into regions. The Jacksonville store is in the southeast region encompassing the states of Florida, Georgia, North Carolina, and South Carolina. Prior to Full Moon's acquisition by Mizar, Otis worked under the oversight of **Rex Ornstein**, regional director for southeast stores. After Mizar acquired Full Moon, Rex was replaced as regional manager by *Bruce Belcher*. Rex was transferred to the advertising department in Atlanta.

The new regional manager visited with Otis shortly after being hired. Belcher told Otis he was very impressed by how Otis had developed the Jacksonville store. He told Otis that Full Moon wanted him to continue as manager. Belcher asked Otis to sign a contract with Full Moon. Previously, Otis had no formal contract with the company. The new contract had a three-year term, running from September 2000 through September 2003. Under the contract, Otis would continue to receive a salary of $75,000.

Otis was reluctant to sign the contract. As soon as he learned that Full Moon had been acquired by Mizar, he developed misgivings about his future with the company. Mizar had a reputation in the industry as a company that focuses on the bottom line with little loyalty to its employees. Otis began to explore other job options. One option was presented by local entrepreneur and long-time customer, Izzy Able. Izzy proposed that Otis and Fiona move to Key Largo and set up a kayak sales and rental business. Izzy offered Otis a one-half partnership interest in exchange for Otis' managing the business. Otis and Fiona gave plenty of consideration to Izzy's proposal. Key Largo was a kayaker's paradise and a relatively undeveloped market. They believed a Key Largo business might prove to be highly profitable.

Otis felt comfortable calling Rex Ornstein, his former regional manager, to discuss this important career decision. Rex counseled Otis to "do what's best for you and Fiona." Rex was not as troubled by Mizar's reputation as Otis, but he advised Otis to speak candidly with Belcher. Otis contacted Belcher, who arranged a visit with Otis at the Jacksonville store. When the two met, Belcher was surprised to discover Otis was thinking of leaving Full Moon.

Belcher urged Otis to stay. He offered to increase Otis' salary to $85,000. He emphasized that Full Moon provided Otis "great" job security especially compared to the speculative business venture proposed by Izzy. Although Belcher admitted he had "no room to move" on the three-year term of Otis' contract ("that's the longest term Atlanta is offering to any of its managers"), he stressed that "a guy with your track record shouldn't worry about his future with Full Moon. Jacksonville is your store as long as you want it to be. You can retire here."

Otis was reassured and signed the contract.

3.   Bad News

One month after Otis signed, Belcher introduced him to **Sid Shockley**. Shockley was to be department manager for the new extreme sports section of the Jacksonville store. The Jacksonville store was going to "invest big" in the extreme sporting goods business. Otis had never heard of Shockley and had an immediate aversion to him. According to Otis, "Shockley came off as a self-absorbed jock. He wore an earring and had several tattoos. Although an expert in most 'board' sports, he showed little interest in outdoor activities like camping and sea kayaking—he said they were 'boring.'" Shockley had tested extreme sports equipment for Edge Performance prior to working for Full Moon. He had no prior retail sales experience.

From 2000 through mid-2003, Otis and Shockley worked fairly well together. Shockley listened to Otis and largely followed his directions for running the extreme sports department. He learned the retail sporting goods business quicker than Otis had expected. The store's extreme sporting goods sales increased to the point where they accounted for 30% of the store's profits. Still, Otis sensed an uneasiness in their relationship that, at the time, Otis thought was just a "generational difference."

In July, 2003, regional manager Belcher came to Otis with bad news: Full Moon was initiating a corporate downsizing. About 20% of its work force was being terminated and Full Moon was "re-shuffling" store management. What this meant for the Jacksonville store was (a) the elimination of about 10 of the store's employees, and (b) the possible replacement of Otis as store manager. Belcher asked Otis to consider how the Jacksonville store might reduce its staff. He also asked Otis to consider his own career goals and whether there was another Full Moon store he wanted to manage. Belcher promised to work with Otis to make the downsizing "as painless as possible," but emphasized that final personnel decisions would be made by management in Atlanta.

Otis later recommended to Belcher that the Jacksonville store target newer employees for its reduction in force. Most of these employees were lower-wage workers in their late teens and early twenties, and experience suggested they would not stay with the company more than a few years. Otis recommended that Full Moon retain its experienced employees who had "proven their loyalty to the store. They are better producers." Otis also told Belcher he wanted to stay as manager of the Jacksonville store and knew of no other store in the southeast that interested him. As Otis explained to Lane, "There was no way I would push another manager out of his store, and that's what Belcher was asking me to do."

Otis soon learned the worst. His wife, Fiona, was one of the employees who would be terminated. Otis would be retained but would no longer be store manager. Instead, Otis would manage the camping department at a reduced salary of $45,000. Shockley would be the new store manager, effective upon expiration of Otis' contract in September.

4.   The Olmans Respond

Fiona stoically accepted her termination. As she said to Otis at the time, "I think they've been planning to get rid of us ever since Shockley walked into the store. I'd just as soon work someplace else." As part of her severance package, Fiona received one month's salary. In exchange, Fiona was asked to sign a release waiving any legal rights she might have related to her employment. Fiona signed the release even though Otis urged her not to.

Otis was deeply disturbed about his demotion. He called Rex Ornstein in Atlanta. Rex expressed surprise that Full Moon was replacing Otis as store manager. Rex promised to "find out what I can," but told Otis that "frankly, I don't have a lot of influence around here anymore." Later that day Rex called Otis back and confirmed the bad news. Rex then tried to assuage Otis' feelings by telling him: "Otis, you and I have been with the company for a long time. The sporting goods business has changed, and Full Moon has changed, too.

The extreme generation is young. We're not. Maybe it's time to move on. I plan to retire next year." Needless to say, Otis was disappointed in Rex's advice.

Otis sent a strongly-worded letter to president Bertie Lurch in Atlanta. Otis accused the company of "ageism" and wrote that, "While there is still time, I hope we can resolve this dispute amicably, but if the company does not rescind its decision, I will be compelled to take legal action. Given the fact that a substantial amount of our business comes from over-40 customers, it would be bad for business if they learned of management's attitude toward them."

5.   Otis Is Fired

Otis' letter got results. Two weeks later he was told that the offer to make him manager of the camping department was rescinded and he was fired. The termination letter, signed by Bertie Lurch, explained the company's reasons:

> *Full Moon will not tolerate age discrimination in any form. But discrimination has nothing to do with our decision. As you are aware, profits in the Jacksonville store have declined in recent years, with the exception of profits from extreme line products. But for the success of Mr. Shockley in marketing the extreme line, the Jacksonville store might now be slated for closure. We had hoped you would support Mr. Shockley as new store manager just as he has supported you. Regrettably, store employees inform us that you are openly hostile to Mr. Shockley and refuse to cooperate in the transition to new store management. It now seems inconceivable that you could work, in any capacity, with Mr. Shockley.*
>
> *In preparing for the transition to new management in the Jacksonville store, we have also learned that significant quantities of inventory have been reported as "lost, damaged, or unaccounted for." Legal counsel has advised us that these losses might support criminal investigation. As store manager, you are ultimately accountable for these discrepancies.*
>
> *With the hope that we can conclude your association with the Full Moon family on amicable terms, we are offering you six months severance pay to enable you to pursue a new career direction. If our proposal is acceptable, please sign the enclosed release and return it to me at your earliest convenience. I will need a response within 10 days.*
>
>   *Bertie Lurch*
>   *President*

6.   The Olmans Take Legal Action

Otis had no intention of signing the release. Otis told Eleanor Lane that, given the circumstances, he had conducted himself very professionally in his dealings with Shockley. If there was a personnel problem in the Jacksonville store, it was caused by Shockley. According to Otis, Shockley had told several employees that Otis was "too old" to be running an extreme sports store and was being "put out to pasture" in the camping department. As soon as Shockley learned of his promotion, he immediately began behaving as if he were already store manager. This had put employees in an awkward position. Belcher did nothing to help the situation.

As for the missing-inventory threat, Otis assured Lane that all sporting goods stores suffer a certain amount of theft and loss. He also explained that, when a store uses its own inventory for rentals and instruction, there is an unavoidable increase in lost or damaged goods. Lurch's suggestion that a "criminal" investigation was warranted; however, it was nothing more than an attempt to intimidate Otis into signing the release.

Lane questioned Otis carefully about his story. She was especially interested in his reasons for believing age discrimination motivated Full Moon's decision to replace him. Otis gave these reasons:

(1)   His replacement by Shockley was proof in itself. Shockley was in his early thirties. Shockley had learned most of his management skills directly from Otis. And the increased sales in extreme sporting goods had little to do with Shockley. After Mizar acquired Full Moon in 2000, the company promoted extreme lines more than conventional sporting goods. In short, Otis was being replaced by a younger manager who was less qualified to run the store.

(2)   Otis suspected that regional manager Belcher (who was in his mid-thirties) played a big part in the downsizing decisions made by management in Atlanta. Otis recalled that Belcher occasionally made semi-humorous ageist remarks when visiting the store. And Belcher was "tight" with Shockley.

(3)   Older managers and employees seemed to be a primary target of Full Moon's downsizing. Of the ten employees terminated in the Jacksonville store, four were over 40. That left only two employees over 40. Fiona's position as manager of the kayak department had been filled by her former assistant-manager, who was under 40. In addition, Otis knew of at least

one older manager in another Full Moon store who had recently been replaced by a person under 40.

B.   Lane's First Steps

Lane asked the Olmans what they wanted from Full Moon. They were adamant about *not* returning to work for the company. The Olmans wanted Full Moon to compensate them for their losses and, if possible, they wanted to punish the company for its wrongdoing.

A Note Concerning:
REMEDIES

It may seem like an obvious question, but many lawyers often neglect to ask their clients "what do you want?" Most clients have general goals in mind when they consult a lawyer. But they may need their lawyer's guidance in specifying these goals, and may sometimes need painful advice about the likelihood of attaining them. Model Rule of Professional Conduct 1.2(a) emphasizes that lawyers must ultimately defer to their clients' decision concerning the "objectives" of representation.[3]

The complaint Lane filed would request the remedies sought by the Olmans. Federal Rule 8(a)(3) requires that a party asserting a claim expressly make "a demand for judgment for the relief the pleader seeks," and allows a party to seek more than one type of relief. A full consideration of the law of remedies is beyond the scope of a course in Civil Procedure. However, some common forms of relief sought in litigation include:

(1)   <u>Compensatory Damages</u>: Compensatory damages are monetary awards designed to put the plaintiff into the position she would have occupied but for the defendant's unlawful conduct. Common examples of compensatory damages include recovery of economic losses like lost wages or medical expenses, as well as recovery for non-economic harm like pain, suffering, and other "psychic" injuries.

---

[3]Rule 1.2(a) provides that "a lawyer shall abide by a client's decisions concerning the objectives of representation. . . ."

(2)   Punitive Damages: Unlike compensatory damages, punitive damages are designed to punish the defendant for its unlawful conduct and to deter such conduct in the future. Punitive damages are generally not available for claims like breach of contract or negligence. When recoverable, punitive damages are usually authorized by statute. They are a fairly common feature of civil rights legislation.

(3)   Injunctive Relief: An injunction is a court order either requiring a defendant to take some action or precluding a defendant from taking action. Traditionally, a plaintiff is not entitled to injunctive relief unless she can demonstrate that money damages will not be adequate. An injunction is enforced by a court's power to hold a non-complying defendant in contempt. Had the Olmans wanted to resume working for Full Moon, they would have sought injunctive relief.

(4)   Ancillary Relief: Finally, there are certain types of remedies that are categorized as ancillary or extra. Perhaps the most important ancillary remedy is an award of attorney's fees. Absent authorization of the recovery of attorney's fees by statute or contract, the "American rule" usually requires each party to pay her own lawyer's fee.

Lane advised the Olmans that, based on their factual representations, they appeared to have claims for age discrimination under employment discrimination laws. Lane explained, however, that the Olmans could not immediately sue Full Moon for employment discrimination, as was the case with many legal claims. Employment discrimination laws generally require that, as a *pre-condition* of filing suit in a court of law, employees first file charges with the administrative agencies that enforce these laws.[4] This provides the

---

[4]Pre-suit filing requirements are common. For example, many states require that, prior to suing a governmental entity, plaintiffs give the entity notice of their grievance and defer legal action until the entity has sufficient time to attempt to resolve the grievance. In the private sector, plaintiffs may be required by contract or law to pursue "alternative dispute resolution" mechanisms like mediation and arbitration before filing suit. Lane found no alternative dispute resolution mechanism in the Olmans' contracts. The only pre-suit requirement applicable to the Olmans' claims was their statutory obligation to exhaust administrative procedures before suing for age discrimination.

administrative agencies an opportunity to attempt to resolve the dispute expeditiously out of court.

You can study the operation of administrative agencies in upper-level courses like Administrative Law. To understand the Olmans' dispute, it is *not* important that you understand what occurred during the administrative proceedings where their charges were considered. You need only appreciate two things: (1) the Olmans' legal suit could not be filed until the administrative process was completed, and (2) the administrative process resulted in a few deadlines the Olmans had to satisfy in order to prosecute their suit.

Federal employment discrimination law is usually enforced by the United States Equal Employment Opportunity Commission (EEOC). The Olmans would have to file their charges against Full Moon with the EEOC. Probably nothing would come of their filing, but the Olmans had to "exhaust" this administrative remedy as a prerequisite to suing. The sooner the Olmans filed their charges the better, but in no event could they file more than 300 days from the date of their termination.[5] Lane agreed to assist them in preparing charges for filing with the agency.

In the meantime, Lane would contact Full Moon and explore the possibility of settling the dispute. To guide her in these settlement discussions, Lane explored with the Olmans their financial situation as well as the amount of money they required to settle the dispute. As was often the case, Lane provided a check on her clients' unrealistic expectations about what they might recover at trial. If settlement discussions were unsuccessful, Lane would prepare to file suit.

Finally, Lane needed to formalize the attorney-client relationship in a contract. Lane's standard contract briefly summarized her responsibilities in representing the Olmans. As important as these contractual commitments, however, was the extensive set of professional rules that governed Lane's attorney-client relationship.

---

[5]29 U.S.C. § 626(d)(2). As discussed later, "statutes of limitation" often give clients several *years* in which to file conventional tort claims. *See infra* pages 32–33. The much shorter limitation period found in most employment discrimination laws emphasizes that clients and lawyers must act diligently in challenging unlawful behavior.

A Note Concerning:
LAWYERS' ETHICAL RESPONSIBILITIES TO CLIENTS

Each state adopts its own code of professional responsibility to regulate members of the bar. Most states have adopted some version of the American Bar Association's "Model Rules of Professional Conduct." Some of Lane's more important responsibilities under the Model Rules included:

- Prosecuting the suit diligently, Model Rule 1.3. Lack of diligence through lawyer neglect or delay is the most common client grievance.

- Communicating with the Olmans about the suit, Model Rule 1.4. Lawyers are required to keep clients informed of the status of their suit and to respond promptly to their clients' inquiries (*e.g.,* they must return clients' phone calls).

- Letting the Olmans make fundamental decisions in the suit, Model Rule 1.2(a). As mentioned earlier, clients generally set the goals of representation. Lawyers may determine the best "means" to achieve these goals after "reasonable" consultation with clients. Model Rule 1.4(a)(2). Most decisions arising under the Federal Rules of Civil Procedure are "means" decisions which will be made by a lawyer with little if any client consultation.

- Keeping communications with the Olmans confidential, Model Rule 1.6(a). Lawyers owe a duty of confidentiality to both clients and *prospective* clients. Therefore, regardless of whether the Olmans retained Lane as their lawyer, their private communications with Lane were confidential.

The Olmans' principal responsibility was to cooperate with Lane and pay any expenses they were obligated to pay under their contract. The most costly aspect of litigation is usually attorney's fees. Lane knew that employment discrimination statutes allowed the Olmans to recover their attorney's fees and other costs *if* they prevailed at trial. So, they were not limited by the traditional "American Rule" under which litigants must pay their own attorney's fee even if they prevail in court.[6] But Lane also knew that most cases settle before trial.[7] Lane proposed the following arrangement.

First, the Olmans would pay all litigation "costs," which included items like court filing fees, expert witness fees, and court reporter fees.[8] These costs were relatively minor, particularly compared to attorney's fees. As for her fees, Lane was willing to invest time in the case without asking the Olmans to pay her normal hourly rate. She would take the risk that the Olmans would recover something from Full Moon. If the Olmans recovered money from the defendants through either settlement or litigated judgment, the Olmans would pay Lane a "contingent fee." The contingent fee would equal a specific share of the Olmans' recovery, as limited by Lane's professional code.[9] Lane's code generally limited her fee to 40% of the Olmans' recovery if the case proceeded to trial.[10] If the Olmans recovered nothing from the defendants, Lane would go unpaid for her labor.

---

[6]Prevailing *plaintiffs* can recover their fees under 29 U.S.C. § 626(b). The Age Discrimination in Employment Act does not expressly authorize fee recovery by prevailing defendants, and most courts deny such fees unless a plaintiff's suit is frivolous. *See, e.g., Turlington v. Atlanta Gas Light Co.*, 135 F.3d 1428 (11th Cir. 1998). Lane advised the Olmans of this risk and opined that it was minimal if the Olmans' story checked out during pre-suit investigation.

[7]The percentage of federal civil cases resolved by trial fell from 11.5% in 1962 to 1.8% in 2002. *See* Marc Galanter, The Vanishing Trial: An Examination of Trials and Related Matters in Federal and State Courts, 1 J. Empirical Legal Studies 459 (2004). That does not mean that 98.2% of filed cases settle. A portion of this 98.2% of cases are resolved through adjudication short of trial; this includes successful motions to dismiss and motions for summary judgment, discussed later in the Guide. The precise percentage of cases ending in settlement is difficult to determine. However, it is certainly a majority. *See, e.g.*, David A. Sklanskey and Stephen C. Yeazell *Corporate Law Without Leaving Home: What Civil Procedure Can Teach Criminal Procedure, and Vice-Versa*, UCLA School of Law Public Law & Theory Research Paper 05-9, available at http://ssrn.com/abstract=706601, at 12 n. 32 (discussing settlement statistics).

[8]Under Rule 54(d) the court could award "costs other than attorney's fees" to the Olmans if they prevailed. These recoverable costs are defined in 28 U.S.C. § 1920.

[9]Although lawyers and clients can determine by contract the fee, under the Model Rules the fee must be "reasonable." Model Rule 1.5. This rule provides a list of factors to consider in determining whether a fee is reasonable. Broadly speaking, these factors center on the difficulty of the representation and the actual work performed by the lawyers. Contingent fees, though historically disapproved by the bar, are now permitted subject to limits on the percentage that can be charged.

[10]*See* Fla. Bar Rule 4-1.5(4)(B)(i) (contingent fee limited to 40% of recovery up to $1 million).

Even though the Olmans' contract contained a contingent fee provision, the Olmans' would still demand in their complaint that Full Moon pay their attorney's fees. If the Olmans prevailed at trial, the contingent fee they owed Lane would be reduced by the amount of any fee Full Moon was ordered to pay by the court. If the court-ordered fee met or exceeded the contingent fee owed Lane, the Olmans would pay her nothing.

Lane also felt obligated to warn the Olmans about the intangible costs of filing a lawsuit. As Lane explained, once the Olmans filed suit they would be subject to various demands of the court and the defendants, and would surrender an appreciable amount of personal privacy. They could, among other things, be compelled to attend depositions, hearings, and trial.[11] These events might, or might not, be scheduled at a time convenient for the Olmans. They might also be required to answer questions and produce personal records that they considered "private" (*e.g.*, their income tax returns). Virtually no party enjoyed the litigation process, and many parties came to strongly dislike it. On this point, Lane shared the observation of one of the twentieth century's leading jurists, Judge Learned Hand. Judge Hand once observed, "After now some dozen years of experience I must say that . . . I should dread a lawsuit beyond almost anything else short of sickness and death."[12]

After the Olmans left her office, Lane began work on their case. She immediately took several steps that would make litigation more organized and efficient. First, Lane dictated a summary of the notes she had taken during the initial interview. These notes were a useful reminder of the Olmans' basic story as well as a valuable check to determine if the Olmans' story changed down the road. Lane also prepared a chronology of events and a "cast of characters" to which she would periodically refer. These are included in Appendix A. Finally, she copied and organized the various documents she obtained from the Olmans. These documents included the employment contract Otis had with Full Moon, the release Fiona signed, the release Otis refused to sign, and the letter to Otis from Full Moon's president. These documents could prove critical to the case and Lane wanted to make sure she knew exactly where they could be found.

Lane also had to do a "conflict check" to verify that her firm had no conflict of interests that might prevent her from representing the Olmans in a suit against the likely defendants. A conflict of interests might arise if any defendant was a current or former

---

[11]We explore these obligations in a later chapter on discovery. *See infra* Chapter 5.

[12]Learned Hand, 3 Lectures on Legal Topics, Association of the Bar of the City of New York 106 (Macmillan, 1926).

client of Lane's firm.[13] Lane confirmed that her firm had never represented any of the potential defendants.

C.   Preparing to File Suit

Before filing suit, Lane needed to be as well informed as possible about the facts of the dispute and the applicable law. As discussed below, this was required by both her professional code and the Rules of Civil Procedure.

1.   Investigating the Facts

Lane had heard her clients' version of the facts and had no specific reason to question their credibility. She knew, however, that clients' memories are imperfect and some clients are less than forthright with their lawyers. Under Rule 11, when Lane filed suit she would be personally certifying to the court that (1) she had made "inquiry reasonable under the circumstances," and (2) the allegations in the complaint had "evidentiary support" or, so long as such allegations were specifically identified in the complaint, were "likely to have evidentiary support after a reasonable opportunity for further investigation or discovery." Because the Olmans' own testimony would be evidentiary support, could Lane reasonably rely solely on what the Olmans had told her?

Based on judicial interpretation of Rule 11[14] and good sense, Lane knew she should at least investigate other sources of evidence readily available to her. Therefore, she would review any important documents to which she had access. As explained earlier, Lane had already obtained some of these documents from the Olmans. These included the Olmans' employment contracts and the releases they had been asked to sign. Lane had also asked the Olmans for copies of any communications they had with Full Moon related to the dispute (*e.g.*, letters and e-mails). In addition, Lane would try to obtain copies of the Olmans' employment records from Full Moon. Because some of these had already been provided to

---

[13]*See* Model Rule 1.7 (lawyer should not represent a client if responsibilities to existing or former client creates significant risk of impaired representation).

[14]*See, e.g.,Worldwide Primates, Inc. v. McGreal*, 87 F.3d 1252 (11th Cir. 1996) (a lawyer who failed to conduct inquiry into truth of client's allegations was subject to sanctions under Rule 11 when he had time to conduct an inquiry and did not have to rely on client).

the EEOC by Full Moon during earlier administrative proceedings,[15] they were available as "public records."[16]

Lane would also attempt to speak to some of the key witnesses identified by the Olmans and perhaps take witness statements.[17] She might even use a private investigator to gather information. By conducting such an investigation, Lane would satisfy her professional responsibility under Rule 11 and her professional code.[18] She would also be in a much better position to draft a good complaint. Finally, economic self-interest supported a sound investigation of the facts. Because Lane and Quincy would be paid for their time only if the Olmans recovered monies by settlement or judgment, the lawyers would be invested in the suit.

2.   Determining the Applicable Law

When Lane signed the Olmans' complaint she would be certifying under Rule 11 that their claims were "warranted by existing law" or a plausible argument for changing the law. Lane could not rely on the Olmans or anyone else to make this certification. She would use her acquired knowledge and legal research skills to determine what legal claims she could fairly allege in the complaint. To some extent, Lane would be doing the same thing she had done on a law school exam when asked to determine the legal rights of a hypothetical plaintiff.

a.   Sources and Types of Law

To properly research the Olmans' legal claims, Lane needed to consider all possible *sources* of law. Lane knew the principal sources governing employment discrimination

---

[15]*See supra* pp. 14–15 (discussing administrative proceedings required before filing suit).

[16]Governmental records are usually available to the public under "freedom of information" or "public records" acts.

[17]Under Model Rule 4.2, Lane could not speak about the suit with parties or persons already represented by a lawyer without the lawyer's consent. Consequently, Lane would communicate with Full Moon through its lawyer.

[18]Model Rule 3.1 largely reiterates Rule 11's prohibition of filing legal claims that lack factual or legal support.

were federal and state law.[19] Federal and state lawmakers have overlapping powers in the field of civil rights, which includes employment discrimination. Although Congress has passed laws to remedy age discrimination in the workplace, most state legislatures have supplemented those laws. The principal limit on states is that they may not contradict or undermine the protections given by Congress.[20]

Lane also needed to consider the various *types* of federal and state law. Among the more commonly-used types of law are (1) constitutions, (2) statutes, (3) administrative regulations, and (4) common law. Lane was aware that neither the United States Constitution nor the Florida Constitution[21] regulates workplace discrimination in the private sector. She was aware, however, that both federal and state statutes prohibit age discrimination in private employment. Federal statutory law is found in the Age Discrimination in Employment Act (ADEA);[22] and applicable state law is found in the Florida Civil Rights Act.[23] The Olmans would probably want to assert claims under both statutes.

Lane also considered whether administrative regulations might apply in the Olmans' suit. Administrative regulations are a type of legal rule issued by governmental agencies that have responsibility for interpreting and enforcing particular statutes. The EEOC has responsibility for the ADEA. Lane knew from past experience that EEOC regulations would be important in processing the Olmans' employment discrimination claims in the administrative proceedings.

Finally, Lane considered whether common law—judge-made law—might apply to the Olmans' suit. Lane knew what first-year law students learn during their study of the

---

[19]Local government (cities and counties) may also share lawmaking authority with the United States and the states. Neither the city nor the county in which the Olmans had been employed had laws prohibiting age discrimination by private employers.

[20]Under the Supremacy Clause of Article VI of the U.S. Constitution, federal law "preempts" inconsistent state law. Preemption may also exist when federal law "occupies" a subject area and preempts state law, whether or not inconsistent with federal law. *See Metropolitan Life Ins. Co. v. Taylor,* 481 U.S. 58, 63–64 (1987).

[21]In Appendix B, we explain why Lane concluded that the law of Florida rather than that of some other state would likely apply to the Olmans' suit.

[22]29 U.S.C. § 621.

[23]Fla. Stat. §§ 760.01–760.11.

"Erie" doctrine: federal courts have very little authority to make common law.[24] State courts, by comparison, have extensive common law-making authority. In the Olmans' suit, state common law might provide the Olmans rights or remedies in addition to those found in federal and state statutes prohibiting employment discrimination.

"You seem to know something about law. I like that in an attorney."

In summary, to properly research and prepare the suit, Lane needed to consider numerous sources and types of law. She had a professional obligation to be competent in all this law, or to develop such a competence before proceeding too far with the case.[25]

b.   Federal Law Applicable to the Olmans' Dispute

(1)   The Olmans' Claims for Discriminatory Treatment

Evidence indicated that Full Moon management may have had ageist motives for replacing Otis and laying off Fiona. If management's hostility toward, or false stereotypes

---

[24]*See* Appendix B.

[25]Lawyers are not prevented from representing a client simply because they lack expertise in a particular area of law. Model Rule 1.1 only requires that a lawyer *become* competent in that area of law in sufficient time to adequately represent a client's interests. Lawyers, particularly new lawyers, frequently learn an area of law while representing clients.

about, older employees played a determinative role in its decisions,[26] the Olmans would have a *prima facie* case of discrimination under the ADEA.[27]

Tactical Tip ✍

List the Elements of Each Potential Claim:

When you are considering whether a given set of facts supports a claim, it is useful to make a checklist of the *elements* of the claim. You can use the checklist for many purposes during litigation, including (1) assessing whether you have evidentiary support for each element of the claim as required by Rule 11; (2) verifying that you have adequately alleged the elements of a claim in your complaint, *see* Rule 8(a)(2); and (3) framing your plans for discovery and trial.

Lane made a list of the elements of a claim under the ADEA.[28] They are:

1. The plaintiff-employee is age 40 or over;

2. The employer took an adverse job action against the employee;

---

[26]*See Hazen Paper Co. v. Biggins,* 507 U.S. 604, 610 (1993) (discrimination occurs when an employee's age "play[s] a role . . . and [has] a determinative influence on the outcome.")

[27]Age discrimination differs historically from discrimination based on race or national origin. Age discrimination is based less on animosity toward older workers than on false stereotypes about their ability. An employer who takes job action against an employee because of false stereotypes about age violates the ADEA even though the employer lacks animosity toward older workers. *See, e.g., Hazen Paper Co. v. Biggins,* 507 U.S. 604, 610 (1993) ("It is the very essence of age discrimination for an older employee to be fired because the employer believes that productivity and competence decline with old age.")

[28]Lists of the elements constituting the parties' claims are found in Appendix A. Statutes typically fail to enumerate the specific elements of a cause of action. The elements of a cause can usually be found, however, in either case law or a text discussing the subject area. *See, e.g.,* Andrew Ruzicho & Louis Jacobs, LITIGATING AGE DISCRIMINATION CASES (2000).

3.   The employer took the adverse job action "because of" the employee's age; and

4.   The employee suffered damages.

Task 1.1

Determine whether, under Rule 11(b)(3), Lane has sufficient evidentiary support to allege ADEA claims on behalf of both Otis and Fiona Olman. Be sure to identify all evidence supporting *each* element of an ADEA claim.

---

(2)   Otis' Claim for Retaliation

Evidence indicated that when Otis complained to the company president about age discrimination, Full Moon responded by terminating him. This suggested to Lane that Full Moon might be liable for retaliation. A claim of retaliation consists of the following elements:[29]

1.   An employee engaged in statutorily protected expression;

2.   The employee suffered adverse employment action; and

3.   The adverse action was causally related to his protected expression.

Importantly, Otis' retaliation claim might succeed even if his age discrimination claim did not. A retaliation claim required only that Otis show he had a *reasonable belief* Full Moon was engaged in age discrimination when he opposed the company's conduct.

---

[29]29 U.S.C. § 623(d).

Task 1.2

Determine whether, under Rule 11(b)(3), Lane has sufficient evidentiary support to allege a claim for retaliation on behalf of Otis. Be sure to identify all evidence supporting *each* element of a retaliation claim.

(3)   Federal Law Remedies

The Olmans sought monetary relief. Obviously, Lane wanted to demand all types of damages to which the Olmans were entitled. Many civil rights statutes permit plaintiffs to recover full *compensatory* damages, which include economic losses as well as damages for "psychic" injuries like emotional distress and humiliation. Typically, these statutes also typically permit the recovery of *punitive* damages if the defendant's wrongdoing is sufficiently egregious.[30]

The law of damages under the ADEA, however, was more limited. The Olmans could recover back pay. They could also recover future pay and earnings for the jobs they had lost. But the Olmans could *not* recover compensatory damages for their emotional distress and humiliation. This reduced the economic value of their suit considerably.[31] Nor could the Olmans recover punitive damages *per se.* Instead, if they proved that Full Moon acted in "reckless disregard" of their rights, their award of back pay (not future pay) would be doubled.[32] This doubling of back pay is called "liquidated damages." Under the ADEA, even if a jury believed Full Moon deserved greater punishment than double back pay it could not award additional damages.

Lane was aware of another limit to ADEA remedies. While Full Moon as employer could be sued under the ADEA, its *employees*—even employees like Shockley and Belcher who may have been the worst culprits—could not be sued. Under the ADEA, the employer

---

[30]For example, employees alleging racial or ethnic discrimination under Title VII may recover both compensatory damages and punitive damages. *See* 42 U.S.C. § 1981A(a)(1).

[31]*See* Andrew Ruzicho & Louis Jacobs, LITIGATING AGE DISCRIMINATION CASES §§ 5.02, 5.05 (2000).

[32]*See id.* § 5.06.

alone is liable for workplace discrimination.[33] Consequently, if the Olmans wanted to sue Shockley or Belcher for their role in Full Moon's discriminatory action, they would have to base their claims on state law (if it existed).

In addition, it would be very difficult to sue Mizar, Inc., even though Mizar owned Full Moon and probably had considerable influence over its subsidiary. Federal law honored the distinct legal identities of Full Moon, Inc. and Mizar, Inc. In essence, Full Moon's status as a corporation served as a warning to the world that it—and not its parent corporation, officers, or shareholders—was liable for its wrongdoing. Although the "corporate veil" can be "pierced" in certain circumstances, Lane knew that Mizar's mere ownership of and influence over Full Moon were not enough to justify joining Mizar as defendant.[34]

c.   State Law Applicable to the Olmans' Claims

Because remedies available to the Olmans under the ADEA were limited, state law might be important in their suit. Lane considered whether the following state-law claims should be included in the complaint.

(1)   Statutory Claims for Age Discrimination and Retaliation

The Florida Civil Rights Act (FCRA) prohibits age discrimination in employment, as well as retaliatory action. In fact, Florida courts interpret the FCRA so that it prohibits essentially the same actions prohibited by the federal ADEA.[35] Florida law, however, provided the Olmans additional *remedies*.

Most important, the FCRA allowed the Olmans to recover full compensatory damages. They would include psychic damages like emotional distress and humiliation that could substantially increase the jury's verdict. The FCRA also authorized the award of

---

[33]Similarly, Title VII prohibiting employment discrimination based on race or gender authorizes suit against the employer but not against individual managers or employees.

[34]*See, e.g., Lusk v. Foxmeyer Health Corp.*, 129 F.3d 773 (5th Cir. 1997) (presumption that parent company is not liable for its subsidiary's ADEA violations can be rebutted only by showing that parent company exercised undue control over subsidiary and was final decisionmaker in actions constituting violation of ADEA).

[35]*See Florida State Univ. v. Sondel*, 685 So.2d 923, 925 n.1 (Fla. Dt. Ct. App. 1997).

punitive damages up to $100,000. This monetary punishment might exceed the "double back pay" punishment provided under the ADEA.

Like the ADEA, however, the FCRA failed to provide the Olmans a remedy against individual employees like Shockley or Belcher. To sue them, Lane would have to find a remedy in state common law.

(2)   State Common Law Claims

Lane knew that Florida common law provided no remedy for age discrimination in the workplace *per se*. So, she considered whether the facts suggested some other common law cause of action.

Lane considered, and rejected, breach-of-contract claims. First, like many other states, Florida is an "employment-at-will" jurisdiction, and courts will not infer unwritten employment obligations.[36] Fiona had no written contract with Full Moon and consequently had no contract claim. Otis, on the other hand, had been a party to a three-year contract. But Lane discovered that Otis' contract gave him no right of renewal. At worst, Full Moon had terminated Otis' contract a few weeks prematurely. Because Full Moon had paid Otis for the weeks remaining on the contract, he suffered no damages as a result of his premature termination.[37]

Lane next considered possible tort law remedies. She recalled that, in 1999, Belcher had told Otis that he had job security if he stayed with Full Moon and could "retire" as manager of the Jacksonville store. In relying on Belcher's representation, Otis had passed up a lucrative partnership with Izzy Able in Key Largo and, instead, signed a three-year contract with Full Moon. Otis felt Full Moon had lured him into staying with the company through fraud. The elements of a common law fraud action under Florida law are:

---

[36]*See, e.g., Smith v. Piezo Technology and Professional Adm'rs,* 427 So.2d 182, 184 (Fla. 1983) (employment relationship that is either discretionary or for indefinite term can be terminated for any reason). *See generally* Wrongful Discharge of an At-Will Employee, 31 Am. Jur. Trials 317 (2004).

[37]Rule 8(a)(2) requires that a plaintiff allege a "statement of the claim showing that the pleader is *entitled to relief*," and Rule 8(a)(3) requires that a plaintiff allege "the *relief* the pleader seeks." Unless Otis could allege that Full Moon's breach entitled him to some remedy, he could not allege a viable claim for breach of contract.

1.   The defendant (or its agent) made a false representation of fact;

2.   The defendant knew the representation was false when made;

3.   The defendant made the false representation to induce the plaintiff to rely; and

4.   The plaintiff justifiably relied on the false representation to his detriment.[38]

Further, Otis could assert his fraud claim against *both* Full Moon and the actual agent of fraud, Belcher.[39]

As mentioned earlier, when Lane filed the complaint, she would be certifying that all claims were "warranted by existing law or by a nonfrivolous argument for the extension, modification, or reversal of existing law. . . ."[40] Consider the following problem related to Otis' fraud claim.

---

[38]*Gandy v. Trans World Computer Technology Group*, 787 So.2d 116 (Fla. Dt. Ct. App. 2001).

[39]*See, e.g., Salit v. Ruden, McClosky, Smith, Schuster & Russell*, 742 So.2d 381 (Fla. Dt. Ct. App. 1999) (employer liable for intentional torts of employee committed within the scope of employment).

[40]Fed. R. Civ. P. 11(b)(2).

Question 1.1

Assume that Lane discovers a Florida Supreme Court decision issued in 1978 stating that a fraud claim cannot be based on a promise that contradicts the terms of a written contract. Lane believes the Court's position is both harsh and obsolescent and also believes that Otis' complaint presents a compelling case for changing precedent. However, she can discover no precedent signaling the Supreme Court is ready to recede from its older decision.

A.   Will Lane violate Rule 11 if she asserts the fraud claim in the complaint? Why or why not?

B.   Must Lane point out this adverse precedent to the trial court in her complaint? To answer this question, consider Model Rule of Professional Conduct 3.3:

(a) A lawyer shall not knowingly:

. . .

(3) Fail to disclose to the tribunal legal authority in the controlling jurisdiction known to the lawyer to be directly adverse to the position of the client and not disclosed by opposing counsel. . . .

C.   Regardless of Lane's legal obligation to notify the court of this adverse precedent, can you think of a strategic reason why she might want to?

Lane next considered the implications of the letter terminating Otis, in which Full Moon's president insinuated Otis might be connected to criminal acts involving missing store inventory. Lane's research revealed that the common law tort of libel generally requires:

1.   A written statement;

2.   Made by the defendant;

3.   Containing false and defamatory statements of fact concerning the plaintiff; which are

4.   Communicated to a third party.

Task 1.3

Review Otis' letter of termination and Otis' discussion of the comments made in that letter. See *supra* page 11. Why, in light of her obligations under Rule 11(b)(3), might Lane decline to assert a claim for libel? Make sure you focus on the specific elements constituting libel and the evidence presently available to Lane.

For reasons you will have recognized when considering Task 1.3, Lane concluded she lacked a good faith basis for alleging a claim of libel. That meant she would draft a complaint alleging statutory claims of age discrimination and retaliation, and a common law claim for fraud. To complete her factual and legal research, Lane prepared a table summarizing the claims she intended to allege against each of the defendants in the Olmans' complaint:[41]

---

[41]This same type of table of parties and claims is also valuable when, in your study of Civil Procedure, you have to apply the rules to a complex set of facts. For example, a table is helpful when applying the rules of claim and party joinder, and when determining whether there is a jurisdictional basis for multiple claims and parties.

Lane also had to address the issue of "joinder" when deciding which parties and claims might be included in the Olmans' suit. We have deferred discussion of joinder to Chapter 6. If you are interested in how the joinder rules permitted Lane to assert all these claims in one complaint, feel free to preview these materials.

Plaintiff	Defendant	Claim
Otis Olman	Full Moon	Discrimination under ADEA
Otis Olman	Full Moon	Retaliation under ADEA
Otis Olman	Full Moon	Discrimination under FCRA
Otis Olman	Full Moon	Retaliation under FCRA
Otis Olman	Full Moon and Bruce Belcher	Common Law Fraud
Fiona Olman	Full Moon	Discrimination under ADEA
Fiona Olman	Full Moon	Discrimination under FCRA

D.   Final Considerations Before Drafting the Complaint

Having fulfilled her obligation to investigate the Olmans' claims, Lane felt confident she could draft a sound complaint. But Lane had three final decisions to make before drafting and filing the complaint. First, she had to decide upon the best geographic locale for the suit. Should she bring suit in Full Moon's home state of Georgia where employment decisions affecting the Olmans had been made, or in the Olmans' home state of Florida where they had worked? Second, Lane had to decide whether to file suit in a federal or state court. Third, she had to determine the proper time to file the suit.

1.   Determining Jurisdiction and Venue

In selecting the geographic locale for the suit, Lane had to consider issues of *personal jurisdiction* and *venue*. In deciding whether to file suit in federal or state court, Lane had to consider the issue of *subject matter jurisdiction*. Lane's analyses of these issues can be found in Appendix B. Those of you who have already studied the topics of personal jurisdiction, venue, and subject matter jurisdiction in Civil Procedure are ready to examine the appendix materials. Those of you who have not yet studied these topics should defer consideration of Appendix B until later in your course.

For reasons explored more fully in the appendix, Lane chose to sue in a federal court located in Jacksonville, Florida, where the Olmans had been employed by Full Moon and where they currently lived. Specifically, she chose to file suit in the "United States District Court for the Middle District of Florida, Jacksonville Division."

2.   Determining the Time to File Suit

The final question Lane needed to consider was *when* to file the Olmans' suit. As mentioned earlier, the Olmans had to "exhaust" administrative remedies before suing Full Moon for employment discrimination. On Lane's advice, the Olmans had previously filed claims with the governmental agency that administers employment discrimination laws.[42] The administrative process was now complete,[43] and the Olmans' age discrimination claims were ripe for filing in federal court.[44] Notice that Otis had not been required to exhaust any administrative proceeding or other pre-suit requirement before filing his state law claim for fraud. As is typical of most common-law tort claims, Otis was permitted to file suit for fraud once he was injured. However, Lane had sensibly deferred filing Otis' fraud claim until *all* the Olmans' claims were ready for filing and she could join them in one complaint.

The other time limit applicable to the Olmans' suit was the relevant *statute of limitations*. Statutes of limitation typically give an aggrieved party a specific period of time after wrongful conduct has occurred in which to file suit. In the case of most legal claims, this window of opportunity extends for several years. For example, the statute of limitations governing Otis' fraud claim gave him four years after he was defrauded to file suit. However, a lawyer *cannot* assume that the relevant statute of limitations provides the luxury of waiting years before filing suit. Federal employment discrimination laws vividly illustrate how short statutes of limitations can be. According to federal law, the Olmans had only 90 days in which to file suit once administrative proceedings were exhausted.[45] This

---

[42]As mentioned earlier, the federal agency in charge of the Olmans' age discrimination claims is the Equal Employment Opportunity Commission or "EEOC."

[43]*See infra* note 45.

[44]Based on Rule 9(c), Lane would allege in her complaint that these "conditions precedent" had been satisfied. *See infra* at p. 37.

[45]29 U.S.C. § 626(e).

90-day limitation began to run on the date the federal agency considering the Olmans' claims issued them a "right to sue" letter.[46] Lane had recently received a copy of this "right to sue" letter and would need to file suit expeditiously.

A Concluding Note Concerning:
SOURCES OF PROCEDURAL LAW

As the Olmans' case illustrates, a lawyer must litigate with numerous sources and types of law in mind. We have already identified the substantive law underlying the Olmans' dispute, including statutory provisions, administrative rules, and common law. But lawyers also have to juggle numerous sources of *procedural* law. In a federal court suit, applicable procedural law may include:

- Federal constitutional provisions (*e.g.,* the due process clause requirements);

- Federal statutory provisions (*e.g.,* jurisdictional and venue statutes);

- Federal rules of civil procedure;

- Federal rules of evidence (to be discussed later); and occasionally

- Judge-made procedural law. *See, e.g., Chambers v. NASCO, Inc.,* 501 U.S. 32 (1991) (recognizing trial court's inherent power to assess sanctions for bad faith conduct during litigation).

To all these must be added two other sources of procedural law that can be important in litigation. First, there are local rules of civil procedure. Federal Rule 83 states that "each district court . . . may . . . make and amend rules governing its practice." *See also* 28 U.S.C. § 2071 (recognizing right

---

[46]When the EEOC issues a "right-to-sue" letter, it means that (1) the agency has declined to file suit against an employer, and (2) the employee is now free to file his own suit. A right-to-sue letter does not mean the EEOC has determined that an employee's charge has or lacks merit. For a variety of reasons, the EEOC files suit in only a small fraction of the complaints it considers. When the EEOC does occasionally elect to sue an employer, it is usually because the issue raised by the employee has important policy implications.

of local district courts to prescribe additional procedural rules). According to Rule 83, these local rules must be "consistent with" the federal rules. Second, many federal judges adopt standing orders for civil cases that set out procedures unique to that judge. Such standing orders also should be consistent with the federal rules. A lawyer should *always* become familiar with both the local rules in the district in which a case is filed and any standing orders of the individual judge assigned to the case.

We will occasionally refer to local rules promulgated by the United States District Court for the Middle District of Florida. Though knowledge of these local rules is not important in your Civil Procedure course, appreciation of their role will better prepare you for the task of rule management in practice.

CHAPTER TWO:
COMMENCING THE LAWSUIT

Chapter Rule References: *3, 8, 9, 10, 11,* 15, 26, 54

A.   The Complaint

Federal rules governing the drafting of a complaint are indulgent. Rule 8 requires a "short and plain" statement of the court's subject-matter jurisdiction, a "short and plain" statement of the plaintiff's claims, and a demand for relief. Rule 10 sketches a format for the complaint that requires little more than a standard heading at the beginning, followed by numbered paragraphs containing the plaintiff's allegations.

This approach is called "notice" pleading. The plaintiff need only give the defendant general notice of the events prompting the suit, the legal claims the plaintiff wants to assert, and the remedy sought. There is no requirement that the plaintiff allege specific legal theories or even the elements of a claim.[1] As Rule 8 states, "no technical forms of pleading are required," and "all pleadings shall be . . . construed as to do substantial justice."[2]

The Supreme Court has illustrated the simplicity of a complaint. Official Form 9[3] demonstrates how a routine personal injury action can be alleged in a few paragraphs:[4]

> 2.   On June 1, 1936, in a public highway called Boylston Street in Boston, Massachusetts, defendant negligently drove a motor vehicle against plaintiff who was then crossing said highway.

Iqbal — plausibility

---

[1]*See Kirksey v. R.J. Reynolds Tobacco Co.*, 168 F.3d 1039, 1041 (7th Cir. 1999) ("the courts keep reminding plaintiffs that they don't to have to file long complaints, don't have to plead facts, don't have to plead legal theories"); *Sparrow v. United Air Lines, Inc.*, 216 F.3d 1111, 1113 (D.C. Cir. 2000) (plaintiff did not have to "make out a prima facie case of discrimination" in his complaint).

[2]Rule 8(e)(1), (f).

[3]Rule 84 confirms that these sample forms "are sufficient under the rules and are intended to indicate the simplicity and brevity of statement which the rules contemplate."

[4]Paragraph 1 of this form also contains an allegation of federal court subject matter jurisdiction.

3.   As a result plaintiff was thrown down and had his leg broken and was otherwise injured, was prevented from transacting his business, suffered great pain of body and mind, and incurred expenses for medical attention and hospitalization in the sum of one thousand dollars.

Wherefore plaintiff demands judgment against defendant in the sum of _____ dollars and costs.

This model complaint does not specifically allege all the elements of the tort of negligence (*e.g.,* duty, breach, causation, and injury). It does not even allege what the defendant did that was negligent. Was he speeding, intoxicated, or driving against a red light? It does not give any information about the time of the accident or the conditions at the scene of the accident. The greatest detail concerns the plaintiff's injuries and tells no more than the plaintiff suffered a broken leg and "other" injuries, and was prevented from transacting some unidentified "business." According to the Supreme Court, these short paragraphs satisfy Rule 8's requirement that the defendant be given notice of the facts underlying plaintiff's suit and the relief he seeks.

With Form 9 as an example, Lane could probably state the Olmans' case in a page or two. The gist of their suit was this: Otis and Fiona lost their management positions at the Jacksonville store because of their age. When Otis complained, Full Moon retaliated by firing him. In addition, Full Moon reneged on its promise to provide Otis job security. The plaintiffs wanted money for their losses and additional money to punish Full Moon.[5]

Although Rule 8 seemed to endorse a "minimalist" approach to pleading, Lane followed a different approach. Here is the complaint she filed:[6]

---

[5]*See, e.g., Bennett v. Schmidt,* 153 F.3d 516, 518 (7th Cir. 1998) (an employment discrimination complaint alleging, "I was turned down for a job because of my race" would satisfy federal pleading rules.)

[6]A note about the form documents we have drafted is in order. As we mentioned earlier, in addition to the federal rules, litigation is also governed by local rules for the particular federal court in which an action is filed. Those local rules need to be consistent with the federal rules, but they also provide important additional detail about how you should conduct litigation. For example, they may specify the form of certain documents such as the size of margins or line spacing. We have *not* made a conscious effort to comply with any particular court's local rules. In practice, you should always consult the local rules to ensure that your drafting, and general litigation conduct, comports with them.

**IN THE UNITED STATES DISTRICT COURT
FOR THE MIDDLE DISTRICT OF FLORIDA
JACKSONVILLE DIVISION**

OTIS AND FIONA OLMAN,

       Plaintiffs,

vs.   Case No. _____

FULL MOON SPORTS, INC.,
& BRUCE BELCHER

       Defendants.

COMPLAINT [AND DEMAND FOR JURY TRIAL]

[Preliminary Allegations]

1. This is an action based upon the Age Discrimination in Employment Act, 29 U.S.C. § 621 *et seq.* ("ADEA"), the Florida Civil Rights Act, Fla. Stat. § 760.01 *et seq.*, and Florida common law.

2. The court has jurisdiction of all ADEA claims under 28 U.S.C. § 1331 and 29 U.S.C. § 216, and supplemental jurisdiction of all state law claims under 28 U.S.C. § 1367. The court also has jurisdiction based on 28 U.S.C. § 1332. The Plaintiffs are both citizens of Florida, Defendant Full Moon is incorporated in Delaware and has its principal place of business in Georgia, and Defendant Bruce Belcher is a citizen of Connecticut. Each of the Plaintiffs seeks more than $75,000 in damages, exclusive of interest and costs, from each of the Defendants.

3. The Plaintiffs have satisfied <u>all conditions</u> precedent to bringing this action under the ADEA and the Florida Civil Rights Act. Specifically, Plaintiffs filed <u>timely</u> claims with the EEOC and the Florida Human Relations Commission on October 1, 2003, and the EEOC subsequently issued Plaintiffs a right-to-sue letter on April 1, 2004.

[Parties]

4. Otis Olman ("Olman") is former manager of the "Full Moon Outdoor Center," a retail sporting goods store located in Jacksonville, Florida, and owned by defendant, Full Moon Sports, Inc. ("Full Moon"). Olman was

[37]

employed by Full Moon from 1982 through August, 2003, and served as store manager of the Jacksonville store from 1990 to 2003. At the time of his termination, Olman was 53 years old.

5. Fiona Olman ("Fiona Olman") is the wife of Otis Olman. She was employed by Full Moon at the Jacksonville store from 1995 through August, 2003. From 1998 through 2003, she served as manager of the store's kayak department. At the time of her termination, Fiona was 49 years old.

6. Full Moon Sports, Inc. is a Delaware corporation that owns and operates retail sporting goods stores throughout the United States. It is a wholly-owned subsidiary of Mizar, Inc. ("Mizar"). Full Moon's principal place of business and executive headquarters are in Atlanta, Georgia.

7. Bruce Belcher ("Belcher") was employed by Full Moon as regional manager of all retail stores located in the states of Florida, Georgia, North Carolina, and South Carolina from 1999 through early 2004.

General Allegations

8. Olman began working for Full Moon in 1982, when he became assistant manager for its store in Burlington, Vermont. Olman was promoted to store manager in 1985.

9. In 1990, Full Moon asked Olman to become manager of its store in Jacksonville, Florida. At the time, the Jacksonville store was a marginally-profitable business.

10. Olman accepted the manager's position at the Jacksonville store.

11. Under Olman's management, the Jacksonville store became a highly-profitable store which featured high-end sporting goods, instruction in popular activities like sea kayaking, and guided outdoor adventures.

12. In 1995, Fiona Olman began working for the Jacksonville store. In 1998, she became manager of the store's kayak department when its existing manager moved to another state.

13. In 2000, Full Moon was acquired by Mizar. Mizar made numerous changes in Full Moon's management and began advertising and selling "extreme" sporting goods in many Full Moon stores.

Rule 10(c) states that allegations in a pleading are to be made in "numbered paragraphs," and that each paragraph "shall be limited as far as practicable to a statement of a single set of circumstances." As you will see later, this enumeration of allegations in separate paragraphs is useful when the parties or the court needs to refer to specific allegations. For example, defendants usually respond to each numbered allegation when answering the complaint. *See infra* pp. 77–82.

One approach to pleading, not set forth in the rules, is "to tell the plaintiffs' story" in an introductory section. Ask yourself: Does this section tell a compelling story? Does it provide sufficient detail? Too much detail?

14. In 2000, defendant Belcher was made regional manager of Full Moon's southeast region, which included the Jacksonville store.

15. When Belcher first met Olman in August, 2000, he admitted to being very impressed by Olman's work at the Jacksonville store. Belcher asked Olman to sign a three-year contract to continue as store manager.

16. In prior years as store manager for Full Moon, Olman had no formal contract with the company.

17. At the time Belcher proposed the contract, Olman was considering a business offer from a local entrepreneur. The entrepreneur offered Olman a one-half partnership interest in a new business to be located in Key Largo, Florida, a proposal Olman believed would be highly profitable.

18. Olman told Belcher of his interest in the Key Largo business partnership.

19. With the intent of inducing Olman to remain as manager for the Jacksonville store and decline the Key Largo partnership offer, Belcher promised Olman "great" job security and also promised him that he could "retire" as manager of the Jacksonville store if he liked.

20. In reliance on Belcher's promise of job security, Olman agreed to remain as store manager, executed the contract with Full Moon, and declined to join in the Key Largo partnership.

21. Shortly after Olman agreed to remain as manager of the Full Moon store, the company opened an "extreme sports" department in the Jacksonville store. To run the department, Full Moon hired Sid Shockley, an extreme sports athlete with no retail sales experience.

22. From 2000 until mid-2003, Olman trained Shockley in retail sales and management skills.

23. In July, 2003, Belcher informed Olman that Full Moon intended to implement a corporate downsizing. As part of this downsizing, Full Moon's overall workforce would be reduced by 20%, and the Jacksonville store would terminate 10 employees. Belcher sought Olman's advice in implementing the downsizing. Belcher also asked Olman if he was interested in managing some other Full Moon store.

24. Olman subsequently recommended to Belcher that the company retain its most experienced employees because of their greater productivity and loyalty to the store. Olman also advised Belcher he was not interested in managing another Full Moon store.

25. On August 5, 2003, Belcher informed Olman that Full Moon had decided to terminate many of its more experienced employees at the Jacksonville store, including several employees over the age of 40. One of these terminated employees was Fiona Olman.

26. Belcher also informed Olman that he was being re-assigned to the position of manager of the camping department, and his salary would be reduced from $85,000 to $45,000. Belcher stated that Full Moon intended to replace Olman with Sid Shockley, the 32-year-old manager of the extreme sports department.

27. Olman immediately contacted his former regional manager for advice. This advisor was now employed in Full Moon's executive headquarters. Olman was told that "Full Moon has changed," the market for extreme sporting goods required "younger" employees, and it might be time for Olman to "move on."

28. Olman protested Full Moon's discriminatory downsizing decisions in a letter to company president, Bertie Lurch, and told Lurch he would take legal action if Full Moon did not cease its discrimination. Two weeks later Olman received a letter of termination from Lurch. The letter offered severance pay to Olman in exchange for his signing a liability release. Olman did not sign the release.

29. Immediately prior to Olman's termination, newly-designated store manager Shockley told store employees that Olman was "too old" to be running the store and that he was being "put out to pasture" through his demotion to the store's camping department. Regional manager Belcher was aware of Shockley's improper behavior but did nothing to correct it.

30. Since their termination by Full Moon, Otis and Fiona Olman have obtained other employment in the Jacksonville area but have suffered a substantial reduction in compensation and other employment benefits.

Rule 10(c) permits a party to "adopt by reference" matters alleged in another part of a pleading. Notice how Lane simplifies the pleading of specific counts by adopting prior allegations in the introductory fact section.

COUNT ONE:
Disparate Treatment under the ADEA
(Otis Olman vs. Full Moon)

31. Plaintiff Otis Olman re-alleges paragraphs 8–30.

32. At the time of Full Moon's corporate downsizing, Olman was 53 years of age, qualified for retention as store manager, and was interested in remaining as store manager.

33. Notwithstanding Olman's qualification and interest, he was replaced by a 32-year-old assistant manager and eventually terminated.

34. Full Moon's decision to demote and terminate Olman was motivated by age-discriminatory animus and stereotypes, including those of assistant manager Shockley and regional manager Belcher.

35. Upon information and belief, Full Moon's discriminatory action against Olman was part of a pattern and practice of age discrimination affecting company-wide downsizing.

36. Full Moon's discriminatory treatment of Olman was in reckless disregard of his rights under the ADEA.

WHEREFORE, Plaintiff Otis Olman demands of Full Moon back pay, future pay and lost earnings, liquidated damages of double back pay, prejudgment interest, costs, attorney's fees, and any other relief the court deems appropriate.

COUNT TWO:
Retaliation under the ADEA
(Otis Olman vs. Full Moon)

37. Plaintiff Otis Olman re-alleges paragraphs 8–30.

38. Upon learning of his demotion from store manager and other downsizing decisions in violation of the ADEA, Olman objected to Full Moon's discriminatory actions in a letter to the company's president.

39. Olman's protest was made in good faith based on objectively reasonable information indicating Full Moon was violating the ADEA in the course of its downsizing.

Such "Wherefore" paragraphs are a standard method for demanding relief under Rule 8(a)(3).

Although Rule 54(c) states that the Court "shall" grant all relief to which a party is entitled regardless of whether the relief is demanded in the pleading, most lawyers allege the relief sought with great care.

Rule 10(b) requires that "each claim founded upon a separate transaction or occurrence" be stated in a "separate count." In practice, however, most lawyers plead separate counts for each *legal* cause of action, even though those separate counts arise out of the same transaction or occurrence.

Notice how Lane qualified this allegation. Can you see how the language "upon information and belief" responds to Lane's obligation under Rule 11(b)(3)?

Notice how Count One demands specific remedies authorized by the ADEA. These remedies are discussed in greater detail in Chapter One.

Take a moment to review the elements of a cause of action for retaliation under the ADEA. *See* Appendix A. Can you see how Lane has drafted Count II to show all elements are present?

40. In direct response to Olman's good faith objection, Full Moon terminated him.

WHEREFORE, Plaintiff Otis Olman demands of Full Moon back pay, future pay and lost earnings, liquidated damages of double back pay, prejudgment interest, costs, attorney's fees, and any other relief the court deems appropriate.

COUNT THREE:
Disparate Treatment under the Florida Civil Rights Act
(Otis Olman vs. Full Moon)

41. Plaintiff Otis Olman re-alleges paragraphs 8–30.

42. The previously-described discriminatory action of Full Moon against Olman violates the Florida Civil Rights Act, Fla. Stat. § 760.01 *et seq.*

WHEREFORE, Plaintiff Otis Olman demands of Full Moon compensatory damages, punitive damages, prejudgment interest, costs, attorney's fees, and any other relief the court deems appropriate.

> Again, notice how the demand for relief in Count III reflects the remedies authorized by applicable state law. Can you identify the difference in remedies authorized by federal law in Count I and state law in Count III?

COUNT FOUR:
Retaliation under the Florida Civil Rights Act
(Otis Olman vs. Full Moon)

43. Plaintiff Otis Olman re-alleges paragraphs 8–30.

44. The previously-described retaliatory action of Full Moon against Olman violates the Florida Civil Rights Act, Fla. Stat. § 760.01 *et seq.*

WHEREFORE, Plaintiff Otis Olman demands of Full Moon compensatory damages, punitive damages, prejudgment interest, costs, attorney's fees, and any other relief the court deems appropriate.

COUNT FIVE:
Common Law Fraud
(Otis Olman vs. Full Moon and Belcher)

45. Plaintiff Otis Olman re-alleges paragraphs 8–30.

> The allegations of fraud in Count V must satisfy the more demanding pleading requirements of Rule 9(b). Do they?

46. In August 2000, Bruce Belcher, acting as regional manager and agent of Full Moon, promised Olman he could remain as manager of the Jacksonville store until he retired. These promises were made for the purpose of inducing Olman to remain as store manager and dissuading Olman from entering into the business partnership in Key Largo, Florida.

47. At the time Belcher made these promises, he knew that neither he nor Full Moon had any intention of honoring them.

48. Belcher made these promises with the intent that Olman rely on them.

49. Olman reasonably relied on Belcher's promises.

50. As a result of Olman's reliance, he forfeited the opportunity to be a partner in a successful business venture.

> Paragraphs 47 & 48 allege defendant Belcher's intentions. What is Lane's factual basis for imputing intention? Are these allegations consistent with Lane's Rule 11 obligations?

WHEREFORE, Plaintiff Otis Olman demands of Full Moon and its agent, Bruce Belcher, compensatory damages, punitive damages, prejudgment interest, costs, attorney's fees, and any other relief the court deems appropriate.

COUNT SIX:
Disparate Treatment under the ADEA
(Fiona Olman vs. Full Moon)

51. Plaintiff Fiona Olman re-alleges paragraphs 8–30.

52. At the time of Full Moon's corporate downsizing, Fiona Olman was 49 years of age, qualified for retention as manager of the store's kayak department, and interested in remaining in that position.

53. Notwithstanding Fiona Olman's qualification and interest, she was replaced by a subordinate employee aged 28.

54. Full Moon's decision to demote and terminate Fiona Olman was motivated by age-discriminatory animus and stereotypes.

55. Upon information and belief, Full Moon's discriminatory action against Fiona Olman was part of a pattern and practice of age discrimination affecting company-wide downsizing.

56. Full Moon's discriminatory treatment of Fiona Olman was in reckless disregard of her rights under the ADEA.

WHEREFORE, Plaintiff Fiona Olman demands of Full Moon back pay, future pay and lost earnings, liquidated damages of double back pay, prejudgment interest, costs, attorney's fees, and any other relief the court deems appropriate.

COUNT SEVEN:
Disparate Treatment under the Florida Civil Rights Act
(Fiona Olman vs. Full Moon)

57. Plaintiff Fiona Olman re-alleges paragraphs 8–30.

58. The previously-described discriminatory action of Full Moon against Fiona Olman violates the Florida Civil Rights Act, Fla. Stat. § 760.01 *et seq.*

WHEREFORE, Plaintiff Fiona Olman demands of Full Moon compensatory damages, punitive damages, prejudgment interest, costs, attorney's fees, and any other relief the court deems appropriate.

Jury Demand

Plaintiffs Otis and Fiona Olman demand a jury trial on all claims.

> Rule 38(b) permitted Lane to demand a jury trial in her complaint.

Respectfully submitted,

_____

Eleanor Lane
Lane & Quincy, P.A.
Trial Counsel for Plaintiffs
Fla. Bar No. 0937304
100 Cook Street
Jacksonville, Florida 32210
(904) 555-5364
Fax: (904) 555-3307

> Among other things, Lane's signature implicates her ethical obligations under Rule 11. Notice that Rule 11(a) does not require that the plaintiff or defendant also sign the pleadings.

Dated: May 1, 2004

B.   Pleading Beyond the Notice Requirement of Rule 8

Could Lane have drafted a simpler, shorter complaint and still satisfied her obligations under the federal rules? Yes. In fact, an appreciable number of lawyers prefer a "minimalist" approach to pleading and disapprove of the amount of detail contained in Lane's complaint. There are sound arguments for adopting a minimalist approach, particularly when the facts of a dispute are unclear. First, it might be unwise to commit to a detailed version of the facts in the complaint. Courts tend to assume that parties can prove their allegations. When they cannot, they may lose credibility. Second, detailed factual allegations can unintentionally provide fodder for pretrial challenges and discovery disputes.[7] This can undermine a client's ability to obtain expeditious, cost-effective relief. Third, a lawyer must always keep in mind her obligation to plead in good faith under Rule 11. Her good faith obligation takes precedence over the desire to tell a compelling story in the complaint. Fourth, the minimalist approach may provide a needed check on lawyers' tendency to draft verbose documents.

A lawyer's decision whether to follow a more minimalist approach to pleading will usually reflect a combination of factors, including her philosophy of pleading and the nature of the case. Lane obviously did not follow the minimalist approach to pleading in the Olmans' complaint. We will next examine Lane's reasons for pleading more detail than required by Rule 8. As you consider these reasons, ask whether they might still be addressed using the minimalist approach. Your Civil Procedure professor likely has well-thought-out views on this question.

---

[7]In Chapter 3 we will see how Lane's detailed pleading resulted in at least one unintended consequence.

Tactical Tip ✍

Relying on Form Books or "Model" Complaints

Whatever your philosophy of pleading, it is best not to rely uncritically on "model" pleadings drafted by others. There are many sources for model pleadings, including commercial "form" books, pleadings developed by your associates or partners in previous litigation, and, increasingly, pleadings found in electronic databases of actual court filings. These pleadings can provide useful guidance when you are considering what claims and remedies to allege, and can also provide valuable clues to drafting. But there may be significant shortcomings to relying on these form pleadings. First, they will seldom be tailored to the specific facts and legal issues presented in your case. Second, too often they are poorly drafted and inculcate poor lessons about legal writing.

If you have access to high quality forms (for example, those provided by an experienced lawyer with writing skill), you are fortunate. If not, develop your own. While it may take a bit of courage in the beginning, try to draft pleadings based on your own sound knowledge of the law and the facts. And trust your own judgment about good legal writing. Write simply, clearly, and persuasively, while avoiding legalese. You can often improve the quality of "model" pleadings and take pride in your own authorship.

Lane knew from experience that the complaint serves many functions during the litigation process, few of which are suggested by Rule 8. Lane drafted the Olmans' complaint with these functions in mind. They include:

- Preparing for the defendants' anticipated responses;

- Preserving the opportunity to fully litigate the plaintiffs' case, at a minimum of procedural cost;

- Preserving clients' legal rights;

- Pinning down the defendants;

- Telling a "good story" to the court, the defendants, and (perhaps) the public; and

[46]

•   Complying with a lawyer's ethical obligations.

Let's briefly examine each of these considerations. To do this, we need to think ahead to aspects of the litigation process you will study more fully later in Civil Procedure.

1.   Preparing for the Defendants' Anticipated Responses

A useful litigation tactic is to consider how you would respond to the complaint if you represented the defendant. Lane was aware that defendants in civil rights suits commonly file a Rule 12(b)(6) motion seeking to dismiss one or more of the plaintiff's counts[8] because they fail "to state a claim upon which relief can be granted." As we will see in the next chapter, a Rule 12(b)(6) motion enforces Rule 8(a)'s requirement that the complaint allege a "claim showing the pleader is entitled to relief." Lane was also aware that, despite the Supreme Court's unequivocal conclusion that Rule 8(a) permits "notice" pleading, many courts continue to require "heightened pleading" in civil rights suits.[9]

Anticipating a possible Rule 12(b)(6) motion, Lane alleged greater detail than is required by notice pleading. She alleged facts specifically supporting each element of the claims in the complaint, i.e., she pled "*prima facie*" claims, even though Rule 8(a) does not require this.[10] Not only did Lane want all counts to survive a motion to dismiss, if possible she wanted to *preclude* such an attack and the needless time and cost her client would incur in responding to it.

---

[8]In the Guide, the terms "claim" and "count" are used synonymously; occasionally, we also use the term "cause of action."

[9]*See, e.g.,* Christopher M. Fairman, The Myth of Notice Pleading, 45 ARIZ. L. REV. 987, 996, 1027-33 (2003) (noting persistence of heightened pleading requirements among many federal circuits notwithstanding the Supreme Court's contrary interpretation of Rule 8(a)(2)).

[10]In *Swierkiewicz v. Sorema N.A.*, 534 U.S. 506, 512 (2002), the Supreme Court specifically held that an ADEA plaintiff did not have to allege a *prima facie* claim of age discrimination in his complaint. According to the Court, Rule 8's "simplified notice pleading standard relies on liberal discovery rules and summary judgment motions to define disputed facts and issues and to dispose of unmeritorious claims." *See also Conley v. Gibson*, 355 U.S. 41, 45-6 (1957) ("a complaint should not be dismissed for failure to state a claim unless it appears beyond all doubt that the plaintiff can prove no set of facts in support of his claim which would entitle him to relief.")

Tactical Tip ✍

Alleging the Elements of a Cause of Action

When pleading a cause of action or "count," think about a table. In order to stand, a table must have all its legs. The "legs" of a count can be envisioned as the elements of the cause of action you are trying to plead. To show the court you have an adequately supported table, you may want to allege that *all* legs exist. If your count omits a leg, the defendant may argue that the table must fall, *i.e.,* that the cause of action should be dismissed for "failure to state a claim upon which relief can be granted." Rule 12(b)(6). While not literally required by Rule 8, recital of all the elements may help forestall a time-consuming motion to dismiss.

2.   **Preserving the Opportunity to Fully Litigate the Case, with a Minimum of Procedural Cost**

Lane knew that the scope of her pleadings would be important when she used other procedural rules later in the suit. Specifically, a more comprehensive complaint would facilitate her efforts to obtain the broadest *discovery* and the most comprehensive *relief* for the Olmans.

Rule 26(b)(1) permits parties to obtain discovery of any matter "relevant to the claim or defense of any party." When this limiting language was added to Rule 26, the drafters stated that "[t]he rule . . . signals to the court that it has authority to confine discovery to the claims and defenses asserted in the pleadings, and signals parties that they have no entitlement to discovery to develop new claims or defenses not already identified in the pleadings."[11]   So, Lane wanted a comprehensive complaint to support broad discovery.[12]   For example, Lane made sure to allege that Full Moon's discriminatory treatment of the Olmans was part of a "pattern or practice" of discrimination affecting company-wide downsizing. This allegation would provide a pleading foundation for

---

[11]2000 Advisory Committee Note to Rule 26.

[12]Of course, this rule is a two-way street. To the extent a plaintiff is concerned about broad discovery directed at it, it may have an incentive to plead in a minimalist way. For example, if Lane had pled that the Olmans suffered from "extreme emotional distress, pain and suffering" as a consequence of their termination, they might make their mental condition and history fair game for discovery. *See infra* Chapter 5.

inquiring into the company's treatment of other older workers, which Full Moon might otherwise contend had no relevance to the Olmans' individual claims.[13]

A more detailed complaint would also support more comprehensive relief for the Olmans. Rule 54(c) tells the court that "every final judgment shall grant the relief to which the party . . . is entitled, even if the party has not demanded such relief in the party's pleadings." But a defendant can still object to the award of a remedy not alleged in the complaint by arguing that it was unaware during discovery or trial that the particular remedy was in issue. If lack of notice sufficiently prejudices the defendant's opportunity to argue the merits of the remedy, the remedy may be denied.[14] Consequently, Lane made a habit of specifically alleging every form of relief her clients were entitled to and wished to obtain.

Finally, Lane knew there was a chance she would want to amend the complaint at a later date, possibly adding new claims.[15] A complaint that contains only minimal detail can provide the defendant a basis for objecting to later amendment of the complaint. For example, if Lane sought to add a new claim after the statute of limitations applicable to the claim expired, she would need to show that the new claim "arose out of the conduct . . . set forth or attempted to be set forth in the original pleading" in order to circumvent the limitations bar.[16] Consequently, the more comprehensive the allegations in the original

---

[13]Similarly, the scope of a party's duty to provide "mandatory disclosure" of information under Rule 26(a) is determined by what is alleged in the pleadings. *See, e.g.,* Rule 26(a)(1)(A) (duty to disclose persons with discoverable information that party may use to supports its "claims or defenses").

[14]*See Albermarle Paper Co. v. Moody,* 422 U.S. 405, 424 (1975) (a party may not be "entitled" to a specific form of relief under Rule 54(c) if its conduct of litigation has prejudiced the opposing party).

[15]*See infra* Chapter 6, Part B (discussing Lane's later consideration of amending the complaint).

[16]*See* Rule 15(c). For example, in *Marsh v. Coleman Co.,* 774 F. Supp. 608 (D. Kan. 1991), a plaintiff suing under the ADEA was prohibited from amending his complaint to add a fraud claim, even though his termination led to both the ADEA and the fraud claims. According to the court, the original complaint failed to give the defendant notice that fraud might be an issue in the case.

complaint, the better disposed Lane would be to argue that an amended claim "arose" out of those allegations.[17]

A more detailed complaint would better enable Lane to fully investigate her clients' case and obtain the broadest relief for them. She did not want to find, at some later point in the suit, that a lack of detail in the complaint gave her opponents reason to claim "surprise" and so limit her clients' recovery.

3.   Preserving a Client's Legal Rights

Under a doctrine called "claim preclusion" by federal courts,[18] a plaintiff suing a defendant based on a specific transaction or occurrence must usually assert all legal claims arising out of that transaction or occurrence.[19] If such a claim is neither included in the complaint nor introduced later by amendment, the plaintiff is usually "precluded" from asserting that claim in a later suit. The litigation maxim that captures the concept of claim preclusion is "use it or lose it."

In the Olmans' complaint, Lane asserted all claims related to their termination that had factual and legal support. She did so even though it was possible the Olmans might be fully compensated under a single claim in the complaint, and even though some claims might be weaker than others. Lane knew that if she did not assert all supportable claims, those omitted would likely be lost when the suit was over.

4.   Pinning Down the Defendants

Every allegation in the complaint requires a specific response from the defendant.[20] In this respect, the complaint serves an investigative function by requiring that a defendant admit or deny each alleged fact. Facts admitted by the defendant need not be investigated

---

[17]Broader allegations might also help deter objections to evidence at trial. According to Rule 15(b), when a party presents trial evidence "not raised by the pleadings" it may be objected to if it will "prejudice" an adversary's case.

[18]*See Davis v. Dallas Area Rapid Transit*, 383 F.3d 309, 313 (5th Cir. 2004) (a party is barred from asserting a claim that, *inter alia*, arises from the same transaction or same "nucleus of operative fact" that was the subject of litigation in a prior suit).

[19]*See, e.g., Olmstead v. Amoco Oil Co.*, 725 F.2d 627, 629 (11th Cir. 1984).

[20]Rules 8(b), 10.

during discovery or proven at trial. Lane knew that the more specific the complaint's allegations, the less room a defendant has to avoid admitting matters that are not really in dispute. In other words, the complaint is a useful tool to narrow the scope of issues in dispute.

5.   **Telling a Good Story to the Court, the Defendants, and (Perhaps) the Public**

The complaint is not evidence *per se*[21] and will seldom be seen by the jury. Nonetheless, the complaint can serve an important storytelling function.

To begin with, the complaint will often be read by the court and certainly will be studied by the defendants and their lawyers. The court's first impression of the merits of the suit will usually be derived from the complaint. That impression can influence how the court decides the array of motions typically filed before trial. At the very least, it will set an initial tone for the litigation. In this regard, Lane knew she had a slight advantage under the pleading rules: the Olmans were permitted to narrate their version of the facts in the complaint, while Full Moon and Belcher were largely limited to responding to this narration in terse admissions or denials. *See* Rule 8(b).

So, Lane wanted to use the complaint to preview her story of the Olmans' misfortunes to the court. Lane also knew a strong complaint sends a message to the defendants. It shows that the plaintiffs' lawyer has competently investigated the law and facts before filing suit. The complaint would say something about the strength of the Olmans' case and about the quality of their lawyer. In a fair number of cases, a well-prepared complaint can be the catalyst that settles the suit.

Finally, court files are usually open to inspection by the general public, including the press.[22] A lawyer should assume that what is said in a complaint will be a matter of public record. Consequently, a plaintiff may sometimes allege more in a complaint than is

---

[21]There is one important qualification to this statement. Factual allegations made in pleadings are generally deemed to be "judicial admissions" that bind that party in litigation unless the pleading is amended or withdrawn. *See, e.g., In re Worldcom Inc. Securities Litigation,* 308 F. Supp. 2d 214, 232 (S.D.N.Y. 2004).

[22]*See Nixon v. Warner Communications, Inc.,* 435 U.S. 589, 598 (1978) (recognizing a common-law right to inspect and copy judicial records, subject to discretion of supervising judge to prevent inspection for an "improper purpose").

required by the rules of procedure in order to tell a story that the public will understand.[23] And certainly a lawyer should not allege something in a complaint that she would not want the public to read.

6. Complying with a Lawyer's Ethical Obligations

As discussed earlier, Lane was required by both her professional code and Rule 11 to adequately investigate the facts and law before filing suit. The allegations in the complaint would reflect the results of her pre-suit investigation. Lane was required to sign the complaint, and her signature would certify her compliance with Rule 11. A well-pled complaint could signal that she had conducted the requisite investigation.[24]

Two ethical questions may arise when pleading a case whose facts are uncertain at the time of pleading. First, may a lawyer ethically allege a claim when concrete evidence to support it is not presently available but may be available through formal discovery? Second, may a lawyer allege claims that are factually inconsistent? These questions can be important when, in a case like the Olmans', the plaintiff is alleging that the defendants acted with improper motive but has nothing at the outset of litigation other than suspicion and circumstantial evidence to support allegations of motive.

Rule 11(b)(3) is relevant to the first question. Rule 11(b)(3) permits a lawyer to allege matter that is "likely to have evidentiary support after a reasonable opportunity for further investigation or discovery" provided the complaint "specifically . . . identifie[s]" the matter requiring investigation. Examples of such exploratory pleading are found in paragraphs 35 and 55 of the complaint, where Lane alleges that Full Moon's age discrimination was "part of a pattern and practice of age discrimination affecting company-wide downsizing."

Regarding the second question, Rule 8(e) permits multiple allegations "regardless of consistency," and the inconsistent allegations are not considered "admissions" by the

---

[23]There are limitations on using the complaint for "public advocacy" purposes. For example Rule 11(b)(1) requires that the complaint not be "presented for any improper purpose . . ." In addition, there may be ethical concerns related to using the complaint for publicity. *See, e.g.,* Model Rule 8.4(d) (generally prohibiting conduct prejudicial to the administration of justice).

[24]Lane's obligations under Rule 11 would come into play whenever she "later advocate[d]" any matter alleged in the complaint. For example, if Lane later relied on the complaint in responding to a motion, she would again be certifying to the court that the complaint allegations had proper factual and legal support.

plaintiff.[25] However, Rule 8(e)(2) specifically states that the right to plead inconsistent claims is "subject to the obligations set forth in Rule 11."

Consider how these rules might apply in the question below:

Question 2.1

Count one of the complaint alleges that Otis was terminated because of *age discrimination*, while count two alleges he was terminated in *retaliation* for his letter of protest to Full Moon.

A.   Was Lane obligated under Rule 11(b)(3) to identify these allegations as matters "likely to have evidentiary support after a reasonable opportunity for further investigation or discovery" since she obviously did not know when drafting the complaint exactly *why* Full Moon terminated Otis? Did she do this?

B.   Assume that Fiona Olman recalls that Belcher sometimes made sexist remarks when he visited the Full Moon store. Assume also that Fiona was replaced by a male employee. Based on this information alone, can Lane allege that Fiona's termination was prompted by gender discrimination without violating Rule 11?

C.   Specificity in Pleading

The only "special matters" in the Olmans' complaint *requiring* greater specificity under Rule 9 were the fraud allegations in count four, and possibly some of the remedies the Olmans sought.[26] It is worthwhile considering what, exactly, Rule 9 requires.

---

[25]*See Schott Motorcycle Supply, Inc. v. American Honda Motor Co., Inc.*, 976 F.2d 58, 61 (1st Cir. 1992).

[26]Some courts have held, for example, that attorney's fees and damages for emotional distress are "special" damages. *See, e.g., National Liberty Corp. v. Wal-Mart Stores, Inc.*, 120 F.3d 913, 915 (8th Cir. 1997) (attorney's fees); *Smith v. DeBartoli*, 769 F.2d 451, 542–53 n.2 (7th Cir. 1985) (emotional distress).

To begin with, not everything associated with a common law fraud claim needs to be pled with specificity. For example, Rule 9 states that allegations of the defendants' motive and intent in making allegedly fraudulent statements need only be "averred generally."

When considering whether your claim of fraud satisfies the heightened pleading requirements of Rule 9(b), think about the five W's: Who, What, When, Where, and Why. If your fraud claim alleges (1) who committed fraud; (2) the substance of the fraudulent comments; (3) the time when the fraudulent comments were made; (4) the place where the comments were made; and (5) why the comments resulted in harm to the plaintiff, the claim will pass muster.[27]

D.   Filing and Serving the Complaint

With the complaint in final form, Lane filed it with the federal court and "commenced" the suit under Rule 3. The filing of a complaint is accomplished most often by physically taking the complaint to the office of the clerk of court and paying a filing fee.[28] The clerk accepts the complaint and fee, assigns the case a "case number,"[29] starts a file on the case, and randomly assigns the case to a United States District Court Judge.

What obligations did Full Moon and Belcher have after the complaint was filed? None. Although the filing of the complaint serves as the "commencement" of the action, filing alone does not require a response by the defendant. In order to trigger a defense obligation, the plaintiff must "serve" the defendant with the complaint or get the defendant to agree to waive service.

---

[27]*See, e.g., Schaller Tel. Co. v. Golden Sky Sys., Inc.*, 298 F.3d 736, 746 (8th Cir. 2002); *Ziemba v. Cascade Int'l, Inc.*, 256 F.3d 1194, 1202 (11th Cir. 2001).

[28]Certain other documents specified by the local rules of the various district courts are often required to be filed with the complaint. For example, federal courts require the filing of a "civil cover sheet" containing basic information about the case. Also, several federal courts, including the Middle District of Florida, now require the filing of pleadings and other documents electronically rather than in paper form.

[29]Note that the Olmans' complaint has a blank space where the case number will be inserted after the case is filed and a number assigned. In many jurisdictions, the case number reveals information like the date of the complaint's filing, the judge to whom the case is assigned, and the nature of the case (*e.g.*, civil or criminal), provided one knows the codes used by the clerk of court.

Those of you who have already studied service of process understand what Lane was required to do and are ready to consider the materials in Appendix B. Other students should defer these materials until later. We will assume in coming chapters that service has been accomplished.

"Some people say you can't put a price on a wife's twenty-seven years of loyalty and devotion. They're wrong."

Rule References: 5, *8, 9, 11, 12*, 13, 15, 41, 56

A.   Full Moon Responds to the Complaint

Bart Tweedy was a seventh-year associate at the Atlanta law firm of Lord, Amercey & Taylor, which served as outside counsel for Mizar and its subsidiaries like Full Moon. Tweedy had assumed the defense in *Olman* at the request of senior partner, Harrison Ames. Ames was the partner in charge of Full Moon's account and was ostensibly lead counsel in *Olman;* however, Tweedy knew he would do almost all the work on the case prior to trial.[1]

After meeting with Ames, Tweedy immediately went to work developing a formal response to the Olmans' complaint. Fortunately, Tweedy had represented Full Moon during the EEOC investigation. Defense lawyers are often at a disadvantage when called to represent clients who have been sued. They must respond quickly to a complaint on which

---

[1]In order to appear as counsel in the district court in which the Olmans filed their suit, Tweedy was required either to be a member of the court's bar, or to obtain special permission to appear in the suit by the court. Tweedy sought such special permission by filing a motion requesting the right to appear "*pro hac vice*." The court had granted Tweedy's motion and now he was authorized to, among other things, file motions or pleadings in response to the Olmans' complaint. As a condition of his *pro hac vice* admission, Tweedy had to associate with an attorney already admitted to practice before the court. Because Ames was a member of the court's bar, Tweedy satisfied the association requirement. Tweedy also had to comply with any of the district court's local rules, including its rules of professional responsibility.

the plaintiff's lawyers may have worked for some time.[2] Despite this disadvantage, defense lawyers have the same ethical obligation as plaintiff's counsel to adequately investigate the facts and relevant law before filing any document with the court.[3] The fact that Tweedy had been involved in the EEOC investigation meant that he had essentially conducted his Rule 11 investigation and was prepared to go forward with Full Moon's defense.

At the outset of the EEOC investigation, Full Moon had offered Otis $85,000 to settle the charges (one year's salary for Otis). Tweedy thought this a mistake and recommended against it. But Full Moon's president, Bertie Lurch, seemed concerned that the Olmans' charges could snowball. Already, a few other employees laid off during Full Moon's downsizing had filed charges of age discrimination with the EEOC. Tweedy suspected that Eleanor Lane was counseling some of these ex-employees.

Full Moon had offered nothing to settle Fiona Olman's complaint. Full Moon had sensibly realized that any settlement offer to Fiona would signal the company's doubts about the enforceability of liability releases that Fiona and many other former employees had signed. The generous settlement offer to Otis Olman was intended to appease Fiona as well; however, it had not worked.

Tweedy felt fairly confident he could prove Full Moon management in Atlanta had not acted with discriminatory motive. His conversations with executive decisionmakers convinced Tweedy that Full Moon's downsizing decisions were profit-driven. Under prior management, Full Moon had been overpaying its store managers. A manager with Otis Olman's qualifications merited a salary of no more than $50,000–$60,000. Sid Shockley, for example, was now being paid a base salary of $50,000 with a bonus tied to annual sales.

The potential Achilles' heel for Full Moon's case was Bruce Belcher. During the EEOC investigation, Belcher had provided an affidavit supporting Full Moon's position that it had not discriminated against the Olmans. His affidavit stated that, at the time he made recommendations for downsizing, he acted in good faith based on the company's economic needs and guidelines developed by management in Atlanta. Belcher also denied Otis' assertions that he had made ageist comments at the workplace.

---

[2]A defense lawyer faced with an impractical deadline has the option of requesting an extension of time from opposing counsel, or the court. *See* Rule 6(b) (authorizing motion for "enlargement" or extension of time). As a matter of professional courtesy, opposing counsel usually consents to such a request.

[3]*See* Rule 11(b).

That was *before* Belcher left Full Moon. Belcher was now working for another company in Connecticut and would have separate defense counsel in the Olmans' suit. Belcher had left the company under a cloud. For some time, Full Moon had suspicions about Belcher's expense accounts. Things came to a head when Belcher was arrested for soliciting a prostitute in Atlanta, and Full Moon's accountants began scrutinizing invoices for room service and "bath supplies." Full Moon had severed its relationship with Belcher with as little acrimony as possible. Still, Belcher was unreliable and was the Olmans' best means of tying Full Moon to age discrimination. Atlanta management had considered the recommendations of regional managers like Belcher when making downsizing decisions. A jury might possibly believe the Olmans' allegations that Belcher acted with ageist motives and, in turn, tainted management decisions in Atlanta.

Shockley was also a problem. Shockley had openly professed to other employees that he was better suited than Otis to manage the Jacksonville store as it continued to expand into the youth-oriented, extreme sporting goods market. He also expressed his belief that Full Moon had already saturated the market of older customers who identified with Otis. While Full Moon agreed with Shockley's marketing views on extreme sporting goods, the company disavowed his ageist stereotypes about Otis. The company had even given Shockley a written reprimand for his indiscrete statements and required Shockley to attend special "diversity training" to insure that he managed the Jacksonville store with greater sensitivity to older employees and customers. But Shockley remained as store manager.

Assuming Tweedy could show that the decision to replace Otis as store manager was profit driven, he still faced significant hurdles defending Otis' claim of retaliation. Company president, Bertie Lurch, had acted rashly in sending a termination letter to Otis on the heel's of Otis "protest" letter. Although Lurch had legitimate reasons for terminating Otis, the timing of his action might look suspicious to a jury. If a jury found that retaliation was a "motivating factor" in Otis' discharge, the company might be liable.

Tweedy had identified several substantive defenses to the Olmans' suit. He would move to have *all* of Fiona's claims thrown out based on the release she signed. He would also move to dismiss Otis' fraud claim based on its patent legal insufficiency: How could Otis have "reasonably relied" on a promise of lifetime job security when his contract stated that his employment was for three years?

Tweedy had other statutory defenses under the ADEA. He thought he could show that Full Moon targeted higher-paid management during its downsizing, not older workers *per se.* Replacement of management for economic reasons would show Full Moon based its decisions on "reasonable factors other than age," which is a defense under the ADEA.[4] Tweedy also intended to show Full Moon had "good cause" to terminate Otis, another defense under the ADEA.[5] Several employees would testify that Otis had behaved poorly after receiving notice that he was being replaced by Shockley. This insubordination showed that Otis could no longer continuing working for the Full Moon Sports Outdoor Center. Even worse, Shockley had told Tweedy about what amounted to theft by Otis. In Spring 2003, Shockley had observed Otis loading two costly fiberglass kayaks onto an SUV owned by Otis' son. Shockley could find no records indicating Otis' son had paid for the boats. The apparent theft of this, and possibly other store inventory, provided Full Moon good cause for terminating Otis.

Fortunately for Tweedy, he did not have to navigate litigation strategy through counsel for Full Moon's insurance company. Tweedy had reviewed Full Moon's commercial liability policy and found it excluded coverage for "intentional" wrongdoing by employees, which expressly encompassed violations of "employment discrimination laws." Full Moon's insurer had repudiated any obligation to indemnify or defend the company, and Tweedy concluded the insurer's response was well-supported.

Procedural rules provided Tweedy two general options in responding to the complaint. First, Tweedy could file a "pre-answer motion" attacking some aspect of the complaint or the case. Second, Tweedy could respond to the complaint's allegations by filing an answer. We discuss both of these responses below.[6]

---

[4] Even if an employer's decision has adverse impact on older employees, the decision is lawful if it is based on "reasonable factors other than age." *See* 29 U.S.C. § 623(f)(1).

[5] It is not unlawful to discharge an older employee "for good cause." *See* 29 U.S.C. § 623(f)(3).

[6] Rule 7.1, a relatively new addition to the rules, also requires that private corporations like Full Moon file a "disclosure statement" that identifies, among other things, "any parent corporation." Full Moon was required to file this disclosure statement with its "first appearance pleading, petition, motion, response, or other request addressed to the court." By requiring Full Moon to disclose its parent corporation, Mizar, Inc., the rule would enable the judge to identify potential conflicts of interest including any conflict the judge might have (*e.g.*, if the judge was a shareholder of Mizar).

1.   Pre-Answer Motions

If Tweedy chose to respond to the complaint by first filing an answer, he could include virtually all of Full Moon's defenses to the suit. His answer could include challenges to the court's power to hear the case as well as challenges to the adequacy of the complaint's allegations.[7] However, an answer merely *preserved* these defenses for later litigation. The court would normally not rule on them until Tweedy later filed a motion asking the court to rule.[8]

The Federal Rules provided Tweedy a more aggressive option: he could assert some of Full Moon's strongest defenses in a pre-answer motion thereby asking the court to rule on them at the outset of the suit.[9] Over the years Tweedy had developed a checklist of

---

[7] Rule 12(b) states that "every defense, in law or fact . . . shall be asserted in the responsive pleading" but also permits defenses enumerated in sub-sections (1) through (7) to be asserted by motion. On rare occasions, however, an objection *must* be asserted before filing an answer. The best example is a Rule 12(e) motion for more definite statement. This motion must be filed before answering the complaint, since the ground for seeking a more definite statement is that the complaint is so vague that the defendant "cannot reasonably be required to frame a responsive pleading."

[8] A party who has asserted a Rule 12 defense in its answer will typically file a motion at some point asking the court to decide the merits of the defense. Rule 12(d) states that most Rule 12 defenses "shall be heard and determined before trial on application of any party. . . ." The "application" usually takes the form of a motion. Although it might seem more expeditious to assert Rule 12 defenses in a pre-answer motion, a party may want to defer action on the defense when, for example, it needs to obtain further information before asking the court to rule. If, say, a defendant suspects the plaintiff's citizenship prevents the court from exercising subject matter jurisdiction, but needs to conduct discovery to verify its suspicion, the best tack is to include an objection to subject matter jurisdiction in the answer. Upon confirming its suspicion through discovery, the defendant can then file a motion asking the court to rule on its defense.

[9] In most federal courts, motions are not literally placed on the judge's desk for decision when filed. Motions, as well as supporting and opposing memoranda, will often be given to the judge's clerk for review. Most judicial clerks are recent law school graduates who are hired by individual judges to provide research and writing support. (Judicial clerks should be distinguished from "the clerk of court," an administrative officer involved with the administration of the court's business.) The clerk will read the parties' submissions, review necessary parts of the record, do legal research to independently assess the parties' characterizations of the law, and—usually—draft opinions for the judge. *See* Richard A. Posner, THE FEDERAL COURTS: CHALLENGE AND REFORM 143 (1999) (discussing the clerk's role as a "judicial ghostwriter."). This process takes time, and a motion may not be decided for months after its filing. However, a defense merely asserted in the answer has not

possible defenses to assert in a pre-answer motion, most of which are found in Rule 12. His checklist included the following:

(A) *"Power" motions*: These are objections to the court's power to hear the case. They include challenges under Rule 12(b)(1)-(5) to the court's subject matter jurisdiction, personal jurisdiction, venue, and service of process.[10]

(B) *"Pleading" motions*: These are challenges to the form or content of the complaint, and include the motion to dismiss for failure to state a claim under Rule 12(b)(6), the motion for a more definite statement under Rule 12(e), and the motion to strike improper allegations (*e.g.,* "impertinent" or "scandalous" statements) under Rule 12(f). In addition, Rule 9(b) sets forth heightened pleading requirements for certain matters; the failure to meet these requirements can serve as the basis for a pre-answer motion, as we will discuss later in this chapter.

(C) *"Substantive" motions*: In appropriate cases, the defendant may seek to have some or all of the plaintiff's claims thrown out on the ground that they will inevitably fail on the merits. This "summary judgment" motion is authorized by Rule 56 and can be sought by a defendant "at any time." *See* Rule 56(b). We will discuss summary judgment motions in much greater detail in a later chapter.[11] Suffice it to say that if the defendant has incontrovertible evidence that the plaintiff's case must fail—for example, a release of liability signed by the plaintiff, or a bankruptcy court judgment discharging defendant of all debts—the defendant may present this evidence to the court and avoid further litigation by obtaining summary judgment.

(D) *"Miscellaneous" Motions*: There are other pre-answer motions not specifically addressed in the federal rules. For example, a defendant can seek to transfer the case to another federal court.[12] Or, in the right circumstances, the defendant might

---

even activated the judicial decisionmaking process and so will inevitably delay its decision.

[10]These power motions also included a challenge under Rule 12(b)(7) and Rule 19 to the plaintiff's failure to join an indispensable party.

[11]*See infra* Chapter 7.

[12]*See, e.g.,* 28 U.S.C. 1404 (authorizing a motion to transfer a case to another federal district court "for the convenience of parties and witnesses" and "in the interest of justice.").

ask the trial judge to disqualify opposing counsel from handling the plaintiff's case, or even ask the trial judge to "recuse" herself from hearing the case.[13]

a.   Power Motions

Detailed discussion of the "power" motions available to Tweedy requires background knowledge of the concepts of subject matter jurisdiction, personal jurisdiction, service of process, and venue. We discuss these concepts in Appendix B, and you will want to consider this material at the appropriate point in your study of Civil Procedure. For now we focus on an important procedural aspect of power motions: Many challenges to a court's power to hear a case can be *forfeited* early in litigation through a lawyer's inadvertence.

The Federal Rules establish numerous time periods for taking various procedural action. Often a lawyer's failure to comply with these time limitations can be excused by the court for good reason.[14] At other times, however, failure to comply with these limitations is fatal and results in the procedural waiver of a party's right to take action. Such waivers can even result in a party's loss of the right to assert an otherwise valid defense. Among the defenses that can be irrevocably waived by a lawyer's failure to act timely are objections to personal jurisdiction, venue, and service of process. *See* Federal Rule 12(g) & 12(h). To help you understand how a lawyer can inadvertently waive his or her client's right to make these objections, consider the following questions. Make sure you carefully read Rule 12 when answering them.

---

[13]For example, if the plaintiff's lawyer had previously represented the defendant in another matter, a motion to disqualify the lawyer might be proper. Similarly, if there was ground for suspecting the judge lacked impartiality (for example, the judge had a personal bias against the defendant), the defendant might ask the judge to recuse himself. *See, e.g.,* 28 U.S.C. § 455 (a judge "shall disqualify himself in any proceeding in which his impartiality might reasonably be questioned.").

[14]As we will see later in this chapter, if a defendant fails to file a timely answer to the complaint and default is entered, the court may set aside the default for "good cause."

Question 3.1

A.   Assume that Tweedy files a Rule 12(b)(6) motion to dismiss Otis' fraud count on the ground that it "fails to state a claim." He later discovers that service of process on his client was defective. Tweedy's Rule 12(b)(6) motion has not yet been ruled on by the court. Can Tweedy now file a second motion under Rule 12(b)(5) challenging service of process if he acts promptly?

B.   Can Tweedy avoid the procedural waiver discussed above by simply asserting his objection to service of process later in Full Moon's *answer*? Why not?

---

b.   Pleading motions

The Olmans had alleged *prima facie* cases of age discrimination and retaliation, and Tweedy saw no plausible ground to attack the sufficiency of these allegations. Otis' fraud claim was a different matter.

Rule 9(b) states that when pleading fraud "the circumstances constituting the fraud . . . shall be stated with particularity." As discussed earlier,[15] Rule 9(b) alters the minimal notice pleading standard set out in Rule 8(a). Tweedy carefully considered whether Otis' fraud claim satisfied Rule 9(b)'s pleading requirements and, if it did not, what he could do about it. Consider the question below.

---

[15]*See supra* at 53–54.

Question 3.2

A.   Review the earlier discussion in chapter two regarding the "particularities" required in a fraud allegation, and re-read count five of the complaint alleging fraud. Do the allegations in the fraud claim satisfy the special pleading requirements of Rule 9(b)?

B.   If Tweedy concludes that Otis' fraud count is not pled with sufficient particularity, what Rule 12 motions can he file to assert his objection? (*Hint*: There are at least two available motions.) Which motion do you think preferable? Why? Can both options be used?

Tweedy ultimately declined to challenge the factual sufficiency of the fraud allegations. He chose instead to make what he considered to be a stronger challenge to the fraud count: on its face the count's allegations showed Otis Olman could not recover for fraud. Rather than challenging the degree of particularity in the fraud count, which the court might permit Olman to cure by filing an amended complaint offering greater detail,[16] Tweedy decided to argue that, regardless of how well Otis pled his fraud claim, it had to fail as a matter of law.

The fraud count alleged that Otis was defrauded by Belcher's promise of a *lifetime* job, but also alleged he had entered into an employment contract limited to *three years*. *See* Complaint ¶¶ 15, 20. All legal precedent disclosed by Tweedy's research indicated that a victim of fraud has no claim if he has not "justifiably" relied on a promise. When, as in Otis' situation, the fraudulent promise contradicts the express terms of a contract, reliance is unjustifiable as a matter of law.

---

[16]Most jurisdictions give a party whose pleading is insufficient at least one chance to cure the defect by filing an amended pleading. This reflects the philosophy that cases should be decided on their merits and not as the result of technical pleading errors.

"No, Billy, I distinctly said that if you mow
the lawn you can *halve* your allowance.
That's why we ask for things in writing."

Tweedy, too, had come to visualize a legal claim as a table, whose "legs" consist of each of the required elements making up the claim. A fraud claim was supported by four "legs" that included (1) a false representation, (2) which the promisor (Belcher) knew was false, (3) made to induce reliance by the promisee (Otis), and (4) on which the promisee justifiably relied to his detriment. In order to prevail on a Rule 12(b)(6) motion, Tweedy only had to show that the fraud count, taken at face value, was missing a leg. Somewhat ironically, Lane had actually alleged the fatal deficiency in Otis' fraud count by simultaneously pleading that he was promised a lifetime job and yet signed a contract obligating Full Moon to only three years of employment. If the allegations in Otis' complaint were accepted at face value, case law indicated that his fraud claim must fail because the element of justifiable reliance was missing.

Tweedy chose to file a motion under Rule 12(b)(6) seeking to dismiss Otis' fraud count for failure to state a claim. Below is an excerpted version of Tweedy's motion and supporting memorandum.[17] When you consider these filings, note that Tweedy does not introduce facts beyond those alleged in the complaint. This is the hallmark of the motion

---

[17] Rule 5(b) requires that motions "state with particularity" the grounds supporting the motion. Federal courts typically require that written motions by accompanied by a memorandum or brief explaining the supporting grounds. *See, e.g.*, Local Rule 3.01(a) for the Middle District of Florida.

to dismiss for failure to state a claim. Tweedy and the court assume that Otis will be able to prove everything he alleges. However, these allegations, Tweedy argues, are not sufficient under the law to support all the elements needed to establish the claim.

IN THE UNITED STATES DISTRICT COURT
FOR THE MIDDLE DISTRICT OF FLORIDA
JACKSONVILLE DIVISION

OTIS AND FIONA OLMAN,

        Plaintiffs,

vs.   Case No. 03-2222-CIV-M-46-B

FULL MOON SPORTS, INC.,
& BRUCE BELCHER

        Defendants.

Rule 7(b)(2) requires that motions and other "papers" include the same caption required for pleadings.

Notice that the clerk has now assigned a case number to be included in all later documents submitted to the court in the case.

DEFENDANT FULL MOON SPORTS, INC.'S
MOTION TO DISMISS FOR FAILURE TO STATE A CLAIM

      Defendant Full Moon Sports, Inc., moves this Court for an order dismissing the fraud claim of plaintiff Otis Olman for failure to state a claim upon which relief can be granted. In support of this motion, Full Moon Sports, Inc., submits the accompanying memorandum of law.

                    Respectfully submitted,

_____

Harrison Ames, Esq.
Bart A. Tweedy, Esq.
Counsel for Full Moon Sports, Inc.
[Address, phone number, etc. omitted.]

Certificate of Service

      Undersigned counsel hereby certifies that a true copy of this motion was served on plaintiff's counsel, Eleanor Lane, 100 Cook St., Jacksonville, Florida, 32210, and on defendant Bruce Belcher, 4 Cedar Tree Lane, Stamford, Connecticut, 59438, this 20th day of May, 2004.

_____

Bart A. Tweedy, Esq.

Rule 5(d) requires that "all papers after the complaint" include a certificate of service. This certificate informs the court that all parties have been properly served, as required by Rule 5(a).

[68]

IN THE UNITED STATES DISTRICT COURT
FOR THE MIDDLE DISTRICT OF FLORIDA
JACKSONVILLE DIVISION

OTIS AND FIONA OLMAN,

      Plaintiffs,

vs.   Case No. 03-2222-CIV-M-46-B

FULL MOON SPORTS, INC.,
et. al.

      Defendants.

DEFENDANT FULL MOON SPORTS, INC.'S
MEMORANDUM IN SUPPORT OF ITS
MOTION TO DISMISS FOR FAILURE TO STATE A CLAIM

Defendant, Full Moon Sports, Inc. ("Full Moon") submits this memorandum in support of its motion to dismiss plaintiff Otis Olman's count for fraud because it fails to state a claim upon which relief can be granted. Full Moon's motion should be granted because, as a matter of law, Olman could not have justifiably relied on Full Moon's alleged promise to offer him lifetime employment when he contemporaneously executed a written contract guaranteeing him employment for only three years.

Otis Olman's fraud count (count five in the complaint) alleges he was defrauded when Full Moon's regional manager "promised specifically that [Olman] could remain as manager of the Jacksonville store until he retired." Complaint ¶ 46. Olman alleges he "reasonably relied" on this promise in renewing his employment with Full Moon and declining the opportunity to become partner in another business. *Id.* ¶¶ 49, 50.

An earlier allegation in Olman's complaint, however, repudiates his assertion that he "reasonably relied" on the promise of lifetime employment allegedly made by his regional manager. Paragraph 15 alleges—correctly—that Olman signed "a three-year contract to continue as store manager" at the same time he was supposedly promised he "could remain as manager of the Jacksonville store until he retired." Both common sense and applicable precedent confirm that Olman could not have

Is this an example where pleading more than is required by Rule 8(a) has unintended consequences for the pleader? Would Lane have been better off leaving this detailed allegation out of the complaint?

[69]

reasonably relied on an oral representation that directly contradicted the terms of a written contract he signed.

In order to state a claim for fraud, a plaintiff must allege (1) a false statement of material fact, (2) made by a person who knew or should have known the statement was false, (3) with the intent that the plaintiff rely on the false statement, and (4) on which the plaintiff justifiably or reasonably relies to his detriment. *See Taylor Woodrow Homes Florida, Inc. v. 4/46-A Corporation*, 850 So.2d 536 (Fla. 5th DCA 2003). A long line of Florida decisions affirms that a party alleging fraud cannot "reasonably rely" on a promise that directly contradicts the term of a contract entered into after the alleged fraudulent statement is made. As one Florida court recently observed in *Taylor Woodrow, supra*, "a party may not recover in fraud for an alleged false statement when disclosure of the truth is subsequently revealed in a written agreement between the parties." Similarly, the court in *Wilson v. Equitable Life Assurance Society of the United States* affirmed that "a party cannot maintain an action in fraud if the alleged misrepresentation is explicitly contradictory to a specific and unambiguous provision in a written contract." 622 So.2d 25, 28 (Fla. 2d DCA 1993).

The decision in *Eclipse Medical, Inc. v. American Hydro-Surgical Instruments, Inc.,* 262 F. Supp. 2d 1334 (S.D. Fla. 1999) is directly on point. In *Eclipse*, the plaintiffs alleged they were defrauded when the defendant "gave false assurances that [it] intended and agreed to a long-term relationship," but terminated their distributorship upon expiration of the written contract term. *Id.* at 1342. The court rejected the plaintiff's fraud claim as a matter of law because "the clear and unambiguous language of the Agreement itself specifically contradicts any of [the] alleged misstatements. . . ." As the court commented, "Florida courts have made clear that no action for fraud in the inducement will lie when the alleged fraud contradicts the subsequent written contract." *Id*; *see also Pettinelli v. Danzig*, 722 F.2d 706, 709–10 (11th Cir. 1984) (reliance was unjustified when alleged misrepresentations were contradicted by subsequent contract terms); *Barnes v. Burger King Corp.*, 932 F. Supp. 1420, 1428 (S.D. Fla. 1996) (reliance on promises contradicted by the terms of a franchise agreement was "unreasonable as a matter of law"); *Hillcrest Pac. Corp. v. Yamamura,* 727 So.2d 1053, 1056 (Fla. 4th DCA 1999) ("a party cannot recover in fraud for alleged oral misrepresentations that are adequately covered or expressly contradicted in a later written contract.").

Accordingly, Olman's fraud count fails to state a claim under Florida law because his complaint admits he unreasonably relied on a promise that was clearly and unambiguously contradicted by the employment contract he signed. Count five of the complaint should be dismissed.

Conclusion

For the foregoing reasons, Full Moon respectfully requests that the Court dismiss with prejudice count five of the complaint against Full Moon on the ground that this count fails to state a claim upon which relief can be granted.

Respectfully submitted,

_____

Harrison Ames, Esq.
Bart A. Tweedy, Esq.
Counsel for Full Moon Sports, Inc.
[Address, phone number, etc. omitted.]

Certificate of Service

[omitted]

c.   Other Possible Motions

Tweedy considered two other possible pre-answer responses to the complaint. Full Moon had provided him a copy of Fiona's signed release in which she waived all legal claims against the company in exchange for severance pay. Tweedy believed this document was irrefutable evidence defeating Fiona's claims of age discrimination.

Tweedy could not, however, assert this defense through a Rule 12(b)(6) motion. A motion under Rule 12(b)(6) is based on the assumption that the facts alleged in the complaint are true but legally insufficient. Tweedy wanted to interject a *new* fact never mentioned in the complaint—the release—which he believed was conclusive evidence that his client could not be found liable for age discrimination. A motion to dismiss is not the proper tool to attack a claim when the movant intends to rely on facts not alleged in the complaint. In order to have Fiona's claims thrown out based on the release, Tweedy would have to use a Rule 56 motion for summary judgment.[18] This motion would allow Tweedy to introduce the release as evidence and seek to have Fiona's claims disposed of without further litigation. We will later examine in detail the form and content of a Rule 56 motion for summary judgment.

There might be another, simpler way to eliminate Fiona's claims. When Lane filed the complaint, she certified under Rule 11(b)(3) that she had made a "reasonable" inquiry into the facts underlying the Olmans' claims and that the claims had evidentiary support. Either Lane had failed to make a reasonable inquiry or Fiona had failed to disclose the release to her lawyer. In any event, once Tweedy brought to Lane's attention the signed release, Lane could not persist with Fiona's claims without risking sanctions.[19] When Lane recognized her ethical duty to dismiss Fiona's claims, Tweedy would achieve victory for his client with minimum cost.

If Tweedy had known Lane better or had an amicable professional relationship with her, he might simply have called Lane and advised her of the release. Among the lawyers Tweedy knew, it was considered good decorum to give one's adversary the opportunity to

---

[18]At the same time, Rule 12(b) permits a challenge to the complaint to be "treated as one for summary judgment" when matters outside the pleading are presented to the court.

[19]According to Rule 11(b), if Lane later "presented" or "advocated" Fiona's claims contained in the complaint, she would be certifying to the court that they had adequate evidentiary support. Unless Lane had some ground for invalidating the release, she could no longer advocate Fiona's claims in good faith.

correct obvious mistakes.   Judges also prefer to have lawyers fix obvious problems informally without involving the court.   But Tweedy's prior dealings with Lane had been a bit contentious and he decided to follow the formal procedures set out in Rule 11.

Question 3.3

Describe the actions that Tweedy must take under Rule 11 if he wants to use that rule to induce Lane to voluntarily dismiss Fiona's claims.   Why can't Tweedy simply file a Rule 11 motion for sanctions with the court and bring Lane's mistake to the court's direct attention?

2.   Full Moon's Answer

A defendant's second general option for responding to the complaint is to file an answer.   According to Rule 12(a), a defendant has twenty days after being served[20] with the summons and complaint to serve a responsive answer.[21]   As discussed earlier, this 20-day deadline can place defense counsel not already familiar with the case at quite a disadvantage, because counsel is expected to research the law and the facts and draft an answer that complies with his ethical obligations under Rule 11.   For this reason, many defendants do not in fact serve their answers within 20 days.   One means of avoiding this deadline is to file a motion for "enlargement of time" under Rule 6(b).   Most district courts require that the lawyer seeking an enlargement of time (more commonly referred to as an "extension" of time) confer with opposing counsel before filing this motion.   When the request for an extension is reasonable, standards of professionalism usually dictate that opposing counsel consent.   Cooperation also makes good sense given the likelihood that opposing counsel may herself need an extension at some point during the suit.

*NEW RULE

---

[20]According to Rule 5(a), most documents filed with the court—including pleadings and written motions—"shall be *served* upon each of the parties."   The service of documents, rather than their filing, is the act that typically triggers an opponent's responsive obligation.

[21]As explained in Appendix B, the deadline for responding to a complaint is extended to 60, or even 90, days when the defendant agrees to waive service of process.

There is another way in which the 20-day deadline for serving an answer can be deferred. Consider the following question:

Question 3.4

A.   According to Rule 12(a)(4), what effect does Full Moon's service of its motion under Rule 12(b)(6) have on the deadline for filing its answer? What is the new deadline for filing the answer?

B.   Does the impact of Rule 12 motions on the deadline for filing an answer suggest a tactical reason why a defendant might want to file *some* pre-answer motion? According to Rule 11(b), is it unethical to file a motion solely for the purpose of obtaining more time in which to serve the answer?

Although Tweedy's filing of a Rule 12(b)(6) motion extended the time he had to serve his answer, Tweedy decided he would file Full Moon's answer anyway. He had fully investigated the case and knew how he would respond to the complaint allegations. In addition, he intended to assert a counterclaim against Otis in the answer that would put Otis on the defense, undermine his credibility, and likely improve Full Moon's litigation (and settlement) posture.[22]

Over time, Tweedy had developed a mental checklist for items to include in the answer. That checklist included the following:

---

[22]Tweedy's decision was also influenced by other factors. First, he knew something about how Judge Sarah Goodenough, to whom the Olmans' case had been assigned, managed litigation. Goodenough usually required defendants to file an answer to the complaint despite a pending motion to dismiss. Second, Tweedy was pleased that the Olmans' case had been assigned to Judge Goodenough and he wanted to insure that she continued to preside over the case. According to Rule 41(a)(1)(i), a plaintiff has the right to dismiss her case "at any time before service by the adverse party of an answer or of a motion for summary judgment." By filing Full Moon's answer, Tweedy could eliminate the risk that Lane might voluntarily dismiss the suit and attempt to obtain a different judge when she re-filed. Although such attempts to "judge shop" are not common, Tweedy had witnessed them in prior litigation.

(A) *"Admit, deny, or DKI"*: Under Rule 8(b), Full Moon was obliged to respond to each specific allegation in the Olmans' complaint. Full Moon could (1) admit the truth of an allegation, (2) deny the allegation, or (3) state that it did not have knowledge or information sufficient to determine the allegations's truth (summarized by the acronym "DKI" standing for "deny knowledge or information"). Tweedy knew that it was quite important that Full Moon deny all allegations it believed were untrue. If Full Moon failed to deny an allegation it would be deemed admitted.[23]

(B) *Affirmative defenses*: Rule 8(c) contained a non-exhaustive list of special defenses Full Moon needed to assert in its answer. These affirmative defenses are generally thought of as defenses that go beyond mere denial of liability allegations in the complaint. Affirmative defenses provide reason to deny the relief sought by a plaintiff regardless of whether the complaint's allegations are true. Full Moon was obliged to give the Olmans and the court notice in its answer that it intended to rely on these affirmative defenses. Although Full Moon might later seek to amend its answer to include affirmative defenses omitted from its original answer, Tweedy knew that courts were more reluctant to permit amendment of the answer to include them—especially when the facts underlying an affirmative defense were known at the time the original answer was filed.

(C) *Counterclaims and crossclaims*: Rule 13 authorizes a defending party to go on the offensive by asserting its own claims in its pleading. Under Rule 13(a), Full Moon was *required* to assert counterclaims against the Olmans if these "compulsory" counterclaims arose from the occurrences alleged in the Olmans' complaint. Under Rule 13(b), Full Moon was *permitted* to assert counterclaims not arising from the occurrences alleged in the Olmans' complaint. Rule 13(g) also permitted Full Moon to assert a cross-claim against its co-defendant Belcher, provided the cross-claim arose from the occurrence alleged in the Olmans' complaint.[24]

Tweedy had conducted a careful investigation of the Olmans' charges and was prepared to answer the complaint consistent with his obligations under Rule 11. Full Moon would deny all allegations of legal liability. In addition, Full Moon would assert a few

---

[23]*See* Rule 8(d). The exception is an allegation of the "amount of damages" claimed by the plaintiff, which does not require an explicit denial.

[24]*See infra* Chapter 6 (discussing joinder of counterclaims and crossclaims).

"affirmative" defenses to liability including: (1) that Full Moon's downsizing decisions were based on "reasonable factors other than age," and (2) that Fiona had executed a release absolving Full Moon of all liability.[25]

Question 3.5

Recall that Full Moon has filed a Rule 12(b)(6) motion seeking dismissal of Otis' fraud count. Assume for purposes of this question that Full Moon had *not* filed this pre-answer motion. How, in its answer, would Full Moon assert the defense that the fraud count failed to allege a legally sufficient claim? Is this an "affirmative defense" that must be specifically pled in Full Moon's answer? Or can Full Moon assert this defense by simply denying allegations in the fraud count?

Finally, Tweedy intended to assert a counterclaim against Otis. He would base this claim on the tort of "conversion," and ask that Otis reimburse Full Moon for the cost of the kayaks he had apparently "given" to his son together with the cost of any other inventory Otis had taken. The counterclaim would also support Full Moon's affirmative defense that it had non-discriminatory "good cause" to terminate Otis, and would lessen Otis' credibility in court.[26]

Tweedy decided not to assert a cross-claim against Belcher. Although Belcher might have a duty to indemnify Full Moon if the company was found liable for fraud, Tweedy did not want to make Belcher an adversary at this time. He could always amend Full Moon's answer to include a cross-claim at a later date, assuming the claim survived Full Moon's motion to dismiss.

---

[25] Only the release is specifically identified in Rule 8(c) as an affirmative defense. However, the list of affirmative defense in Rule 8(c) is not exhaustive. Tweedy decided to plead that Full Moon acted based on "reasonable factors other than age" because case law was still unsettled as to whether this constituted an affirmative defense. *See, e.g., Smith v. City of Jackson*, 125 S. Ct. 1536 (2005).

[26] At first glance, one might think that a defendant who denies allegations in the complaint has a ready-made counterclaim for *libel*. The prevailing rule in American law, however, is that allegations in pleadings are "privileged" and cannot serve as the basis for a libel claim so long as they are relevant to the subject matter of the suit. *See* 50 Am. Jur.2d Libel & Slander § 305 (2004).

Below is the answer Tweedy filed on behalf of Full Moon. Note how the answer uses the various procedural responses discussed above.

IN THE UNITED STATES DISTRICT COURT
FOR THE MIDDLE DISTRICT OF FLORIDA
JACKSONVILLE DIVISION

OTIS AND FIONA OLMAN,

     Plaintiffs,

vs.   Case No. 03-2222-CIV-M-46-B

FULL MOON SPORTS, INC.,
et al.

     Defendants

ANSWER AND COUNTERCLAIM
OF DEFENDANT FULL MOON SPORTS, INC.

Defendant, Full Moon Sports, Inc., answers the complaint as follows:

Preliminary Allegations

1. Admitted.

2. Defendant admits that it is incorporated in Delaware and that it has its principal place of business in Georgia. Defendant further admits that the Court has jurisdiction of Plaintiffs' ADEA claims. Defendant is without knowledge or information sufficient to admit or deny the remainder of Plaintiffs' jurisdictional allegations.

3. Defendant is without knowledge or information sufficient to admit or deny the allegations in paragraph 3.

Parties

4. Admitted.

5. Admitted.

Sidebar (left): Notice how the complaint's use of numbered allegations, and Full Moon's specific response to each allegation, has made it easier to determine what issues are in controversy.

Sidebar (right): Rule 8(b) permits a party to confess that it is unable, in light of available information, to either admit or deny an allegation. This confession "has the effect of a denial," thus permitting the party to challenge the allegation at a later time.

6. Admitted.

7. Admitted.

General Allegations

8. Admitted.

9. Defendant admits Olman became store manager in 1990, but denies the Jacksonville store was a marginally-profitable business.

10. Admitted.

11. Denied insofar as Plaintiffs imply Olman was responsible for the Jacksonville store's increased profitability.

12. Admitted.

13. Admitted.

14. Admitted.

15. Defendant is without knowledge or information sufficient to admit or deny the allegations in paragraph 15.

16. Admitted.

17. Defendant is without knowledge or information sufficient to admit or deny the allegations in paragraph 17.

18. Defendant is without knowledge or information sufficient to admit or deny the allegations in paragraph 18.

19. Denied.

20. Denied.

21. Admitted.

22. Admitted.

> **Rule 8(b) requires that a party specify what part of an allegation it denies when at least part of the allegation is true.**

23. Defendant is without knowledge or information sufficient to admit or deny the allegations in paragraph 23, insofar as they are based on conversations between Belcher and Olman.

24. Defendant is without knowledge or information sufficient to admit or deny the allegations in paragraph 24, insofar as they are based on conversations between Belcher and Olman.

25. Defendant is without knowledge or information sufficient to admit or deny the allegations in paragraph 25, insofar as they are based on conversations between Belcher and Olman. Defendant admits Fiona Olman was terminated.

26. Defendant is without knowledge or information sufficient to admit or deny the allegations in paragraph 26, insofar as they are based on conversations between Belcher and Olman.

27. Denied.

28. Defendant admits that Olman wrote a letter to Full Moon's president and that Full Moon's president responded to the letter. Defendant states that these letters speak for themselves and, therefore, denies the allegations of this paragraph to the extent inconsistent with those written documents. Defendant admits that Full Moon terminated Olman.

29. Defendant is without knowledge or information sufficient to admit or deny the allegations in paragraph 29, insofar as they are based on conversations between Shockley and Olman. The remainder of the allegations are denied.

30. Defendant is without knowledge or information sufficient to admit or deny the allegations in paragraph 30.

COUNT ONE:

31. Defendant re-alleges its responses to paragraphs 8–30.

32. Denied.

33. Denied.

34. Denied.

35. Denied.

36. Denied.

COUNT TWO:

37. Defendant re-alleges its responses to paragraphs 8–30.

38. Defendant denies allegations that it violated the ADEA.

39. Denied.

40. Denied.

COUNT THREE:

41. Defendant re-alleges its responses to paragraphs 8–30.

42. Denied.

COUNT FOUR:

43. Defendant re-alleges its responses to paragraphs 8–30.

44. Denied.

COUNT FIVE:

45. Defendant re-alleges its responses to paragraphs 8–30.

46. Denied.

47. Denied.

48. Denied.

49. Denied.

50. Denied.

COUNT SIX:

51. Defendant re-alleges its responses to paragraphs 8–30.

52. Denied.

53. Denied.

54. Denied.

55. Denied.

56. Denied.

COUNT SEVEN:

57. Defendant re-alleges its responses to paragraphs 8–30.

58. Denied.

FIRST AFFIRMATIVE DEFENSE

59. Full Moon based all employment decisions affecting the plaintiffs on "reasonable factors other than age."

SECOND AFFIRMATIVE DEFENSE

60. Fiona Olman previously executed a release waiving all claims of liability against defendant Full Moon Sports, Inc.

DEFENDANT'S FIRST COUNTERCLAIM FOR CONVERSION AGAINST OTIS OLMAN

Note that Rule 8(a) requires that a party allege the jurisdictional basis for all claims, including counterclaims.

61. The Court has supplemental jurisdiction of this counterclaim for conversion because it arises out the same occurrences alleged in Otis Olman's complaint, namely his termination by Full Moon and its reasons for his termination.

62. Early on the morning of March 6, 2003, prior to the opening of the Jacksonville store, Otis Olman was observed loading expensive kayaks and related equipment onto the vehicle of his son.

63. Subsequent review of store records indicates that neither Otis Olman nor his son paid the store for this merchandise, or otherwise made any record that this merchandise had been removed from store premises.

64. Based upon information and belief, Otis Olman has converted store merchandise on several occasions during the time he served as store manager, including the occasion alleged in paragraphs 62–63.

WHEREFORE, defendant Full Moon Sports, Inc. demands of Otis Olman compensatory damages, punitive damages, costs and attorney's fees.

Respectfully submitted,

_____

Harrison Ames, Esq.
Bart A. Tweedy, Esq.
Counsel for Full Moon Sports, Inc.
[Address, phone number, etc. omitted]

Certificate of Service

[omitted]

B.   Belcher's Belated Response to the Suit

Even though Full Moon had terminated Belcher, for tactical reasons it offered to provide him legal counsel in response to the Olmans' suit. Belcher had somewhat rashly declined this offer.

After being served with the Olmans' summons and complaint in Connecticut (where Belcher now lived), Belcher still neglected to hire a lawyer to respond the complaint. Lane waited more than a month to receive some response from Belcher. When she received no response, she asked the trial court to enter default against Belcher.

Question 3.6

A.   According to Rule 55, what steps must a plaintiff take in order to have default entered against a non-responsive defendant?

B.   What is the consequence of entry of default?

C.   What should a defendant do in response to entry of default if he intends to defend the suit? What must the defendant show the court in order to have entry of default set aside?

D.   What is the difference between "default" and "default judgment?"

E.   According to Rule 55, could Lane have been asked the clerk of the court to enter default judgment against Belcher? Why or why not?

The clerk entered default against Belcher. When Belcher was notified that default had been entered, he immediately hired a lawyer in Jacksonville. Belcher's lawyer quickly contacted Lane and asked her consent to have the entry of default set aside.[27]

---

[27]Local federal court rules typically provide that, prior to filing most motions with the court, counsel for the moving party confer with opposing counsel to see if she will consent to the relief sought in the motion. *See, e.g.,* Local Rule 3.01(g) for the Middle District of Florida. In the subsequently-filed motion, the moving lawyer must certify that he has complied with this requirement

Lane knew that the trial court would inevitably grant Belcher's expeditious motion to set aside the entry of default and so she consented to the motion. Belcher's lawyer then filed an "Unopposed Motion to Set Aside Entry of Default," which was granted by the trial court. After Belcher's default was set aside, his lawyer filed a motion to dismiss the complaint against Belcher based on the identical ground alleged in Full Moon's earlier motion to dismiss—the complaint failed to state a claim for fraud.

---

and state whether opposing counsel has consented.

CHAPTER FOUR:
PRELUDE TO DISCOVERY

Rule References: 7, 8, 11, 12, *16, 26,* 54

A.   Lane Responds to the Defendants

Lane now had to make several decisions about what to do in light of the defendants' responses to the complaint. These responses included: (1) the defendants' motions to dismiss Otis' fraud claim; (2) Full Moon's demand that Lane voluntarily dismiss Fiona's claims or be the subject of a sanctions motion; and (3) Full Moon's answer and counterclaim.

Lane had anticipated the defendants' motion to dismiss Otis' fraud claim. Her own research had uncovered the same case law cited by Full Moon in its motion, which seemed to say that Otis could not rely on an oral promise that contradicted the express provision of his employment contract. Yet, Lane still believed she had a plausible argument that this precedent should not be followed in Otis' situation. After all, the Florida Supreme Court—the ultimate authority on Florida common law of fraud—had not specifically held that a fraud claim is precluded by conflicting contract language.[1] Further, Lane believed the facts of Otis' situation supported an exception to the prevailing rule. Otis, a long-term employee, had been lied to by his regional manager and fraudulently induced to sign an employment contract. Lane had discovered several cases from other jurisdictions recognizing that, in appropriate circumstances, an employer should not be permitted to make false promises to an employee and then evade liability by relying on contract language.

Lane expected the trial court would grant the defendants' Rule 12(b)(6) motion, but she believed assertion of the fraud claim was both ethically and tactically sound. If need be, she could raise this issue on appeal and seek to make new law.[2] At the same time, Lane had made a point of explaining to the Olmans that the fraud claim would likely be dismissed by the trial court. She always thought it advisable to prepare clients for bad news.

---

[1] Note that the state of Florida Supreme Court precedent is different from that you were asked to assume in Question 1.1, *supra.*

[2] A party is usually prohibited from raising an issue on appeal if it is not raised in the trial court. This rule is described as the "preservation of error" requirement. The requirement ensures that both opposing counsel and the trial court have an opportunity to respond to a suspected error. So, Lane had to allege the fraud claim despite her conviction the effort would be futile in the trial court.

As for Tweedy's demand that she voluntarily dismiss Fiona's claims because of the release, Lane had written to Tweedy refusing that request. Her refusal gave Lane some small personal satisfaction, as the tone of Tweedy's letter implied either that she did not know what she was doing, or that she did and was acting unethically. However, Tweedy had too readily assumed that the release was in fact enforceable.

According to federal law, the release had to strictly comply with statutory requirements. One requirement is that an employee be "advised in writing to consult with an attorney prior to executing the agreement."[3] When Lane scrutinized her client's release, she noticed that it failed to specifically advise Fiona to consult "an attorney." Instead, it contained a vague, evasive admonition that Fiona consult with her "advisor" before signing. Based on Supreme Court precedent insisting that releases carefully comply with federal law, Lane believed she had an argument that the release was unenforceable.[4] She had explained all this in her response to Tweedy's demand. Lane doubted he would now file a sanctions motion with the court, although he might later seek summary judgment based on the release.

---

[3]*See* 29 U.S.C. 626(f)(4).

[4]*See Oubre v. Entergy Operations Inc.*, 522 U.S. 422 (1998) (a release that fails to contain provisions required by federal law is unenforceable).

The final decision for Lane was how to respond to Full Moon's answer. The answer contained several components including (1) admissions and denials, (2) affirmative defenses, and (3) a counterclaim. Lane recognized that she had to consider the *distinct* procedural obligations pertaining to each component.

Question 4.1

Review Federal Rules 7(a) and 8(d). What pleading, if any, must Lane serve in response to the three components of the answer? If Lane serves no response to Full Moon's answer, what are the consequences? Be specific.

Full Moon's counterclaim had potential to ruin Otis' case. Otis had never mentioned the incident involving the kayaks, although Lane had questioned him closely about whether Full Moon might have legitimate reasons for his firing. When Lane spoke with Otis about the theft allegations, he had an immediate and comforting response.

Otis explained that the kayaks in dispute had *not* belonged to Full Moon. It seems that the store had an annual "used equipment" sale at which customers could bring their sporting equipment to the store and offer it at a flea-market-like sale held in the parking lot. When one customer brought in the two fiberglass kayaks in question to offer at the sale, Otis immediately called his son and told him he might want to consider buying them. His son contacted the owner and made an offer that was accepted before the day of the sale. Apparently, Shockley had misunderstood what was happening when he saw Otis loading these kayaks onto a vehicle. Although Otis' son had been advantaged by learning about the kayaks before the sale actually took place, in no sense was there a "conversion" of Full Moon's merchandise. As for Full Moon's allegation that Otis had "converted store merchandise on several occasions," Otis assured Lane that discovery would prove this to be a baseless charge. In fact, Otis was quite perturbed by Full Moon's pursuit of its bogus "conversion" allegations.

As you have probably discovered in answering question 4.1, one of Lane's options was to deny Full Moon's allegations of conversion in a reply.[5] But what if Otis directed

---

[5]The reply to Full Moon's counterclaim would look in many respects like Full Moon's Answer to the Olmans' Complaint. Lane would need to admit, deny or "DKI" each allegation. *See* Rule 8(b). In addition, Lane would need to plead any affirmative defense to the counterclaim available to her client. *See* Rule 8(c). Because Otis was a defending party with respect to Full Moon's

Lane to respond more vigorously to Full Moon's allegations? Consider the following question below.

Question 4.2

Assume that Otis is particularly concerned that (a) the allegations of theft against him might damage his reputation if they are reported by the news media, and (b) in any event, Full Moon should not "get away" with making such wild and frivolous charges. Given Otis' insistence that Lane take aggressive action in response to these allegations, what options does Lane have in addition to filing a pleading in response to the counterclaim allegations? Which option would you recommend?

B.   The Pleadings Are Closed . . . Or Are They?

With Lane's serving of a reply to Full Moon's counterclaim, the pleadings were ostensibly closed. Rule 7(a) specifically limits the type and number of pleadings litigants can file. These include:

- a complaint and an answer;

- a counterclaim (to be included in the answer according to Rule 13) and a reply;

- a crossclaim (also to be included in the answer) and an answer; and

- a third-party complaint and an answer to this complaint.

Rule 7(a) states that "no other pleading shall be allowed," although the court can "order a reply to an answer or a third-party answer." One way of understanding pleading under the Federal Rules is to focus on the principle, that for every "offensive" pleading there is a corresponding "defensive" pleading. In other words, pleadings form something of a

---

counterclaim, he could employ all the options made available to defending parties, including the filing of Rule 12 motions. *See, e.g.,* Rule 12(b) (power motions); 12(e) (motion for more definite statement); 12(f) (motion to strike).

matched set of bookends. According to this philosophy, when a party serves a pleading seeking affirmative relief, the defending party must respond to that pleading. However, the pleadings should generally end at this point.

Although Rule 7(a) limits the types of pleadings that may be filed in a suit, Rule 15 adopts a liberal approach to the *amendment* of those pleadings. In the case of pre-trial amendment, Rule 15(a) permits parties to amend their pleadings either (a) as a matter of right, or (b) by permission of one's adversary or the court.

A party's right to amend depends on whether that party has served an "offensive" pleading to which her adversary must respond (*i.e.*, a complaint, a counterclaim, a crossclaim, or a third-party complaint), or instead has filed a "defensive" pleading to which there is no response. When a party has served an offensive pleading, she has the right to amend it "once . . . at any time before a responsive pleading is served." *See* Rule 15(a). When a party has served a purely defensive pleading, she has a right to amend it "once . . . at any time within 20 days after it is served." In light of Rule 15(a)'s provision for amendment by right, consider the following question:

Question 4.3

Recall that at this point in the suit, the Olmans have served a complaint on Full Moon; Full Moon has served an answer to the Olmans' complaint which includes its own counterclaim; and Otis has served a reply to Full Moon's counterclaim. Does any party have the right to amend any of its pleadings at this point?

Rule 15(a) imposes no specific time limit on a party's request for permission to amend a pleading. It states, instead, that a party may amend a pleading "by leave of court or by written consent of the adverse party; and leave shall be freely given when justice so requires." According to the Supreme Court, amendment should normally be permitted unless the party opposing amendment can show either that it will be unduly prejudiced, or that the movant has acted in bad faith.[6]

---

[6]*See Foman v. Davis,* 371 U.S. 178 (1962).

Rule 15(a) would suggest, then, that both the Olmans and Full Moon still had opportunity to amend their pleadings to change the claims or the parties, to allege new defenses, or to otherwise revise their allegations. Later in the Guide,[7] we will see how developments during discovery led the Olmans to consider amending their complaint. But as we learn in the following discussion, the liberality of rules like Rule 15(a) is tempered by the trial court's power to impose its own plan and schedule for the conduct of litigation. We now consider that judicial power of case management.

C.   Case Management

At this point in the Olmans' suit, pre-trial procedures began to reflect a distinct approach to litigation found in the federal rules. In many state courts, lawyers are free to commence the discovery process soon after the case is filed. The lawyers are largely unsupervised by the court during the discovery process and may proceed according to their own plans and schedule. They also have considerable discretion in taking other pre-trial action, including the filing of pre-trial motions and the amending of pleadings. In many cases, this attorney freedom results in a pre-trial process extending over years and a corresponding delay in the trial date.

Federal court practice is often different.[8] Federal rules require that a judge become involved in a suit at an early stage. A federal judge plays an active role in managing the pre-trial process, and much of this process occurs within a framework established by the judge. For example, shortly after Lane filed suit the case was randomly assigned to *Judge Sarah Goodenough*.[9] Judge Goodenough's first action was to order the parties to confer and develop a discovery plan under Rule 26(f). One important implication of the parties' Rule 26(f) conference was that all discovery was *prohibited* until the conference was conducted.[10]

---

[7]*See infra* Chapter 6, Part B.

[8]It merits emphasis that both the judge and the parties can influence whether procedural rules operate as intended. Some judges are more lenient in supervising the pre-trial process, and some lawyers succeed in bending the rules. Consequently, the text portrayal of the pre-trial process reflects the behavior of our hypothetical judge and parties; it may not be an apt description of what occurs in some lawsuits.

[9]The prevailing practice among district courts is to assign cases to judges randomly, often with the aid of computer software.

[10]*See* Rule 26(d) ("a party may not seek discovery from any source before the parties have conferred as required by Rule 26(f)").

Judge Goodenough also scheduled a meeting in her chambers at which the discovery plan and related matters would be discussed.

As required by the judge's order and Rule 26(f), the lawyers for the parties in *Olman v. Full Moon* conferred with each other by correspondence and phone. Because they had experience litigating in federal court, they had a good idea of the type of discovery plan and schedule Judge Goodenough would be willing to approve. They knew that Judge Goodenough would probably approve any reasonable plan, but that she would be extremely reluctant to change the plan once she confirmed it in an order.

The lawyers later met in the judge's chambers for a scheduling conference authorized by Rule 16(b). At this conference, Judge Goodenough was empowered to discuss a variety of matters, including deadlines for conducting discovery and filing motions. To begin the meeting, Judge Goodenough announced that she had reached a decision on the defendants' motion to dismiss Otis' fraud claim. She would grant the motion. This meant that Belcher was dismissed from the case. Although Belcher's lawyer was delighted by the judge's ruling, he silently wondered why he had been required to appear at a conference only to be told that his client was no longer a party.

Lane, on the other hand, now faced the prospect of litigating the case without addressing Otis' fraud claim. She still had some hope that, on appeal, she might persuade the federal circuit court to change precedent and reinstate the claim. But the prospect of appealing *after* the trial and having Otis' fraud claim re-instated was not very attractive; essentially, she would have to try the case a second time. Lane would also lose whatever current settlement leverage the fraud claim had given her.

If Lane had been litigating the Olmans' case in state court, where "interlocutory" appeals are sometimes more liberally authorized, she might have had the option of appealing the judge's decision immediately. But according to the "final judgment" rule prevailing in federal court, Lane had very few options for immediately challenging the court's ruling. As with many other decisions the court would make before and during trial, Lane would probably have to live with the court's ruling until the case ended and final judgment was entered.

A NOTE CONCERNING:
APPEALS

During the course of litigation and trial, the presiding judge will often make several rulings that can alter the outcome of the case. If the judge is mistaken, it might seem sensible to let the losing party immediately appeal the trial court's decision. By giving an appellate court the immediate opportunity to consider and correct the trial court's error, the judicial system may avoid the waste of a flawed trial and the need for a second one.

In federal court, a losing party is generally denied the opportunity to appeal a suspected error until the case is fully adjudicated. This limitation is called the "final judgment" rule and is codified in 28 U.S.C. section 1291 (federal appellate courts have "jurisdiction of appeals from all final decisions"). Although there are some exceptions to the final judgment rule, for the most part the losing party cannot file an "interlocutory" appeal of the trial court's intermittent rulings while the suit is still being conducted. Instead, a party must litigate the case to final judgment and then assert all grounds for appeal collectively. One benefit of the final judgment rule is that litigation is not continually disrupted by piecemeal appeals. Another benefit is that the appellate court can consider an alleged error in the context of the outcome in trial court. For example, the outcome at trial may demonstrate that the alleged error was harmless and any appeal pointless. A final benefit is that the need for an appeal may become moot; if the party claiming error ultimately prevails at trial the party will usually have no incentive to appeal.

One exception to the final judgment rule, potentially available to Lane, permits the trial court to enter a "final judgment" for part of the case. *See* Fed. R. Civ. P. 54(b). For example, Lane could ask the court to enter a *partial* judgment essentially stating that its order on the fraud claim against Belcher, Full Moon, or both was "final." This action would satisfy the statutory requirement limiting appeal to final judgments and permit Lane to seek immediate review of the court's interpretation of the law of fraud. But trial courts are often reluctant to grant partial, final judgments. Further, lawyers are often reluctant to seek such judgments, since this requires that they simultaneously engage in a trial and an appellate proceeding.

After announcing her decision dismissing Otis' fraud claim, Judge Goodenough asked Lane and Tweedy whether they would consider participating in mediation and try to settle the remaining claims in the suit. Both lawyers agreed this was not a good idea at present, because their clients had already attempted to settle the suit and probably were not in a position to alter their positions until more discovery was completed.[11]

Judge Goodenough then queried the lawyers about the witnesses they intended to depose, the documents they intended to inspect, and the time it might take to complete this discovery. She also asked them of their availability for trial in the coming year and similarly told them of her own availability.

After the conference ended, Judge Goodenough drafted a "scheduling order" that would be a template for the suit. According to Rule 16(b), the scheduling order can set time limits for a variety of matters including amending the pleadings, filing motions, conducting discovery, and conducting the trial. Rule 16(b) specifically provides that the schedule developed by the court "shall not be modified except upon a showing of good cause." In effect, this order *supercedes* several federal rules that otherwise give lawyers far greater flexibility in litigating a case.[12] Below are excerpts from Judge Goodenough's scheduling order.

---

[11]Under the local rules for the Middle District, Judge Goodenough could have ordered the parties to mediation, or the parties on their own initiative could have stipulated to engage in court annexed mediation. *See* Local Rule 9.03.

[12]For example, Rule 15(a) does not set a fixed time limit for seeking to amend pleadings. Similarly, Rule 26(d) does not establish a fixed time period for conducting discovery. Scheduling orders, however, routinely establish time limits for these activities. Later, we explore the impact of such orders on lawyers' procedural options.

IN THE UNITED STATES DISTRICT COURT
FOR THE MIDDLE DISTRICT OF FLORIDA
JACKSONVILLE DIVISION

OTIS AND FIONA OLMAN,

    Plaintiffs,

vs.   Case No. 03-2222-CIV-M-46-B

FULL MOON SPORTS, INC.,
& BRUCE BELCHER

    Defendants

CASE MANAGEMENT AND SCHEDULING ORDER

1. **TRIAL:** This case is scheduled for jury trial in Jacksonville, Florida, during the weeks of September 19, 2005.

2. **PRETRIAL CONFERENCE**: A Pretrial Conference will be held Thursday, September 15, 2005 at 2:00 p.m. before the Honorable Matthew Malarkey, United States Magistrate Judge, in the United States Courthouse, Courtroom 3414. Parties are directed to meet the pretrial disclosure requirements and deadlines in Fed. R.Civ. P. 26(a)(3) and to adhere to all requirements in Local Rule 3.02 concerning final pretrial procedures. The parties shall file a **JOINT** Pretrial Statement no later than three (3) days before the date of the Pretrial Conference. Failure to do so, may result in the imposition of sanctions. The Pretrial Conference shall be attended by lead trial counsel who is vested with full authority to make agreements touching on all matters pertaining to the trial.

3. **MOTIONS TO AMEND:** Motions to Amend any pleading or to continue the pretrial conference or trial are distinctly disfavored after entry of the Case Management and Scheduling Order.

4. **DISCOVERY CUTOFF**: All Discovery is to be completed by the parties on or before July 1, 2005.

[97]

5. **<u>DISPOSITIVE MOTIONS CUTOFF</u>:** Dispositive motions shall be filed on or before August 1, 2005.

. . .

DONE and ORDERED at Jacksonville, Florida, this 30th day of June, 2005.

_____

SARAH GOODENOUGH
United States District Judge

CHAPTER FIVE: GATHERING EVIDENCE AND REFINING STRATEGY: THE DISCOVERY PROCESS

Chapter Rule References: 8, *26,* 29, *30,* 31, 32, *33, 34,* 35, 36, *37, 45.*

A.   Preparing for the Discovery Process

Both Lane and Tweedy knew that, with the pleadings and Rule 16(b) conference behind them, they were able to begin the single largest pre-trial stage in federal court litigation: discovery. The parties would now use the discovery tools available under the Federal Rules to assemble the information necessary to establish their claims or defenses. Without good use of discovery, they knew the chances of success in litigation would be greatly diminished. They also knew that the discovery process was an important ingredient in any settlement discussions that might later occur, as the parties would be better able to assess the strengths and weaknesses of their positions in light of information obtained in discovery.

Lane and Tweedy also knew they could take advantage of means to gather information not addressed in the Federal Rules. They could search the Internet for relevant information, file Freedom of Information Act requests with the federal government (or use the state equivalents), or even hire a private investigator. In this case, for example, Full Moon and its parent corporation Mizar were publicly traded companies, and Lane could obtain certain documents the companies were required to periodically file with the United States Securities and Exchange Commission. We will focus our discussion on the Rules, but you should not forget about other important means of obtaining valuable information.

The formal information-gathering process under the Federal Rules essentially proceeds on two tracks. One track focuses on experts while the other focuses on factual information.[1] We will return to expert discovery/disclosure later in this chapter. For now, we focus on factual discovery.

The Federal Rules establish a two-phase process for obtaining factual information. First, the parties are required to exchange certain information, principally concerning matters they may use to establish their claims or defenses,[2] without waiting for a request

---

[1] *Compare* Rule 26(a)(1) (setting forth required disclosures concerning non-expert material) *with* Rule 26(a)(2) (setting forth required disclosures concerning expert testimony).

[2] *See* Rule 26(a)(1).

from the opposing party. This process is one of required "disclosure." Thereafter, the parties may use various methods provided under the Rules for obtaining information from parties and non-parties alike.[3] This latter process is called "discovery."

Before Lane and Tweedy could engage in either disclosure or discovery, they needed to comply with Rule 26(f)'s mandate to prepare a "discovery plan." As we have already seen, they prepared this plan in preparation for their initial meeting with Judge Goodenough.[4] Among other things, the lawyers discussed possible changes in their required disclosures, changes in limits on the use of discovery devices imposed by the Rules,[5] and the content and timing of discovery.[6] Ultimately, the lawyers agreed to abide by disclosure requirements and discovery restrictions stated in the Rules. They also agreed on a discovery completion date that was memorialized in Judge Goodenough's Case Management and Scheduling Order.[7]

---

[3]*See* Rule 26(d).

[4]*See supra* Chapter 4.

[5]We will discuss these limitations throughout this chapter as we review the parties' uses of the various discovery devices.

[6]*See* Rule 26(f). An exemplar "Report of Parties' Planning Meeting" is included as Form 35 of the Appendix of Forms of the Federal Rules.

[7]*See* Chapter 4, pp. 96–97.

Tactical Tip ✍

Party Autonomy in Discovery

Among other things, Rule 26(f) requires that parties confer about changes in disclosure obligations and discovery limitations. This requirement highlights an often underestimated feature of the Federal Rules discovery regime: ~~the rules governing disclosure and discovery are largely default rules~~. Rule 29 allows the parties to "modify . . . procedures governing or limitations placed upon discovery . . . " unless a change would alter court-imposed deadlines governing discovery, hearings, or trial. ~~If the parties do not agree to proceed in a different manner, the Rules govern.~~ You should not lose sight of the ability to craft discovery rules suited to your case.

Lane and Tweedy knew that planning for discovery involved understanding the case inside and out. They needed to understand what facts (good and bad) were in their possession, what additional facts they would need to obtain, what the law required them to prove at trial, and what the other side's case would likely be. Thus, the elements of the various claims asserted in the Complaint became important yet again.[8]

Before we explore the disclosure and discovery process itself, you should try your hand at a bit of planning.

---

[8]The use of summary judgment for resolving claims may also drive the type of discovery taken in a case. This consideration is dealt with more fully in our discussion of summary judgment. *See generally infra* Chapter 7.

Task 5.1

Planning for Discovery:

Put yourself in Lane's position. If you represented Otis on his retaliation and age discrimination claims:

- What information would you want to obtain?
- Why would you want to obtain it?
- From whom would you seek it?

Now put yourself in Tweedy's shoes. If you represented Full Moon as a defendant on the retaliation and age discrimination claims:

- What information would you want to obtain?
- Why would you want to obtain it?
- From whom would you seek it?

As they headed into the disclosure and discovery process, Lane and Tweedy reminded themselves that discovery was a *means* not an *end*. Lawyers can get lost in the process of gathering information, with all its potential for conflict with opposing counsel, instead of keeping the discovery process in perspective. Lane and Tweedy both knew they needed to keep their eyes on the prize: achieving their clients' goals in the litigation process. Discovery was not an end in itself.

B.   The Parties Make Their Required Disclosures

Rule 26(a)(1) generally requires a party to make certain disclosures without awaiting a request from the other party.[9] The Rule sets forth four categories of information

---

[9]Exceptions are recognized in Rule 26(a)(1)(E) (listing "categories of proceedings" exempt from required disclosure obligations), and Rule 26(a)(1) (allowing required disclosures to be avoided by a stipulation or order of the court).

Although making the calculations can be difficult under the Rules, the required disclosures must usually be made within three months of formal service on the defendant or the defendant's agreement to waive service. One reaches this result by starting with Rule 16(b), which requires the

a party is required to disclose. Rather than memorizing these categories, Lane had developed the sound habit of returning to the Rules to confirm her obligations.

Tactical Tip ✍

Read the Rules:

Closely read the Federal Rules each time you use them. Few lawyers have the capacity or inclination to memorize all the detail found in the Rules. It is more important to (1) generally know what Rule addresses the topic at hand, and (2) read the Rule *each time* it is used. If you follow this advice, you will seldom make mistakes when using a Rule.

When drafting the Olmans' disclosures, Lane needed to review both her offensive and defensive theories of the case. First, to identify which documents and witnesses she needed to disclose Lane had to determine which of these she might "use to support [her clients'] claims or defenses."[10] When Lane was unsure whether she might use a given witness or document, she tended to err on the side of disclosure. She reasoned that this information would likely be discovered by Full Moon anyway and, if she did not disclose it, she might be precluded from using the material later at trial.[11]

A second reason Lane needed to review the Olmans' case closely was to develop a more precise figure of the damages her clients would demand. While the complaint made

---

assigned judge to hold a scheduling conference within 90 days after service on the defendant or 120 days after the defendant's appearance. Rule 26(f) keys its requirement for the parties to meet and prepare a discovery plan to the Rule 16 conference, requiring that the Rule 26(f) conference take place "at least 21 days before" the Rule 16 conference. Rule 26(a)(1) provides that the required disclosures be made at the Rule 26(f) conference or within 14 days thereafter. It is not usually necessary to perform this calculation to determine disclosure deadlines. Many judges will include these deadlines in a pre-trial order.

[10]*See* Rule 26(a)(1)(A) and (B).

[11]*See* Rule 37(c)(1) ("A party that without substantial justification fails to disclose information required by Rule 26(a) . . . is not, unless such failure is harmless, permitted to use as evidence at a trial, at a hearing, or on a motion any witness or information not so disclosed.").

a general "demand for judgment for the relief" the Olmans sought,[12] Lane needed to be far more specific in her required disclosure statement.[13] Estimating damages can be particularly difficult in the early stages of a lawsuit, but Lane knew she could supplement her disclosures at a later point.[14]

Before reviewing Lane's disclosures, consider the following hypothetical disclosure issues based on the Olmans' suit:

---

[12]*See* Rule 8(a)(3).

[13]*See* Rule 26(a)(1)(C) (requiring disclosure of "a computation of any category of damages claimed by the disclosing party . . .").

[14]*See* Rule 26(e)(1).

Question 5.1

A.   Assume that Lane had spoken with a former employee at the Jacksonville store. This employee told Lane that she never heard any ageist comments directed against Otis or Fiona. Why would Lane *not* have to disclose the identity of this former employee to Full Moon? Since she will not use this at trial she doesn't need to disclose it.

B.   Assume that, in Question A, Full Moon later asks Otis in an interrogatory to "identify any person known to you who has knowledge concerning whether any ageist comments were made about either Otis or Fiona Olman at the Jacksonville store?" Would Lane have to identify the former employee? Why? Yes, it is reasonable 26(b)(1)

C.   Now assume that Lane was in possession of a tape recording of a meeting in which Bertie Lurch, Full Moon's President, said that he was going to get rid of Otis because he was "too old to handle the job." According to Rule 26(a)(1)(B), what factor determines whether Lane must disclose the recording? What risk does Lane run if she chooses not to disclose? Whether she will use it to support her claims. It could be barred or only used to impeach.

D.   Assume that, after making her required disclosures, Lane discovers a memorandum from Lurch she believes she may use to support Otis' claim of discrimination. What obligation, if any, does Lane have to disclose this memorandum? What risk does she run if she takes no action? Consider Rules 26(e) and 37(c) in answering these questions. She has an duty to update & include this new evidence, risks having it barred.

Excerpts from the disclosure statement Lane served after reviewing her case file and consulting with Otis and Fiona are below.

IN THE UNITED STATES DISTRICT COURT
FOR THE MIDDLE DISTRICT OF FLORIDA
JACKSONVILLE DIVISION

OTIS AND FIONA OLMAN,

    Plaintiffs,

vs.   Case No. 03-2222-CIV-M-46-B

FULL MOON SPORTS, INC.
& BRUCE BELCHER,

    Defendants.

REQUIRED DISCLOSURE STATEMENT
OF PLAINTIFFS OTIS AND FIONA OLMAN

Pursuant to Fed. R. Civ. P. 26(a)(1), plaintiffs Otis and Fiona Olman (collectively "Plaintiffs") hereby submit their Required Disclosure Statement concerning their claims and the counterclaim asserted by defendant Full Moon Sports, Inc. ("Defendant").

I.   **Disclosures Pursuant to Rule 26(a)(1)(A)**

Plaintiffs identify the following individuals who are likely to have discoverable information that Plaintiffs may use to support their claims or defenses:

> Lane used Rule 26(a)(1)(A) as a checklist to determine the information she needed to include in this section of the disclosure statement.

1.   **Otis Olman**, 105 Boxwood Lane, Jacksonville, Florida, 32210, phone: (904) 555-3607. Mr. Olman has information concerning Defendant's unlawful termination of him, including but not limited to the ageist attitude of the company and its representatives and the damages he suffered as a result of that attitude. He also has information concerning the lawfulness of his actions that form the basis for Defendant's counterclaim.

* * * * *

> While Lane was not required to identify Rex in the complaint, *see* Complaint ¶ 27, she had to identify Rex in her disclosure statement if she planned to use him to support the Olmans' claims.

4.   **Rex Ornstein**, 2702 Skimmer Point Way, Atlanta, Georgia, 30303, phone: (404) 555-1110. Mr. Ornstein has

[106]

information concerning the ageist attitudes of Defendant's employees in Atlanta, Georgia, including its officers and other senior management.

* * * * *

II.   Disclosures Pursuant to Rule 26(a)(1)(B)

Plaintiffs identify the following documents that are in their possession, custody or control that they may use to support their claims or defenses:

1.   Plaintiff Otis Olman's employment evaluations for the period of time he served as manager of the Jacksonville store.

* * * * *

5.   Pay stubs and other related records showing the Plaintiffs' lost pay resulting from Defendant's unlawful activities.

* * * * *

III.   Disclosures Pursuant to Rule 26(a)(1)(C)

Plaintiffs provide the following computation of the categories of damages claimed in the Complaint. In addition, Plaintiffs agree to make available for inspection and copying documents and any other evidentiary material, not privileged or otherwise protected from disclosure, on which their computation is based.

As requested in his Complaint in this action, Plaintiff Otis Olman seeks to recover (1) damages of back pay and future pay; (2) double back pay; (3) other compensatory damages; (4) prejudgment interest; (5) costs; and (6) attorney's fees in this action. Each category of damages is discussed separately below:

> While the Rule does not require an in-depth description of the damages the Olmans sought, it does require more information than Rule 8(a)(3) requires in the complaint.

1.   Damages of Back Pay and Future Pay: Mr. Olman seeks to recover damages in the form of lost income from back pay and future pay. Mr. Olman will request that these amounts be determined based on a salary of $85,000 per year, increased by the cost of living, from the time of his

wrongful termination through and including the year in which he will turn seventy-two, when he had planned to retire.

* * * * *

5.   <u>Attorney's Fees</u>: Mr. Olman will seek to recover the fees reasonably incurred by his attorney in prosecuting and defending this case.

* * * * *

IV.   <u>Disclosures Pursuant to Rule 26(a)(1)(D)</u>

Plaintiffs state that no insurance agreement provides coverage for the matters set forth in Defendant's counterclaim.

Plaintiffs reserve the right to supplement this disclosure statement pursuant to the Federal Rules of Civil Procedure.

OTIS OLMAN
FIONA OLMAN

By their attorney,

_____

Eleanor Lane
Lane & Quincy, P.A.
Trial Counsel for Plaintiffs
[Address, etc. omitted]

Lane's signature on this discovery constituted her certification under Rule 26(g) concerning the legal basis for her requests and her good faith in making them.

Certificate of Service

[omitted]

[108]

Of course, disclosure is not a one-way street. Full Moon also needed to comply with its obligations under Rule 26(a)(1). We have not included excerpts from Full Moon's disclosure statement, but ask that you consider the following question concerning Full Moon's obligations.

Question 5.2

Assume that Full Moon intends to argue at trial that its decisions to replace Otis and some 35 other store managers in the southeast region were motivated by (1) the managers' excessive salaries, and (2) their stores' relatively weak sales records. To support these claims, Full Moon has a substantial body of documents and electronic files showing manager salaries and store sales during the time of the company's downsizing. Under Rule 26(a)(1)(B), must Full Moon disclose this voluminous information? If so, in what manner must it be disclosed? — *doc. list*

After completing their Required Disclosure Statements, the Olmans and Full Moon had to serve them on all parties.[15] However, as with all discovery documents, they were precluded from filing the statements with the court.[16]

---

[15]*See* Rule 5(a).

[16]*See* Rule 5(d). The Rule's general prohibition on filing extends to deposition transcripts, interrogatories and answers, document requests and responses, and requests for admissions and responses unless these documents are "used in the proceeding or the court orders filing." *Id*. The most common ways in which discovery papers may be "used in the proceeding" are as part of a motion to compel further discovery responses, discussed later in this chapter, or as exhibits supporting or opposing motions for summary judgment. *See infra* Chapter 7.

C.   Discovery Devices: Uses and Disputes

1.   General Considerations

a.   Relevance and Privilege

Lane and Tweedy knew that the parameters of discovery were set by Rule 26(b)(1)'s twin requirements. First, they could discover without court permission any matter "relevant to the claim or defense of any party." Second, discovery extended to relevant matters "not privileged."[17]

The first thing to notice is that relevance is defined by reference to the *pleadings*. Allegations in the complaint, answer, and any other pleading essentially set the stage on which discovery will take place. This interconnection between pleading and discovery conveys a simple lesson: At the pleading stage one must be looking forward to discovery, and at discovery one must look back to the pleadings. At the same time, the Rules allow a party to seek court *permission*[18] to obtain discovery of matters that are "relevant to the *subject matter* of the action."[19]

The second requirement for discovery is that the information sought not be "privileged." While relevance is concerned more with the content of the matter sought to be discovered, privilege focuses on the *source* from which the information is sought. For example, a commonly-asserted privilege is that between attorney and client. A party seeking discovery is normally not permitted to ask a lawyer what her client told her. That does not mean, however, that the underlying *information* possessed by the client is privileged. The client may be asked to convey information she possesses, provided it is relevant. But any

---

[17]Rule 26(b)(1).

[18]*See* Rule 26(b)(1). One court has opined that the difference in a discrimination case between matters relevant to a "claim or defense of any party" and something merely relevant to "the subject matter of the action" may go to the *type* of discrimination at issue in the case. *See Davis v. Precoat Metals, Inc.*, 2002 WL 1759828 (N.D. Ill. 2002). So, for example, in a race discrimination case information concerning discrimination on the basis of race with respect to other employees would be related to the claims or defenses of a party while information concerning age-based discrimination would relate only to the subject matter of the action (*i.e.*, job discrimination by an employer). *Id.* A party could take discovery of the former on its own initiative but would need permission of the court to take discovery of the latter.

[19]*See* Rule 26(b)(1).

communication with her lawyer *per se* is protected from discovery.[20] Society has made a determination that the attorney-client *relationship* is one worthy of enhanced protection.

---

[20]To illustrate, Full Moon could properly ask Otis Olman how early he complained to Full Moon's representatives about age discrimination. However, Full Moon could not ask Lane to disclose what *Otis conveyed to her* during the course of a privileged conversation about his complaints. The information is relevant and discoverable from Otis but cannot be accessed by asking Lane to breach a privilege.

A Note Concerning:
COMMON PRIVILEGES

In litigation, a "privilege" is a right to prevent the disclosure of information even if relevant. ~~The concept of privilege reflects the belief that some values are more important than resolving the dispute at hand by full disclosure of relevant information.~~ For example, we protect information communicated between a lawyer and her client not because there is something about the *information* that makes disclosure inappropriate. Rather, we protect the information because we value the *relationship*, and want to encourage clients to confide in lawyers and want lawyers to provide full advice to clients. ~~Because of their effect on the litigation process, privileges tend to be narrowly construed~~.

There are numerous privileges. Although there are common law privileges, ~~most privileges are created through legislation~~. ~~According to Federal Rules of Evidence 501, federal courts apply a federal common law of privileges to claims based on federal law, but apply state-law privileges to claims based on state law.~~

You will learn much more about privileges in your evidence class.[21] In the meantime, here are some of the more common privileges you may encounter in your career (in addition to the attorney-client privilege already discussed):

The Marital Privilege: This privilege generally prevents one spouse from giving testimony against the other.

The Fifth Amendment Privilege Against Self-Incrimination: The Fifth Amendment to the United States Constitution allows a person to decline to provide testimony that might lead to or support criminal charges against him.

The Doctor-Patient Privilege: This privilege precludes a doctor from testifying concerning communications she has had with a patient.

The Religious Advisor-Penitent Privilege: This privilege protects communications between priests, ministers, rabbis, mullahs, *etc.* and their congregants.

---

[21]Our descriptions of these representative privileges are accurate but presented at a high level of abstraction. For a more in-depth view of privileges, you should consult one of the many excellent secondary sources in this field. *See, e.g.*, Scott N. Stone & Robert K. Taylor, TESTIMONIAL PRIVILEGES (2d ed. 1995).

Rule 26(b)(3) creates a unique restriction on the scope of discovery that is specifically related to the trial process. This restriction — which is not technically a privilege[22] — extends to "trial preparation" or "work product" and is intended to protect from disclosure "documents and other tangible things . . . prepared in anticipation of litigation or for trial." While the work product protection encompasses materials developed by a party's lawyer, it is not limited the lawyer's product. Rather, it encompasses trial preparation by any "party" or "by or for that . . . party's representative (including the . . . party's attorney, consultant, surety, indemnitor, insurer, or agent. . . .") The key question to ask in determining whether material is protected work product is: Was it prepared in anticipation of litigation or for trial? In other words, the *purpose* for which material was prepared is critical. The Advisory Committee Notes to Rule 26 make this clear. Those notes emphasize that material "assembled in the ordinary course of business, or pursuant to public requirements unrelated to litigation, or for other nonlitigation purposes" are not protected.

If material qualifies as work product, it is generally immune from discovery unless the party seeking it can show that he "has substantial need of the materials in the preparation of the party's case" *and* is "unable without undue hardship to obtain the substantial equivalent of the material by other means." The burden of overcoming a valid claim of work product is heavy. What is more, Rule 26(b)(3) provides absolute immunity to that part of work product containing "mental impressions, conclusions, opinions, or legal theories of an attorney." As a consequence, even if a party makes the compelling case that he should be permitted to discover work product, any parts of that product containing a lawyer's recorded thoughts will be "redacted" prior to disclosure.

Generally, as with privileges, a work product protection cannot be used to conceal relevant information. Thus, a party may object to disclosing a document or report that was prepared in anticipation of litigation, but cannot refuse to answer questions that seek information contained in the work product. For example, a party might authorize its agent to prepare a special accident report and feel secure that the report will be protected work product. However, information obtained while preparing the report (*e.g.*, the names of eyewitnesses, observations at the accident site) will be discoverable through mechanisms like depositions and interrogatories.

The work product privilege is intended to permit parties to prepare for litigation without fear that their preparation materials will be revealed to adversaries. A good lawyer,

---

[22]Work product does not qualify as a "privilege" *per se* because it can be obtained if the party seeking it makes a compelling case. Privileged material, in contrast, is usually immune from any attempt at discovery.

appreciating the value of work product protection, will often take steps to ensure that he or she is in a strong position to argue that material is "work product" when discovery commences. For example, the lawyer may advise his or her client that all materials generated pertaining to a lawsuit (or potential lawsuit) contain a introductory legend with words like, "Attorney Work Product—Prepared at the Direction of an Attorney in anticipation and preparation of litigation." If an adversary later seeks this material, the party will be well positioned to argue that it purposefully developed it "in anticipation of litigation or for trial."

Later in this chapter we will see how Full Moon's claim that material sought by Lane was work product evolved into a discovery controversy.

b.   Tools of Discovery

Lane and Tweedy knew that as long as they sought relevant, unprivileged information, they could choose from a wide array of tools. The following table summarizes those tools and some of the limitations on their use:

A Guide to Gathering Information Under the Rules

Information Gathering Method	Rules' Nomenclature	Rule(s)	Court Permission Required?	Available Against Non-Party, as Well as Party?
Requiring a person to give you documents, data, or objects	"Production of documents and things . . ."	34, 35 and 45	No	Yes (via R.45)
Obtaining entry to land or property	" . . . Entry upon land for inspection and other purposes"	34 and 45	No	Yes (via R.45)
Requiring written answers to questions under oath	"Interrogatory"	33	No	No
Requiring submission to exam by a health professional	"Physical and Mental Examination"	35	Yes	No

Information Gathering Method	Rules' Nomenclature	Rule(s)	Court Permission Required?	Available Against Non-Party, as Well as Party?
Requiring answers to questions orally under oath	"Deposition upon Oral Examination"	30 and 45	No	Yes (via R.45)
Requiring a person to admit whether something is true	"Requests for Admission"	36	No	No

So how were Lane and Tweedy to figure out how to use this panoply of tools in a coordinated way? An interesting feature of the discovery rules is that they simultaneously provide considerable detail about how each tool is to be used while saying little about how these tools are to be used together. There is, for example, no required chronological order for submitting written questions to parties (interrogatories) and questioning the party orally (by deposition). In the end, the choice of the order in which to use discovery tools is based on the needs of the individual case and the experience of the lawyers.

The professional experience of Lane and Tweedy had led them to similar conclusions regarding the relative value of discovery devices. They each saw depositions as the crown jewels of discovery. They devoted greatest preparation to depositions and expected that depositions would yield much of the information important at summary judgment and trial. Therefore, they usually waited until later in the discovery period, after first acquiring information through other discovery tools, to take depositions.[23]

Lane and Tweedy would use "paper discovery" devices early in the process, including document requests and interrogatories. This information might be valuable in its own right and would also prepare them for depositions. They would, however, typically save one form of paper discovery to the end of the process: requests for admission. These requests were designed to take matters out of contention at trial. In order to use this tool

---

[23]This approach was not invariable as each case is unique. For example, Lane had at times taken the deposition of a corporate decisionmaker in discrimination cases early on to lock that person into a single version of events.

most effectively, Lane and Tweedy would seek admissions after assembling information obtained through other forms of discovery.[24]

One final consideration is important before we turn to the parties' use of the various discovery devices. Both Lane and Tweedy knew they needed to consider the prospect of discovery from two perspectives. First, they would consider their opportunity to *seek* discovery to build their own clients' case. Second, they would consider their responsibility to *provide* discovery to assist their opponents in building their case.

There are several reasons for viewing discovery from an opponent's perspective. First, sound litigation practice requires that a lawyer know the weak points of a client's case and the discovery product that will be used to expose these weak points. By thinking about weaknesses early on, a lawyer is often able to anticipate and address problems in her client's case. In addition, by considering the discovery an opponent may seek, a lawyer can engage in some preparatory work such as collecting material on her own schedule instead of one dictated by her opponent.

Yet another reason for defensive consideration of discovery material is that clients and lawyers are under a duty to *preserve* discoverable material once litigation is filed or there is a reasonable prospect of litigation about a given issue.[25] If harmful evidence is lost

---

[24]In appropriate cases, it is also possible to compel a party to undergo a mental or physical examination as part of the discovery process. *See* Rule 35. Unlike the great majority of other discovery devices, a party needs court permission to obtain this type of discovery. *Id.* In certain ADEA cases mental or physical examinations may be allowed because the plaintiff has, in the words of Rule 35(a), placed his "mental or physical condition . . . in controversy." A plaintiff may also place his or her mental condition in controversy, for example, by claiming damages for emotional distress. *See, e.g., Cauley v. Ingram Micro, Inc.*, 216 F.R.D. 241, 243 (W.D.N.Y. 2003) (claim of severe emotional distress in employment discrimination case sufficient to place the plaintiff's emotional condition in controversy under Rule 35). In practice, parties who have placed their mental or physical condition in controversy know that their opponents are entitled to have them examined. Consequently, most mental and physical examinations will be conducted by agreement of the parties rather than by court order.

The Olmans had not placed their mental or physical condition in controversy and, therefore, Full Moon would not seek, nor would it be entitled to compel, a mental or physical examination under Rule 35.

[25]*See, e.g., Silvestri v. General Motors Corp.*, 271 F.3d 583, 591 (4th Cir. 2001) ("The duty to preserve evidence arises not only during litigation but also extends to that period before the litigation when a party reasonably should know that the evidence may be relevant to anticipated

or destroyed, clients and lawyers may pay a steep price for this "spoliation" of evidence.[26] For example, if a court determines that a party has not done enough to preserve relevant evidence it can sanction the party by, among other things, awarding costs to an opponent, or worse, informing the jury of the destruction of evidence and allowing the jurors to draw adverse inferences against the responsible party. Thus, a jury might be allowed to infer that lost or destroyed evidence was extremely harmful to the party responsible for preserving it.[27] As you can imagine, such an instruction is often fatal to a party's case.[28]

The risk of spoliation particularly concerned Tweedy. His client was a large corporation with numerous employees at various locations. The opportunities for inadvertent destruction of documents were quite high. Luckily, Full Moon had taken proper steps to preserve documents from spoliation. As soon as it became clear that the Olmans might sue, Full Moon's general counsel (its in-house lawyer) issued a "litigation hold" to all employees. This litigation hold described the nature of the suit the company faced, specifically identified the types of documents that needed to be preserved, and explicitly directed that those documents be retained.

When Tweedy became involved in the case he reconfirmed the litigation hold. In addition, he personally met with management-level personnel in Full Moon's business divisions to reiterate the importance of the litigation hold. Tweedy's most difficult task was ensuring that Full Moon did not inadvertently destroy any electronically stored documents such as email. Tweedy educated himself about how Full Moon stored electronic material and then issued appropriate directions for recycling or deleting this material while litigation

---

litigation."); *Fujitsu Ltd. v. Federal Express Corp.*, 247 F.3d 423, 436 (2d Cir. 2001) ("The obligation to preserve evidence arises when the party has notice that the evidence is relevant to litigation or when a party should have known that the evidence may be relevant to future litigation."); *Zubulake v. UBS Warburg LLC*, 2004 U.S. Dist. LEXIS 13574 at *31–*43 (S.D.N.Y. July 20, 2004) (discussing counsel's duties to ensure compliance with duty to preserve relevant evidence).

[26]*See, e.g., West v. Goodyear Tire & Rubber Co.*, 167 F.3d 776, 779 (2d Cir. 1999).

[27]*Zubulake v. UBS Warburg LLC*, 2004 U.S. Dist LEXIS 13574 at *51–*62 (S.D.N.Y. July 20, 2004) (discussing range of possible sanctions and setting forth jury instruction concerning spoliation).

[28]*Zubulake v. UBS Warburg LLC*, 220 F.R.D. 212, 219 (S.D.N.Y. 2003) ("In practice, an adverse inference instruction often ends litigation—it is too difficult a hurdle for the spoliator to overcome.").

was pending.[29] Tweedy's efforts at document preservation took time, but he knew that the time was well spent given the potential consequences Full Moon faced if the job was not done right.

2.   Initial Paper Discovery

a.   Lane Begins the Discovery Process[30]

Lane determined that she would start the discovery process by seeking documents from Full Moon and certain non-parties. She would also send interrogatories to Full Moon. Lane would then use the information she obtained to identify the individuals she wanted to depose and begin preparing to take these depositions.

Lane began with documents. Lane's ability to require the production of documents was an exceptionally important tool. She knew from experience that documents often contain important information unavailable elsewhere. She also knew that, at least initially, the relative burden of document production was greater for Full Moon than the Olmans. Lane's clients had few documents relevant to their claims. Full Moon, on the other hand, likely had thousands of potentially-relevant documents. Thus, documentary discovery was an inexpensive way for Lane to obtain quite valuable information. Lane knew, however, that the burden involved in document discovery would shift to her when she began the time-consuming task of reviewing the documents Full Moon produced.

---

[29]For a comprehensive discussion of counsel's obligations concerning document preservation, *see Zubulake v. UBS Warburg LLC*, 2004 U.S. Dist LEXIS 13574 (S.D.N.Y. July 20, 2004).

[30]Full Moon would be engaging in discovery simultaneously with the Olmans. Although we will consider some of Full Moon's discovery requests in this chapter, we will primarily focus on the Olmans' discovery efforts and Full Moon's responses.

Task 5.2

Put yourself in Lane's position:

(1)   What documents, described either specifically or by category, would you want to obtain through discovery? Why would you want these documents?

(2)   From whom would you seek these documents?

(3)   What specific discovery mechanism would you use to obtain these documents from the persons you identified?

Now put yourself in Tweedy's position:

(1)   What documents, described either specifically or by category, would you want to obtain through discovery? Why would you want these documents?

(2)   From whom would you seek these documents?

(3)   What specific discovery mechanism would you use to obtain these documents from the persons you identified?

Lane focused first on obtaining documents from Full Moon. She knew that Rule 34 allowed her to serve a request for production of documents or other tangible things on any party.[31] Before she began drafting the document request, she reminded herself of some of the important features of the Federal Rules governing her request. First, she knew there were no specific limits on the number of document requests she could make, unlike limits restricting the number of interrogatories she might ask. Second, she needed to ensure that

---

[31] In an appropriate case, Rule 34 would also provide the authority for a party to enter another party's property for the purpose of conducting an inspection. *See* Rule 34(a)(2). That provision of the Rule was not likely to be of use in the Olmans' case.

[119]

her document requests complied with Rule 26(b)(1)'s parameters concerning relevance and privilege.

Finally, Lane knew that, although discovery papers are not subject to the requirements of Rule 11,[32] her signature on the document requests constituted a certification similar to that made under Rule 11. According to Rule 26(g), Lane would by certifying that her requests were (1) "consistent with [the discovery rules] and warranted by existing law or a good faith argument for the extension, modification, or reversal of existing law";[33] (2) "not interposed for any improper purpose, such as to harass or to cause unnecessary delay or needless increase in the cost of litigation";[34] and (3) "not unreasonable or unduly burdensome or expensive, given the needs of the case, the discovery already had in the case, the amount in controversy, and the importance of the issues at stake in the litigation."[35] Lane took these certifications seriously and thus paid close attention when identifying the documents she requested from Full Moon.[36]

Here is an excerpted version of the document request Lane served on Tweedy:

---

[32]*See* Rule 11(d) (Rule 11's requirements "do not apply to disclosures and discovery requests, responses, objections, and motions that are subject to the provisions of Rules 26 through 37.").

[33]Rule 26(g)(2)(A).

[34]Rule 26(g)(2)(B).

[35]Rule 26(g)(2)(C).

[36]These three certifications apply to all discovery requests, responses, and objections. *See* Rule 26(g)(2). Similar certifications apply to a party's required disclosures. Rule 26(g)(1).

IN THE UNITED STATES DISTRICT COURT
FOR THE MIDDLE DISTRICT OF FLORIDA
JACKSONVILLE DIVISION

OTIS AND FIONA OLMAN,

    Plaintiffs,

vs.   Case No. 03-2222-CIV-M-46-B

FULL MOON SPORTS, INC.,
& BRUCE BELCHER,

    Defendants.

PLAINTIFFS' FIRST REQUEST
FOR PRODUCTION OF DOCUMENTS

Pursuant to Federal Rule of Civil Procedure 34, Plaintiffs hereby request that Defendant produce for inspection and copying the documents described below.

Definitions

Unless otherwise indicated, the following definitions shall apply to all the requests set forth below.

> Many attorneys include definitions at the beginning of a discovery request to make it easier to understand. Care must be taken, however, to ensure that the definitions do not make the request too broad or burdensome.

1.   The term "concerning" means relating to, referring to, describing, evidencing or constituting.

2.   The term "Defendant" means Full Moon Sports, Inc. and any of its officers, agents, employees or representatives.

3.   The term "Jacksonville Store" means the Full Moon Outdoor Center, a retail sporting goods store located in Jacksonville, Florida, and owned by Defendant.

* * * * * *

Document Requests

1.   The personnel files for Otis Olman and Fiona Olman.

2.   The personnel or employee handbook(s) or manual(s) in effect at the Defendant for the period during which either Otis Olman or Fiona Olman were employed by Defendant.

* * * * *

Notice that Lane sought information beyond that concerning the Olmans. Was this proper? Why?

6.   All documents concerning any investigation performed by Defendant or at its request concerning allegations that any employee, including either Plaintiff in this action, was terminated, demoted, transferred, denied a promotion, or otherwise harmed as a result of such employee's age.

7.   All documents concerning or supporting Defendant's allegation in its Answer and Counterclaim that Plaintiff Otis Olman converted Defendant's property.

Lane used the discovery tools both to support her claims and refute Full Moon's counterclaim.

* * * * *

15.   All communications, including but not limited to email or other electronic communications, concerning the reduction in force at the Jacksonville store.

16.   All documents concerning reductions in force for the period from 2000 to the present at any of the Defendant's retail locations, corporate headquarters, or any other location at which the Defendant conducts its business that indicate the ages of those employees terminated, transferred, or demoted as well as the ages of those persons who replaced such persons in the positions they held prior to the reduction in force.

* * * * *

OTIS OLMAN
FIONA OLMAN

By their attorney,

_____

Eleanor Lane
Lane & Quincy, P.A.
Trial Counsel for Plaintiffs
[Address etc. omitted]

Certificate of Service

[omitted]

Lane also wanted to obtain documents from non-parties. She would use one of the most powerful discovery tools authorized by the Federal Rules. Rule 45 grants lawyers the authority to compel non-parties to produce documents or appear for a deposition, without prior court authorization.[37] Lane knew that it was important that she exercise the power wisely. Consider the following comment:

Tactical Tip ✍

Subpoenaing Non-Parties

Simply having the power to compel a non-party to take a certain action does not mean that a lawyer should automatically use that power. It may be the case that a non-party will be willing to cooperate without a subpoena or that he will be more cooperative if warned ahead of time that a subpoena is on its way. Of course, there will be many situations in which a lawyer knows she should use the subpoena power surely or swiftly. For example, a lawyer may already know a non-party will be uncooperative. Or a lawyer may suspect that evidence will be lost or destroyed if it is not requested formally without advance warning. However, these concerns should not blind a lawyer to the possibility that, in the words of the old saying, you may get more with honey than with vinegar.

There were several non-parties who might provide Lane useful documents or deposition testimony. Key among them was Belcher. Recall that Belcher had been dismissed from the case and was no longer subject to discovery under rules governing parties. Further, Belcher no longer worked for Full Moon and now lived in Connecticut. Absent his agreement to come to Florida, Lane would have to seek discovery from Belcher in Connecticut.[38]

Under the Federal Rules, Lane did not need to initiate any special judicial proceeding in Connecticut to obtain discovery from Belcher. This was so even though the Olmans' case was pending in federal court in Florida. Nor did Lane need to associate herself with a lawyer admitted to practice law in Connecticut. Under Rule 45, an attorney

---

[37]*See* Rule 45(a)(1)(C).

[38]*See* Rule 45(b)(2).

may use the subpoena power to compel production of documents and/or testimony at a deposition in a federal district court in which he or she is admitted,[39] or in *any other* federal district court so long as the attorney is admitted to the bar of the federal district court in which the action is *pending*.[40] Thus, because Lane was admitted to the bar of the Middle District of Florida, where the Olmans' suit was pending, she could issue a subpoena directed to Belcher compelling him to produce documents and appear at a deposition in Connecticut.[41]

"GREETINGS: YOU ARE HEREBY SUBPOENAED TO APPEAR..."

The final form of paper discovery Lane prepared was a set of interrogatories directed to Full Moon. Lane did not consider interrogatories to be a particularly useful

---

[39]*See* Rule 45(a)(3)(A).

[40]*See* Rule 45(a)(3)(B).

[41]You can view a Rule 45 subpoena thorough the web page for the federal judiciary. *See* <www.uscourts.gov/forms/AO088.pdf> (last visited December 29, 2004). Note that, under Rule 45(c)(3)(A)(ii), a person who is subpoenaed may move to quash the subpoena if it requires him to travel "more than 100 miles from the place where that person resides, is employed or regularly transacts business in person."

discovery tool. ~~Interrogatories are written questions that a party may ask another party,~~[42] ~~which must be answered in writing under oath.~~[43] But in practice the answers to interrogatories are most often drafted by a party's lawyer and only reviewed for factual accuracy by the party. The result is that interrogatory answers tend not to be that helpful.[44]

Still, Lane knew that interrogatories had some value for obtaining specific information from Full Moon. For example, Lane could ask for a summary of information contained within Full Moon's business files. Rule 33 requires that a party answering interrogatories provide information *available* to it, like that contained in an electronic database.[45] Similarly, if Full Moon had an officer or employee with knowledge of a matter addressed by an interrogatory, it would have to consult with that person and incorporate his knowledge into its answers. Consequently, Lane would think carefully about how she used the 25 interrogatories permitted her under Rule 33.[46]

---

[42] ~~Interrogatories cannot be served on a non-party (like Belcher).~~ *See* Rule 33(a) ("any party may serve upon any other party written interrogatories").

[43] *See* Rule 33(a) and (b).

[44] Some unscrupulous lawyers submit excessive interrogatories to cause an adversary to spend unnecessary time and incur unwarranted costs. Use of interrogatories for either of these purposes is obviously unethical. *See, e.g.,* Rule 26(g)(2)(B) (A party serving any discovery request certifies that the request is "not interposed for any improper purpose, such as to harass or to cause unnecessary delay or needlessly increase the cost of litigation."); Model Rule of Professional Responsibility 3.4(d) ("A lawyer shall not: . . . (d) in pretrial procedure, make a frivolous discovery request . . .").

[45] *See, e.g., Law v. NCAA*, 167 F.R.D. 464, 476 (D. Kan. 1996) *vacated on other grounds, University of Texas v. Vratil*, 96 F.R.D. 1337 (10th Cir. 1996) (a party responding to interrogatories must provide "composite knowledge" available to it). In comparison, a party answering a question during a deposition need only answer based on information immediately within his knowledge and recollection.

[46] *See* Rule 33(a). Technically, Lane could probably have propounded 50 interrogatories because Otis and Fiona, as separate parties, would each have been able to ask 25 questions.

Task 5.3

A.   Recall that the Olmans allege Full Moon engaged in a "pattern and practice of age discrimination affecting company-wide downsizing." *See* Complaint, ¶ 35, *supra* at p. 41. What interrogatories might Lane frame to obtain information to support this allegation?

B.   Recall that Full Moon has asserted a counterclaim against Otis in which it alleges he "converted store merchandise on several occasions during the time he served as store manager." *See* Answer, ¶ 64, *supra* at p. 82. What interrogatories might Lane frame to obtain information to refute this allegation?

Brief excerpts from the interrogatories Lane drafted for service on Tweedy are below.

IN THE UNITED STATES DISTRICT COURT
FOR THE MIDDLE DISTRICT OF FLORIDA
JACKSONVILLE DIVISION

OTIS AND FIONA OLMAN,

      Plaintiffs,

vs.   Case No. 03-2222-CIV-M-46-B

FULL MOON SPORTS, INC.
& BRUCE BELCHER,

      Defendants.

PLAINTIFFS' FIRST SET OF INTERROGATORIES TO DEFENDANT

> Note that because Full Moon is a corporate defendant it must respond through an officer or agent. *See* Rule 33(a).

Pursuant to Federal Rule of Civil Procedure 33, Plaintiffs hereby request that Defendant, though its officers or agents, answer the following interrogatories under oath.

Definitions

[Definitions omitted]

Interrogatories

1. Identify the person or persons who made the determination to promote Mr. Sid Shockley to manager of the Jacksonville store.

2. Identify the manager or managers of Full Moon's information systems, information management or computer department (or other similar department or organizational structure) for the period from January 2002 to the present.

> Interrogatories such as this one can be useful in determining whom to depose.

* * * *

8. State the age of all managers of all Full Moon retail stores as of January 2003 and January 2004.

[128]

* * * *

15. Identify all facts that support your contention that Otis Olman converted Full Moon's property as Full Moon has alleged in its counterclaim in this action.

* * * *

22. Does Full Moon contend that Otis Olman was unqualified to continue serving as manager of the Jacksonville store at the time of his replacement? If your answer is yes, identify all facts that support this contention.

Interrogatories 15 and 22 are known as "contention interrogatories." They are permitted but courts often allow parties to defer answering until discovery

* * * *

OTIS OLMAN
FIONA OLMAN

By their attorney,

_____

Eleanor Lane
Lane & Quincy, P.A.
Trial Counsel for Plaintiffs
[Address etc. omitted]

Certificate of Service

[omitted]

b.   Full Moon Responds

When Tweedy received the Olmans' document requests and interrogatories, he immediately sent them to his client. Tweedy asked his contact at Full Moon, associate in-house counsel Judy Kaufman, to begin the process of locating and collecting documents requested by the Olmans. He instructed Kaufman to read the requests broadly when making this initial collection. Tweedy knew that he—along with several younger associates—could always remove documents from those initially collected by Full Moon. It would be much more difficult for him to recognize that something was missing and then ask Full Moon to find it. When he and his associates reviewed the documents initially assembled by Kaufman they would have two principal considerations in mind. First, were the documents actually responsive to the requests? Second, was there a proper basis to withhold a document even if it was responsive? One common basis for withholding documents is privilege, a topic to which we will return shortly.

Tweedy also instructed Kaufman to keep good notes about how the company went about locating and assembling responsive documents. In particular, Tweedy wanted a record of who actually looked for documents, what instructions the searchers were given, and where they looked. He knew that such records could be quite useful should Lane claim that Full Moon had not conducted a diligent search. This information would also allow Tweedy to monitor what Full Moon was doing to assemble the documents.

Tweedy also sent the interrogatories to the client. Tweedy asked for specific information he could use to draft responses. Although a representative of Full Moon would have to sign the responses,[47] Tweedy would actually draft them. When he completed his draft he would send it to Full Moon for a careful review to ensure that what he said was accurate.

As with the document requests, Tweedy reviewed the interrogatories to determine whether he could object to any of them. Tweedy kept a list of common discovery objections. These include that requests (1) seek privileged information; (2) seek trial preparation material; (3) seek irrelevant material; (4) are over broad; (5) are vague or ambiguous; (6) are unduly burdensome; (7) will cause undue expense; or (8) will cause undue annoyance or embarrassment. Tweedy used this list to verify he had not missed a viable objection. At the same time he knew that Full Moon's responses to discovery

---

[47]*See* Rule 33(b)(2) ("answers are to be signed by the person making them").

requests, as well as its objections, required his signature certifying that the company's positions were advanced in good faith and were based on solid legal grounds.[48]

As the deadline for serving Full Moon's discovery responses neared,[49] Tweedy was ready to finalize its formal responses. He had younger lawyers and paralegals at his firm prepare the documents for production. Tweedy would never actually give original documents to opposing counsel. Rather, he normally used one of two options. First, he might make the documents available to Lane for her review, after which she could ask that certain documents be copied. Alternatively, if there were relatively few documents to be produced, Tweedy would offer to have his firm make copies (at a reasonable rate) and send them to Lane. In the Olmans' case, Tweedy and Lane had previously agreed that he would make the responsive documents available to Lane for her review.[50]

Excerpts from Full Moon's responses to the document requests and interrogatories appear below.

---

[48] *See* Rule 26(g)(2) (specifying certifications).

[49] Full Moon had 30 days after service of the requests to respond. *See* Rule 33(b)(3) (30 days to respond to interrogatories); 34(b) (30 days to respond to document requests). In many cases, the parties will stipulate under Rule 29 that a longer time may be had to make responses.

[50] Tweedy had another choice about how he produced documents to Lane. He could provide specific documents in response to each of her requests or he could produce the documents as they were "kept in the usual course of business." Rule 34(b). Whichever method he used, Tweedy would place sequential identification numbers on each page so that they could be traced back to Full Moon's production (and provide a useful means of referring to the documents in, for example, later depositions). In the sample responses that follow in the text, we have omitted these identification numbers.

IN THE UNITED STATES DISTRICT COURT
FOR THE MIDDLE DISTRICT OF FLORIDA
JACKSONVILLE DIVISION

OTIS AND FIONA OLMAN,

     Plaintiffs,

vs.   Case No. 03-2222-CIV-M-46-B

FULL MOON SPORTS, INC.,
& BRUCE BELCHER,

     Defendants.

DEFENDANT'S RESPONSES AND OBJECTIONS TO PLAINTIFFS' FIRST REQUEST FOR PRODUCTION OF DOCUMENTS

Pursuant to Federal Rule of Civil Procedure 34, Defendant Full Moon Sports, Inc. ("Defendant") hereby responds to Plaintiffs' First Request for Production of Documents as follows:

General Objections

The following General Objections are applicable to, and incorporated by reference into, each of Defendant's responses to the specific document requests.

> **It is common to begin responses with general objections that are incorporated by reference into specific responses.**

1.   Defendant objects to the Document Request to the extent it demands production of any document protected from disclosure by the attorney-client privilege, the work-product doctrine or any other applicable privilege. To the extent any privileged document is produced by defendant, its production is inadvertent and does not constitute a waiver of any privilege.

2.   Defendant objects to the Document Request to the extent it demands production of information concerning employment actions taken regarding any employee other than Otis Olman and Fiona Olman. Such records are irrelevant and confidential.

[132]

* * * * *

Specific Responses and Objections

Notice that Tweedy first restates the request and then provides a response. While not required, this format is a common one.

Request #1

The personnel files for Otis Olman and Fiona Olman.

Response #1

Subject to and incorporating the General Objections, Defendant states that it will produce all documents in its possession, custody or control responsive to this Request.

Note that Full Moon limited its response to documents "in its possession custody or control." The discovery rules do not require a party or non-party to obtain information that does not come within this description. *See* Rule 34(a)(1).

Request #2

The personnel or employee handbook(s) or manual(s) in effect at the Defendant for the period during which either Otis Olman or Fiona Olman were employed by Defendant.

Response #2

Subject to and incorporating the General Objections, Defendant states that it will produce all documents in its possession, custody or control responsive to this Request.

* * * * *

Request #6

All documents concerning any investigation performed by Defendant or at its request concerning allegations that any employee, including either Plaintiff in this action, was terminated, demoted, transferred, denied a promotion, or otherwise harmed as a result of such employee's age.

Response #6

Defendant objects to Request #6 on the ground that it calls for the production of documents protected from disclosure by the attorney-client

Note that on the basis of these objections Full Moon elects to produce no documents.

[133]

privilege and/or the work-product doctrine. Defendant further objects to this request on the ground that it is over broad and calls for the production of irrelevant material to the extent to calls for the production of information concerning persons other than plaintiffs Otis Olman and Fiona Olman. Based on these objections, Defendant declines to produce documents responsive to this Request.

Request #7

All documents concerning or supporting Defendant's allegation in its Answer and Counterclaim that Plaintiff Otis Olman converted Defendant's property.

Response #7

Defendant objects to Request #7 on the ground that it is vague and calls for the production of documents protected from disclosure by the attorney-client privilege and/or the work-product doctrine. Subject to and without waiving these or any objections, Defendant states that it will produce all non-privileged documents in its possession, custody or control that are responsive to this Request.

Note that Full Moon states its objection but nonetheless agrees to produce some material.

* * * * *

Request #15

All communications, including but not limited to email or other electronic communications, concerning the reduction in force at the Jacksonville store.

Response #15

Defendant objects to Request #15 as being over broad. Additionally, Defendant objects to this Request specifically with respect to the production of "email and other electronic communications" on the ground that compliance with the request would be financially burdensome. Without waiving and subject to these objections, Defendant will produce non-privileged documents in its possession, custody or control that are responsive to this request with the exception of "email and other electronic communications." With respect to "email and other electronic communications" Defendant will make available for plaintiffs' inspection and copying readily available responsive documents. As to other

[134]

responsive "email and other electronic communications" maintained in such a manner as to make retrieval unduly expensive, defendant will make such records available for inspection pursuant to an agreed upon cost sharing agreement concerning the retrieval of such material.

Request #16

All documents concerning reductions in force for the period from 2000 to the present at any of the Defendant's retail locations, corporate headquarters, or any other location at which the Defendant conducts its business that indicate the ages of those employees terminated, transferred, or demoted as well as the ages of those persons who replaced such persons in the positions they held prior to the reduction in force.

Response #16

Defendant objects to Request #16 on the ground that it is over broad and thus calls for the production of documents that are irrelevant to the claims or defenses of the parties. In addition, Defendant objects to this request on the ground that it calls for the production of confidential and private information concerning non-parties. Based on these objections, Defendant declines to produce documents responsive to this Request.

* * * * *

FULL MOON SPORTS, INC.

By its attorney,

_____

Harrison Ames, Esq.
Bart A. Tweedy, Esq.
Counsel for Full Moon
[address etc. omitted]

Certificate of Service

[omitted]

IN THE UNITED STATES DISTRICT COURT
FOR THE MIDDLE DISTRICT OF FLORIDA
JACKSONVILLE DIVISION

OTIS AND FIONA OLMAN,

      Plaintiffs,

vs.   Case No. 03-2222-CIV-M-46-B

FULL MOON SPORTS, INC.
& BRUCE BELCHER,

      Defendants.

DEFENDANT'S ANSWERS AND OBJECTIONS
TO PLAINTIFF'S FIRST SET OF INTERROGATORIES

Pursuant to Federal Rule of Civil Procedure 33, Defendant Full Moon Sport's, Inc. ("Defendant") hereby responds to Plaintiff's First Set of Interrogatories as follows:

General Objections

[omitted]

Answers and Specific Objections

Interrogatory #1

Identify the person or persons who made the determination to promote Mr. Sid Shockley to manager of the Jacksonville store.

Response #1

Subject to and incorporating the General Objections, Full Moon states that the ultimate decision to promote Mr. Shockley was made by Full Moon's Reorganization Committee.

Interrogatory #2

Identify the manager or managers of Full Moon's information systems, information management or computer department (or other similar department or organizational structure) for the period from January 2002 to the present.

Response #2

Subject to and incorporating the General Objections, Full Moon states that Mr. Noah Stephen held the position of Vice-President of Information Management at Full Moon during the specified period.

* * * *

Interrogatory #8

State the age of all managers of all Full Moon retail stores as of January 2003 and January 2004.

Response #8

Note that Full Moon's objection is consistent with the positions it took in responding to the document requests.

Full Moon objects to Interrogatory #8 on the grounds that it is over broad and calls for information that is not relevant to the claim or defense of any party. Accordingly, Full Moon declines to answer.

* * * *

Interrogatory #15

Identify all facts that support your contention that Otis Olman converted Full Moon's property as Full Moon has alleged in its counterclaim in this action.

Response #15

Full Moon objects to Interrogatory #15 as being premature. Further responding, Full Moon states that it will respond to Interrogatory #15 after it has had an opportunity to engage in discovery as contemplated by the Case Management Order in this case.

* * * *

[137]

Interrogatory #22

Does Full Moon contend that Otis Olman was unqualified to continue serving as manager of the Jacksonville store at the time of his replacement? If your answer is yes, identify all facts that support this contention.

Response #22

Yes, Full Moon contends that Plaintiff Otis Olman was unqualified to continue serving as manager of the Jacksonville store at the time of his replacement. Full Moon objects to Interrogatory #22 as being premature to the extent it calls for an identification of "all facts that support this contention." Full Moon states that it will respond to Interrogatory #22 after it has had an opportunity to engage in discovery as contemplated by the Case Management order in this case.

* * * *

As to Objections,

Full Moon Sports, Inc.

By its attorneys

_____

Harrison Ames, Esq.
Bart A. Tweedy, Esq.
Counsel for Full Moon Sports, Inc.
[Address, phone number, etc. omitted]

As to Answers:

_____

Bertie Lurch
President, Full Moon Sports, Inc.

Before me personally appeared Bertie Lurch who swore under the penalties of perjury that the foregoing answers were true and accurate based on a review of the books and records of Full Moon Sports, Inc.

[138]

Thomas Alva
Notary Public, my commission expires: 5/10/2010

Certificate of Service

[omitted]

[139]

After completing the responses to both the document requests and interrogatories, Tweedy served them on Lane. Tweedy was pleased to have completed the work but knew that the ~~Rules required him to supplement these responses should additional responsive information come to light, or if anything contained in the responses later turned out to~~ be "~~incomplete or incorrect~~."[51]

c.   Lane Reacts

Lane immediately reviewed Full Moon's responses to her interrogatories and document requests. As expected, she was unsatisfied with several of the responses. Of course, not all of the responses were deficient. Full Moon had provided substantive responses to many of her interrogatories. In addition, Full Moon had agreed to make available what appeared to be a substantial number of documents. Lane now intended to contact Tweedy to set a mutually convenient time to review those documents and to discuss her disagreement with some of his other responses.

Lane saw ~~three areas in which Full Moon had been unresponsive to her document requests.~~ First, Tweedy had refused to produce documents or answer interrogatories concerning Full Moon's action regarding workers other than the Olmans.[52] Lane knew that such information could be critical to her case.[53] She would try to convince Tweedy to voluntarily disclose this information rather than requiring that she seek a court order compelling disclosure.

Second, Full Moon had withheld a document specifically addressing age-related issues that was prepared in connection with its reduction in force.[54] Lane knew about the existence of this document because Rule 26(b)(5) required Tweedy to identify the document even though Full Moon claimed it was privileged and could be withheld from production. Tweedy had complied with this Rule by preparing a "privilege log," which was intended to

---

[51]*See* Rule 26(e).

[52]*See, e.g.*, Full Moon's Responses to Document Requests Nos. 6 and 15 and Full Moon's response to Interrogatory No. 8.

[53]*See, e.g.*, Andrew J. Ruzicho & Louis A. Jacobs, Litigating Age Discrimination Cases at § 7:02 p. 6 (2002) (noting that such information is "understood to be essential to proving that the plaintiff was treated differently from other employees similarly situated except for age.").

[54]*See* Full Moon's Response to Document Request No. 6.

"enable other parties to assess the applicability of the privilege."[55]   The log disclosed existence of a report dated August 15, 2002, prepared by Samantha Brown, a member of Full Moon's Human Relations Department and entitled "The Personnel Impact of Full Moon's 2002 Reduction in Force." The report had been sent to Full Moon President Lurch, and a copy of the report had been distributed to Full Moon's General Counsel. Lane would try to obtain that report, which might contain evidence damaging to Full Moon's position.

Finally, Tweedy had indicated that Full Moon was willing to produce email relevant to the claims in the case, but only after some agreement had been reached concerning the cost of doing so.[56] In most cases the responding party bears the cost of responding to non-objectionable discovery requests.[57] Lane suspected that Full Moon's concern resulted from the way in which email was stored on its computers and the cost and effort in retrieving it.[58] Because Lane needed access to these communications, she would negotiate with Tweedy some way to reduce these costs.

Lane raised each of the problems she had identified during a phone conference with Tweedy. Lane and Tweedy were able to resolve two of their three disputes. First, Lane and Tweedy resolved the issue of email production by compromising. They agreed that Lane would narrow her request by limiting the emails produced to a briefer time period and to particular individuals or departments. They also agreed, after consulting with their clients, that the Olmans would pay a small portion of the cost of production. Both lawyers knew

---

[55]*See* Rule 26(b)(5) ("When a party withholds information otherwise discoverable under these rules by claiming that is privileged or subject to protection as trial preparation material, the party shall make the claim expressly and shall describe the nature of the documents, communications, or things not produced in a manner that, without revealing information itself privileged or protected, will enable other parties to assess the applicability of the privilege or protection.").

[56]*See* Full Moon Response to Document Request No. 15.

[57]*See, e.g., Oppenheimer Fund, Inc. v. Sanders*, 437 U.S. 340, 358 (1978) ("under [the discovery] rules, the presumption is that the responding party must bear the expense of complying with discovery requests . . .").

[58]There was no question that email is a "document" within the terms of Rule 34. *See* Rule 34(a)(1) (defining "document" to include "data compilations from which information can be obtained . . . "); *see also Zubulake v. UBS Warburg LLC*, 217 F.R.D. 309, 316–17 (S.D.N.Y. 2003) (holding that the term "document" in Rule 34 includes email, including those maintained on back-up storage devices).

that the issue of cost shifting in electronic discovery is filled with uncertainty.[59] Each decided it was better to craft a compromise solution than risk having an unfavorable solution imposed by the court.

Lane and Tweedy also compromised concerning discovery of the impact of Full Moon's reduction in force on workers other than the Olmans. To a considerable extent, the lawyers' disagreement reflected differing views of discovery law. As Lane stressed to Tweedy, courts uniformly recognize that statistics showing a disparity in the ages of employees terminated in a corporate downsizing constitute circumstantial evidence of an ADEA violation.[60] As Tweedy argued in response, Lane's request went too far. Lane had requested company-wide information for all store employees. However, case law generally requires that requests for statistical information target an appropriate group, considering factors such as job title and responsibility, as well as location (both geographically and within the structure of the company).[61]

Lane and Tweedy eventually agreed that Full Moon would produce records showing the ages of those persons in the position of store or department manager, both before and after the company's reduction in force. The parties also agreed to limit the time frame of

---

[59]*See, e.g., Zublake v. UBS Warburg LLC*, 217 F.R.D. 309 (S.D.N.Y. 2003) (discussing difficulties in cost sharing in electronic discovery). The issue of electronic discovery also has drawn the attention of the Standing Committee on Rules of Practice and Procedure of the Judicial Conference of the United States, an important part of the process by which the Federal Rules are amended. The Standing Committee has issued several proposed amendments to the Rules to address issues such as cost sharing and spoliation in the context of electronic discovery. *See* Memorandum from Honorable Lee H. Rosenthal to Honorable David F. Levi re: Report of Civil Rules Advisory Committee, dated May 17, 2004, revised August 3, 2004, available at <www.uscourts.gov/rules/newrules1.html> (last visited December 28, 2004).

[60]*See, e.g., Benson v. Tocco, Inc.*, 113 F.3d 1203, 1208–09 (11th Cir. 1997) (generally discussing circumstances in which statistical information may lead to an inference of intentional discrimination.); *Culley v. Trak Microwave Corp.*, 117 F. Supp. 2d 1317, 1319 (M.D. Fla. 2000) ("A[n ADEA] plaintiff may establish a *prima facie* case through the presentation of evidence by one of three accepted methods: direct evidence of discriminatory intent; statistical evidence; or the familiar test set out in *McDonnell Douglas* . . ."); *see also Sweat v. Miller Brewing Co.*, 708 F.2d 655, 658 (11th Cir. 1983) ("Statistical information concerning an employer's general policy and practice concerning minority employment may be relevant to showing of pretext, even in a case alleging an individual instance of discrimination rather than a 'pattern or practice' of discrimination.").

[61]*See, e.g., Balderston v. Fairbanks Morse Engine Division of Coltec Industries*, 328 F.3d 309, 319–20 (7th Cir. 2003).

the request to the period 2002–2004. Finally, after much resistance Full Moon agreed to provide the data for all its stores, including the information requested in the interrogatories. Tweedy concluded it was highly likely a court would order Full Moon to produce this data if Lane filed a motion to compel.

Tactical Tip ✍

Courts and Discovery Disputes

Some of the willingness of Lane and Tweedy to compromise was driven by a litigation reality: Many judges dislike resolving discovery disputes, which can bring out the worst in lawyers. An experienced lawyer will present a discovery dispute to the court only when it is truly important to the client. Judges appreciate this approach and, over the long term, come to trust a lawyer who is discriminating in seeking the court's involvement.

One issue remained. Despite their best efforts, Lane and Tweedy were unable to resolve their dispute concerning production of the report, "The Personnel Impact of Full Moon's 2003 Reduction in Force." Tweedy was insistent that the document was protected from disclosure either by the attorney-client privilege or the work-product doctrine. Lane was equally insistent that the document was fully discoverable. Lane was able to convince Tweedy to withdraw his objection based on the attorney-client privilege.[62] But Tweedy did not budge on the work-product objection. At the end of their conference, Lane informed Tweedy that she would file a motion to compel seeking the production of this document.

---

[62] Tweedy was wise to abandon the attorney-client privilege objection. That privilege protects (1) communications; (2) between lawyers (including certain of their agents) and clients; (3) made in confidence and remaining private; (4) for the purpose of obtaining legal advice. *See* Edna Selan Epstein, THE ATTORNEY-CLINT PRIVILEGE AND THE WORK-PRODUCT DOCTRINE at 46 (American Bar Association 2001). Ms. Brown, author of the report, was not a lawyer and neither was Mr. Lurch, to whom it was presented. It is true that a copy of the report was sent to Full Moon's general counsel, but simply "copying" a lawyer is not enough. *See id.* at 48 ("Clients and their attorneys often assume, erroneously, that merely conveying something to an attorney will cloak the underlying facts from compelled disclosure. It will not.")

Tweedy good-naturedly responded that he would "see her in court," if they had the opportunity to argue the motion at a hearing.[63]

Before we discuss Lane's action to compel discovery of the report, consider the following hypothetical questions to assess your understanding of the procedural aspects of a motion to compel.

---

[63]Practice varies by court and by judge as to whether oral argument is held on motions, especially those related to discovery.

Question 5.3

A.   What steps should Lane take to properly present her motion to compel to the court? Be sure to cite specific provisions of Rule 37.

B.   Assume that, although Tweedy makes several plausible, good faith arguments that the personnel report is privileged, the court ultimately rules in Lane's favor. What sanctions, if any, can the court award under Rule 37? Is the court required to impose a sanction? Does Rule 26(g) provide the court alternative authority to sanction Full Moon in this situation? Why or why not?

C.   Assume for purposes of this question only that Full Moon simply failed to respond to the Olmans' request for production of the personnel report. What action should Lane take under Rule 37 to compel compliance with her request? What sanctions can the court order against Full Moon?

D.   Assume that instead of seeking the personnel report from Full Moon, Lane issued a subpoena under Rule 45 directing Bruce Belcher to produce the personnel report. (He had apparently retained a copy when he left the company). Recall that Belcher is no longer a party to the suit and currently resides in Connecticut. Belcher fails to respond to Lane's subpoena. What action can Lane take to compel compliance with her subpoena? In which court must Lane proceed to compel production of the report from Belcher?

MOTION TO COMPEL

d.   The Discovery Dispute Is Resolved

After consulting with Tweedy, Lane turned to drafting her motion to compel. Tweedy had originally asserted two bases for Full Moon's refusal to turn over its personnel report: attorney-client privilege and the "work-product doctrine." All that remained was Full Moon's work-product objection.

Under Rule 26(b)(3), work-product, now referred to as "trial preparation material," consists of "documents and tangible things" that are protected from disclosure because they were "prepared in anticipation of litigation or for trial by or for another party or by or for that other party's representative. . . ."[64] It seemed to Lane to be a close call whether the personnel report met the requirements of "trial preparation material."

Consider the following questions concerning work product.

---

[64]Rule 26(b)(3). The Rule goes on to define the term "representative" to include "attorney, consultant, surety, indemnitor, insurer or agent." *Id.*

Question 5.4

A. Assume that Samantha Brown, author of the personnel report, is not an attorney. She was asked by President Lurch to prepare the report immediately after Lurch received Otis' letter complaining of age discrimination. Lurch made this request on his own initiative because "I wanted to see what was going on." Lurch is not a lawyer and did not speak with Full Moon's General Counsel before he ordered the report. In light of these limited facts, what argument might Tweedy make to support his assertion that the personnel report is protected "trial preparation material"? What argument might Lane make to rebut this claim? How should the court rule?

B. Assume for the moment that the report is, in fact, trial preparation material as defined by Rule 26(b)(3). Would there be any way that Lane might still be entitled to it? Please explain.

C. In Document Request number 7, Lane sought "all documents concerning or supporting Defendant's allegation in its Answer and Counterclaim that Plaintiff Otis Olman converted Defendant's property." Tweedy responded that, with respect to some of the documents encompassed within this request, Lane sought material protected by the "work-product doctrine." What might be the basis for Tweedy's objection?

Lane prepared her motion and supporting memorandum with the understanding that the dispute would almost certainly be resolved by **United States Magistrate Judge Matthew Malarkey**.[65] Magistrate judges serve as a form of judicial adjunct to the district court. Unlike district judges who are appointed by the President, confirmed by the United States Senate and serve for life, magistrate judges are appointed to eight year terms by the

---

[65]In the Middle District of Florida, each case is randomly assigned to both a district judge and a magistrate judge. *See* Local Rule 1.03(a). Other federal districts use different methods to assign magistrate judges to cases.

district judges in each federal district.[66] In civil matters, magistrate judges may decide non-dispositive pre-trial matters, such as discovery disputes, if such motions are referred to them by a district judge.[67] A magistrate judge's decision on non-dispositive motions may be reversed by the district judge on appeal, but only if the decision is clearly erroneous.[68]

District judges may also refer dispositive motions, such as motions to dismiss or motions for summary judgment, to a magistrate judge. The magistrate judge will then make a "report and recommendation" to the district judge.[69] If there is an appeal from such a report and recommendation, the district judge decides the matter *de novo* (*i.e.*, without giving any deference to the magistrate's recommendation).[70] Finally, parties may consent to having a magistrate judge conduct all proceedings in a case, including trial.[71] In this case, Full Moon and the Olmans had not consented to such an action.

---

[66]*See* 28 U.S.C. § 631.

[67]*See* 28 U.S.C. § 636(b)(1)(A).

[68]*See* 28 U.S.C. § 636(b)(1)(A). The clearly erroneous standard of review is highly deferential. In other words, the magistrate judge's decision is highly likely to be upheld under this standard.

[69]*See* 28 U.S.C. § 636(b)(1)(B).

[70]*See* 28 U.S.C. § 636(b)(1).

[71]*See* 28 U.S.C. § 636(c).

Judge Goodenough referred Lane's motion to compel to Magistrate Judge Malarkey for resolution. When Tweedy received Lane's motion papers, he prepared an opposition. Tweedy also asked that Lane be sanctioned for making the motion.[72] The matter was now ready to be decided.

As was common practice in the Middle District of Florida, Judge Malarkey did not hold a hearing on the motion. Instead, he issued his decision "on the papers." Lane and Tweedy received his brief decision in the mail. Judge Malarkey denied Lane's motion to compel Full Moon to disclose its personnel report. He ruled that it was a close question whether Full Moon had a strong enough basis to fear litigation when Lurch ordered the report prepared.[73] This "fear" was critical under the Rules because the document could only be considered trial preparation material if it was "prepared in anticipation of litigation."[74] Judge Malarkey ultimately concluded that "anticipation of litigation" was the primary motivating factor in the report's preparation. But he believed that Lane's motion had been "substantially justified." Accordingly, while he denied the motion to compel, he also denied Tweedy's request for sanctions because it would be "unjust."[75]

---

[72] Such a request was common, but probably unnecessary. Rule 37 makes sanctions mandatory unless the court makes certain findings. *See, e.g.,* Rule 37(a)(4)(B) ("If the motion is denied the court may enter any protective order authorized under Rule 26(c) and shall after affording an opportunity to be heard, require the moving party or the attorney filing the motion or both of them to pay to the party or deponent who opposed the motion the reasonable expenses incurred in opposing the motion, including attorney's fees, unless the court finds that the making of the motion substantially justified, or that other circumstances make an award of expenses unjust.").

[73] *See* Edna Selan Epstein, The Attorney-Client Privilege and the Work Product Doctrine at 521-22 (American Bar Association 2001) (discussing work product status concerning documents that could be characterized as "routine investigatory documents"). A document that is prepared as part of the normal course of business simply does not meet Rule 26(b)(3)'s requirement that the trial preparation materials be prepared "in anticipation of litigation."

[74] *See* Rule 26(b)(3).

[75] *See* Rule 37(a)(4)(B).

3.   Depositions

a.   Lane Prepares for Depositions

Now that Lane had reviewed the documentary discovery and answers to interrogatories, she felt ready to begin taking depositions. In a deposition, the lawyers are allowed to question a deponent under oath. All of the questions and answers are recorded for later use at trial or in connection with a summary judgment motion.[76]

Lane knew that depositions can be very important in resolving litigation.[77] In a deposition she could assess how a witness would appear to the jury, explore the meaning of documents, and delve into areas of the case not covered by documents. What is more, she was able to get information unfiltered by a lawyer, as was the case with interrogatories.

The principal downside of depositions is expense. The party taking the deposition must spend the time necessary to review relevant materials and prepare good questions. The person being deposed—particularly if represented by counsel—will try to anticipate likely questions and prepare the best responses. Then, all the parties will need to be present for the deposition itself.[78] Add to these factors the cost of the court reporter's time and the transcript and you can see what an investment in time and resources a single deposition can be. Thus, lawyers and parties need to balance the utility of the deposition against its costs.

---

[76] The most common form of deposition is the "deposition upon oral examination" governed by Rule 30. There is also a seldom used "deposition upon written questions" governed by Rule 31. In a deposition upon written questions one lawyer gives a list of questions to a court reporter. The court reporter then reads the questions to the witness and also records the answers given. The device is not all that useful, principally because it does not allow for follow-up to the answers actually given. Several other rules also concern depositions, including Rule 28 specifying before whom a deposition may be taken, and Rule 32 addressing the use of depositions in court proceedings.

[77] *See, e.g.,* Andrew J. Ruzicho & Louis A. Jacobs, LITIGATING AGE DISCRIMINATION CASES at § 7:13 p. 47 (2002) ("Depositions have taken on additional importance under the ADEA due to the propensity of courts to grant summary judgment.").

[78] Under the Federal Rules a single "deposition day" is limited at 7 hours. *See* Rule 30(d)(2).

The first order of business was for Lane to determine whom to depose. Apart from cost considerations, Lane would have to make her selections carefully. The Federal Rules limited the number of depositions she could take without leave of court to ten.[79]

One of the people Lane clearly wanted to depose was Bruce Belcher. Because Belcher was no longer a party to the suit, Lane had a bit more work to compel his attendance. Had Belcher still been a party, Lane could have simply sent him a "notice of deposition" compelling his attendance. This notice was a one-page document stating the date, time and place the deposition was to be taken. Lane was required to serve the notice on all other parties making sure that she had given a "reasonable" amount of time to prepare for the deposition.[80] However, Belcher was not a party, so in addition to sending the required notice of deposition, Lane would need to serve a subpoena to compel Belcher to appear.[81] Lane prepared the subpoena, which required Belcher to appear for a deposition in Connecticut.

Lane also wanted to depose Kay Bailey, the chairperson of Full Moon's corporate board of directors. Lane believed that Bailey had information relevant to the Olman's claim that Full Moon had discriminated against its older workers. From all Lane could gather, Full Moon had a corporate plan to reduce the number of older workers. Who better to discuss these plans than the leader of the board of directors? An incidental benefit of taking Bailey's deposition was to underscore the seriousness of the Olmans' lawsuit. Lane prepared and served the appropriate paperwork, although she expected that Tweedy might fight it. Time would tell.

---

[79]*See* Rule 30(a)(2)(A).

[80]*See* Rule 30(b)(1) ("A party desiring to take the deposition of any person upon oral examination shall give reasonable notice in writing to every other party to the action. The notice shall state the time and place for taking the deposition and the name and address of each person to be examined, if known . . ."). In most jurisdictions a lawyer noticing a deposition will contact other lawyers (and perhaps the intended deponent) to arrive at a mutually convenient time for taking the deposition. Otherwise, a seriously inconvenienced lawyer will seek a protective order from the court requiring a rescheduling of the deposition. *See* Rule 26(c) (stating grounds for protective orders). The notice of deposition is a single page document that sets out the date, time and place of the deposition. It must be served on all parties.

[81]*See generally* Rule 45.

Finally,[82] Lane wanted to take the deposition of Full Moon itself, something the Federal Rules allowed under Rule 30(b)(6).[83] This procedural device relieved Lane of the obligation of guessing which corporate official might have the information she sought. She would identify what matters she wanted to explore in the deposition, and Full Moon would choose its own spokesperson. This deposition device did not, however, preclude her from taking the depositions of specific individuals in the corporation.[84] So, for example, Lane could still depose Bertie Lurch, Full Moon's president.

When Full Moon received the Rule 30(b)(6) deposition notice, it was required to "designate one or more officers, directors, or managing agents, or other persons who consent to testify on its behalf" to be deposed regarding each matter about which Lane requested testimony.[85] Tweedy knew that he was obligated to prepare any person designated pursuant to Rule 30(b)(6) so that the person was able to "testify as to matters known or reasonably available to [Full Moon]."[86]

---

[82]Lane had many other potential deponents. We limit the text discussion to just a few.

[83]*See* Rule 30(b)(6) ("A party may in the party's notice and in a subpoena name as the deponent a public or private corporation or a partnership or association or governmental agency and describe with reasonable particularity the matters on which examination is requested.").

[84]*See* Rule 30(b)(6) ("This subdivision (b)(6) does not preclude taking a deposition by any other procedure authorized in these rules.").

[85]*See* Rule 30(b)(6).

[86]*See* Rule 30(b)(6).

A Note Concerning:
CORPORATE TESTIMONY

The large majority of litigants in private, civil suits in federal court are business entities like corporations. There are several useful distinctions that can be drawn when seeking deposition testimony from persons employed by a corporate litigant.

First, "apex" officials in the corporation, including *officers, directors, and managing agents*, are equated with the corporation and can be deposed by simply noticing the corporation that you intend to depose the apex person in her "official" capacity. (The discovery rules don't expressly state this, but that is their accepted meaning. *See, e.g., Folwell v. Hernandez,* 210 F.R.D. 169, 172 (M.D.N.C. 2002)). Consequently, Lane could simply notice the deposition of board member, Kay Bailey. As discussed later, however, attempts to depose apex persons can generate dispute during discovery.

Second, as Lane did with Full Moon, you can notify a corporation through a notice or a subpoena of the matters you wish to explore on deposition and permit it to designate its spokesperson. Rule 30(b)(6) states that the corporation may designate an apex person to testify for it ("officers, directors, or managing agents") or may designate "other persons who consent to testify on its behalf."

Third, you can subpoena current or former corporate personnel who are not "apex" persons. While the Rules presume that apex persons speak for the corporation and can be noticed to testify without a subpoena, other persons are not equated with the corporation and may require a subpoena.

The classification of corporate personnel is important for determining how their testimony can be used at trial. According to Rule 32(a)(2), the testimony of an apex person or an employee who consents to testify for the corporation under Rule 30(b)(6) can be used by an opponent "for any purpose." Consequently, the testimony of these persons poses a risk for corporate litigants, and the corporation's lawyer will take pains to properly prepare these persons for deposition.

b.   A Discovery Controversy

Lane and Tweedy had conferred and worked out a schedule for proposed depositions, but they were unable to resolve one issue. Recall that Lane sought to depose Kay Bailey, chairperson of Full Moon's board of directors and an "apex" official. While Tweedy recognized that Bailey's deposition could be noticed under Rule 30, he still objected that she failed to satisfy one of the key requirements of Rule 26 (b)(1): She had no information "relevant" to the issues in contention. Tweedy also wondered whether Lane might be deposing Bailey as a not so subtle means of harassment.

As required under the Rules, Lane and Tweedy discussed Tweedy's reservations about Bailey's deposition.[87] Tweedy referred Lane to several cases in which courts have precluded the depositions of apex corporate officials when the officials lack unique personal knowledge of matters in dispute.[88] For her part, Lane stressed that the decisions leading to her clients' termination were corporate ones, reflecting at some level Full Moon's corporate culture. As Lane asked Tweedy: who better to speak about that corporate culture than the chairperson of the board of directors? Moreover, Lane reminded Tweedy that the Rules gave her a great deal of leeway in using the various discovery tools. Tweedy responded by making two points. First, he underscored for Lane that Bailey had never heard of the Olmans, had never been to Jacksonville, and knew about the facts of the case only through conversations with counsel. Second, Tweedy told Lane that, in his experience, notices of deposition to apex officials such as Bailey were nothing more than a harassment device.

Despite their best efforts, Lane and Tweedy were unable to resolve their disagreement. This time it was Tweedy's turn to seek the court's help. In order to prevent Bailey's deposition, Tweedy turned to Rule 26(c), which allows the court to enter a "protective order" to prevent or limit discovery when "justice requires to protect a party or person from annoyance, embarrassment, oppression, or undue burden or expense. . . ."[89] There was already a protective order in place in the case, but it was of a far different nature.

---

[87]*See* Rule 26(c) (requiring that before seeking the court's intervention to prevent discovery through a protective order the party seeking to prevent the discovery confer in good faith with the other party in an effort to resolve the dispute).

[88]*See, e.g., Evans v. Allstate Insurance Co.*, 216 F.R.D. 515 (N. D. Okla. 2003); *Folwell v. Hernandez*, 210 F.R.D. 169 (M.D.N.C. 2002); *Baine v. General Motors Corp.*, 141 F.R.D. 332 (M.D. Ala. 1991).

[89]Rule 26(c); *see also* Rule 26(b)(2) (conferring similar authority on court as a means to limit discovery more generally).

Early on, Tweedy had proposed and Lane had stipulated to a protective order, later entered by the court, which mandated certain procedures by which Full Moon would produce relevant documents that it claimed were confidential and proprietary business information.[90]

The situation here was quite different because the parties were not in agreement. Tweedy began the formal process of resolving their dispute by preparing, serving on Lane and filing with the court a motion, memorandum of law, and certain supporting papers such as Ms. Bailey's affidavit attesting that she had no personal knowledge of the matters at issue in the complaint. Tweedy once again sought sanctions based on Lane's refusal to withdraw the deposition notice.[91] Tweedy believed that Lane not only was wrong about the law allowing Bailey's deposition, but she had no good faith basis for her argument. Lane responded to the motion with her own memorandum of law opposing entry of a protective order.

Motion Commotion by Charles Fincher

LET ME GUESS... IT'S A MOTION FOR PROTECTIVE ORDERS.

MOTION FOR PROTECTIVE ORDERS

---

[90] *See* Rule 26(c)(7) (providing specific authorization for the court to enter a protective order specifying "that a trade secret or other confidential research, development, or commercial information not be revealed or be revealed only in a designated way.").

[91] *See* Rules 26(c) and 37(a)(4)(A) (concerning award of sanctions in connection with motion for a protective order).

As with Lane's earlier motion to compel, Judge Goodenough referred Full Moon's motion for a protective order to Magistrate Judge Malarkey for resolution. After reviewing the parties' submissions, ~~Magistrate Judge Malarkey issued a brief written order in which he granted the motion. However, he gave Lane the opportunity to seek permission later to depose Bailey should she uncover information suggesting that Bailey did, in fact, have first-hand knowledge of relevant matters.~~ Judge Malarkey ~~also awarded sanctions against Lane and the Olmans, requiring them to reimburse Full Moon for its costs, including a reasonable attorney's fee, incurred in connection with the motion for a protective order.~~[92] Unlike the situation involving the motion to compel, ~~Magistrate Judge Malarkey did not find Lane's position here to be "substantially justified."~~[93]

c.   Preparing Witnesses

Tweedy received Lane's notices and subpoenas and began preparing for the depositions. Lane had subpoenaed Shockley, and Tweedy knew he would have his hands full getting him ready for deposition. Tweedy knew how important this preparation would be.

The lawyer representing a deponent has his principal work to do before the day of the deposition. The lawyer needs to put himself in the shoes of opposing counsel. What questions will she ask? What documents will she use? What style of questioning will she use? To the extent possible, the lawyer preparing a witness wants to ensure the witness is not surprised by any document or line of questioning. The lawyer also wants to prepare the witness for the "experience" of a deposition.

A deposition is a deceptively informal proceeding. It usually takes place in a law office or a hotel conference room. Although a witness is typically nervous at the beginning, after a while the court reporter blends into the background and the questioning seems more and more like a conversation. It was Tweedy's job to make sure that his witnesses were not

---

[92] *See* Rule 26(c) (directing that the provisions of Rule 37(a)(4) concerning the award of expenses apply to motions for a protective order).

[93] *See* Rule 37(a)(4)(A) (directing that the court "shall" impose the shifting of costs as a sanction if a motion is granted unless the court finds that the conduct of the party opposing the motion was "substantially justified"). The Olmans did not appeal Magistrate Judge Malarkey's decision to Judge Goodenough. Lane advised them that, in her experience, Judge Goodenough did not look favorably on such appeals of discovery orders. In this case, the Olmans' legal position was weak. Lane determined that it would be better to save her "judicial capital" for later in the case.

lulled into a sense of false security at their deposition. They needed to be reminded they should remain on their guard for the entire time.

Tweedy also knew it was important to caution his witnesses against the common tendency to say more than is needed to answer a question. He had been amazed in his career how many witnesses actually believe that, if they just explain everything, the other party will see things their way! Tweedy worked with his witnesses so they understood their job was to answer only the question asked. Of course, he began and ended his preparation sessions with the most important rules he wanted deponents to remember: Always tell the truth and don't guess.

d.   Taking a Deposition

The skills involved in taking effective depositions are usually introduced to law students in a pre-trial practice course and later developed through experience. In the following discussion we offer a *very* brief introduction to the subject of taking depositions by focusing on one of Lane's key deponents, Sid Shockley. We begin by offering some practical advice gleaned from experience, which we hope gives you a sense of the personal dynamics involved in a deposition and how the rules of civil procedure come to life in practice. We then offer an illustrative excerpt from Shockley's deposition, which demonstrates how lawyers can respond when deposition questions provoke controversy.

Tactical Tip ✍

Taking Effective Depositions

To take an effective deposition, a lawyer must be thoroughly familiar with the facts of the case. Assuming that foundation, many successful lawyers find the following guidelines useful when deposing a witness:

- Make sure to capitalize on the informal setting of the deposition. Try to engage the witness in small talk before you start. Have coffee, water, and the like available. The more comfortable the witness is the better it will usually be for you.

- Try not to be hostile to the witness. It is usually not to your advantage to come on strong with the witness at a deposition. While there are situations in which a more aggressive attitude will

---

be warranted, this approach usually slows the flow of information. Further, a more laid back approach at a deposition can work to your advantage at trial, when a witness will be expecting a lamb on cross-examination but actually faces a lion.

Establish your mastery of the case for the witness early. To the extent you are able to do so, ask questions early on in the deposition to which you know the answer. It is even better if you have a document to support the answer. By using this technique you are able both to judge the honesty of the witness and to show the witness that you know a fair amount about the case

- Use your knowledge of normal human behavior to your advantage. For example, most people like to hear themselves speak and equally hate the sound of silence. When a witness has finished answering a question, wait a few moments to ask the next question. You will be surprised how often a witness faced with silence will fill it with an "answer" to a question that you have not asked.

- Finally, remember that one of the most important skills at a deposition is listening. No matter what you expect the witness to say, listen closely to the answer and always follow-up.

Shockley's deposition took place on April 1, 2005 at Lane's offices in Jacksonville. Present at the deposition were Lane, Tweedy, Shockley, and a court reporter. Lane had considered having Otis attend the deposition but eventually concluded that it was best not to create a situation in which there could be a "scene." Below are brief excerpts from the transcript of that deposition.

* * * * *

Ms. Lane: Mr. Shockley, have you ever referred to Otis Olman as the old man?

Mr. Shockley: Oh sure, several times. That's what we always called the commander of the ship when I was in the Navy. He . . . Otis was store commander and you know. . . .

Ms. Lane: Did you call Mr. Olman old man to his face?

Mr. Shockley: I can't say for sure, probably not right in his face.

Ms. Lane: Did you believe Mr. Olman would be displeased by your calling him the old man?

Mr. Shockley: Well I don't know, maybe if I said it in front of customers.

Ms. Lane: Did you ever refer to Mr. Olman as the old man in front of customers?

Mr. Shockley: Not that I recall.

Ms. Lane: Did you ever refer to Mr. Olman as the old man when speaking with Bruce Belcher?

Mr. Shockley: I might have. Bruce was cool and you could say things to him.

Ms. Lane: Like you could do a better job running the store?

Mr. Shockley: Yeah.

Ms. Lane: Did you ask Mr. Belcher to give you the job as store manager?

Mr. Shockley: Not exactly. Actually I think he was the one who asked me if I wanted to manage the store. One day he said that Atlanta was going to be making some changes in stores . . . in store managers and maybe I could manage the Jax store.

[159]

Ms. Lane: When was it you spoke with Mr. Belcher about becoming store manager?

Mr. Shockley: It seems like it was month of so before the decision was made. When Atlanta first starting talking about making changes. I'm not sure about the date and all.

Ms. Lane: Did you ever tell Mr. Belcher Otis was too old to be running the store?

Mr. Shockley: No, I never said that. I mean, he wasn't that knowledgeable of extreme sport lines and that's where the store was heading. He was into kayaks and scuba, some camping. He didn't relate to board sports at all.

Ms. Lane: Would you say that extreme sports appeal to younger customers?

Mr. Shockley: For sure. Not too many 40-year-old men like falling onto the sidewalk off a skateboard.

Ms. Lane: Do you believe a younger man like yourself . . . by the way Mr. Shockley, how old are you?

Mr. Shockley: Just turned 32.

Ms. Lane: Well, do you believe a relatively younger man like yourself can do a better job marketing extreme sporting goods?

Mr. Shockley: I don't mean . . . it's not that there's any specific age for selling extreme lines. But if you don't relate to the customers and know the equipment from the point of view of a user you have a harder time selling or even knowing what to stock. Otis had that problem.

Ms. Lane: You mean Otis was better suited for an older customer, boomers for example.

Mr. Shockley: That's right. Otis could sell to a niche customer . . . don't get me wrong. These people have money to spend and are important to the store. They don't have any problem throwing down $1500 for a kayak or $400 for a GPS.

Ms. Lane: You are referring now to older customers?

Mr. Shockley: Yeah, more middle-aged people. Boomers.

Ms. Lane: Did Mr. Belcher share your views?

Mr. Tweedy: Objection.

Notice how limited Tweedy's objection was. He was merely preserving it for trial.

Mr. Shockley: Well I can't speak for Bruce. But I know he was concerned with getting sales figures up and thought extreme lines had more potential over the long run.

Ms. Lane: Did Mr. Belcher indicate whether he thought you were better able to appeal to younger customers?

Mr. Shockley: I'm not clear on what you're asking.
Ms. Lane: Never mind. Mr. Shockley, would you consider Mr. Belcher to be your friend.

Mr. Shockley. Certainly.

Ms. Lane: Have you ever socialized with him outside the store?

Mr. Shockley: Yes.

Ms. Lane: Have you ever observed Mr. Belcher dating a store employee?

Mr. Tweedy: I object Ms. Lane. That is totally irrelevant to any issue in this case.

Ms. Lane: Well, as you know Mr. Tweedy that's an objection you can make at trial if you think it's that important.

Mr. Tweedy: I hope you don't intend to carry this further.

Ms. Lane: Well actually I do. Mr. Shockley, to your knowledge has Mr. Belcher ever had a romantic relationship with a store employee?

Mr. Tweedy: Again I object. Your question calls for irrelevant, private and prejudicial testimony.

[161]

Ms. Lane: Mr. Tweedy, for the record are you instructing Mr. Shockley not to answer my question?

Mr. Shockley: Do I have to?

Tweedy could direct the witness not to answer only if authorized by Rule 30(d).

Mr. Tweedy: For the record, I am not instructing Mr. Shockley to do anything. I am simply making a proper objection to your irrelevant line of questioning.

Ms. Lane: Mr. Shockley, did you discuss your testimony at an earlier meeting with Mr. Tweedy?

Mr. Tweedy: I do object to that question and direct Mr. Shockley not to answer it. You know Mr. Shockley's discussion with me is protected by the attorney-client privilege.

Did Rule 30(d) permit Tweedy's direction to the witness? Why?

Ms. Lane: Well, Mr. Shockley, I'm interested to hear Mr. Tweedy prepared you to testify today. Now let's get back to my earlier question. Do you know whether Mr. Belcher ever had a romantic relationship with a store employee?

Mr. Tweedy: Objection.

Ms. Lane: The witness may answer.

Mr. Shockley: Bruce may have dated an employee a few years ago.

Ms. Lane: Do you remember her name?

Mr. Shockley: Wanda Welcome. She worked as a cashier around 2003.

Ms. Lane: Is she still employed with Full Moon?

Mr. Shockley: No.

Ms. Lane: Do you know why she is no longer employed with Full Moon?

Mr. Shockley: No.

Ms Lane: How old would you guess Ms. Welcome was when she worked at the Jacksonville store?

[162]

Mr. Tweedy: Objection.

Mr. Shockley: I can't say definitely. But I know she had recently graduated from Fletcher High in Jacksonville Beach.

* * * * *

Shockley's deposition occurred outside the presence of a judge. This meant that Tweedy's objections to Lane's questioning could not be resolved during the course of the deposition. ~~To facilitate the uninterrupted taking of depositions, Rule 32 permits lawyers to defer most common evidentiary objections till the objectionable testimony is used later at a hearing or at trial.[94]~~ In addition, ~~Rule 30(d) prohibits a lawyer from instructing a witness not to answer a question except where "necessary to preserve a privilege, to enforce a limitation directed by the court, or to present a motion under Rule 30(d)(4)." The motion authorized in Rule 30(d)(4) permits a lawyer to suspend a deposition and seek court protection when the deposition is being conducted "in bad faith or in such a manner as unreasonably to annoy, embarrass, or oppress the deponent or party. . . ."~~

In light of these Rules, consider the questions below.

Question 5.5

A. When Lane asked Shockley whether Belcher had ever been romantically involved with a store employee, Tweedy objected that the question called for an answer that was "irrelevant, private, and prejudicial." Could Tweedy have deferred making this objection till Lane used the testimony later in court? Could Tweedy have properly instructed Shockley not to answer the question?

B. Why do you think Tweedy felt the need to object to inquiries into Belcher's romantic relationship with a store employee? What relevance might these questions have to the Olmans' suit?

C. Recall that, when Lane asked Shockley whether he had discussed his testimony earlier with Tweedy, Tweedy objected and directed Shockley not to answer the question. Was this proper? If Lane had persisted with this line of questioning, what could Tweedy have done other than directing Shockley to remain silent?

After the deposition the court reporter transcribed what had been said. The transcript was then forwarded to the deponent and, for a fee, counsel in the case. ~~In most~~

---

[94]*See, e.g.,* ~~Rule 32(b).~~

~~cases, deponents will request an opportunity to read the transcript and make any changes in~~ ~~their testimony. The Rules allow for the submission of such an "errata sheet" within 30~~ ~~days of the deponent's being notified that the transcript is available.~~[95] Tweedy had requested an opportunity for Shockley to read and sign his deposition. Given the importance of Shockley's testimony, Tweedy would work closely with him when the time came for the review.

4.   The Second Wave of Paper Discovery: Admissions[96]

A final form of paper discovery Lane and Tweedy needed to consider was the Rule 36 request for admissions. The response to a request for an admission may have greater consequence than the response to other forms of discovery. In particular, if a party actually admits the matter addressed in a request it is no longer in dispute. Both the judge deciding a motion for summary judgment and the jury deliberating its verdict have to accept the admission as true. In comparison, an answer to an interrogatory or a deposition question constitutes evidence the decisionmaker may consider, but is not usually conclusive.[97]

Despite the potential impact of requests for admissions, Lane and Tweedy knew Rule 36 was really most useful for two purposes: (1) to establish the authenticity of documents; and (2) to establish relatively uncontroversial matters or background information for trial (*e.g.*, the number of employees working for Full Moon on a certain date). Neither Lane nor Tweedy had found requests for admissions particularly valuable to establish the more controversial points in litigation; it is usually not difficult for an opposing

---

[95]*See* Rule 30(e) ("If requested by the deponent or a party before completion of the deposition, the deponent shall have 30 days after being notified by the [court reporter] that the transcript of recording is available in which to review the transcript or recording and, if there are changes in form or substance, to sign a statement reciting such changes and the reasons given by the deponent for making them."). The Rules place no limitation on what can be changed in an errata sheet. There are, however, powerful practical limitations on this ability. An opponent can use the uncorrected original answer to impeach, or undermine, later testimony at trial. Thus, it is possible to use the errata sheet to change a "no" to a "yes" but it will not happen with great frequency.

[96]We are treating Requests for Admissions as the "second wave"of paper discovery. It is also possible for a party to serve second, or even third, document requests or sets of interrogatories, assuming that such additional requests are not barred by any limitations in the Rules (such as the limit on the number of interrogatories) or are not otherwise unduly burdensome. Neither the Olmans nor Full Moon made such additional requests in this case.

[97]*See* Rule 36(b) ("Any matter admitted under this rule is conclusively established unless the court on motion permits withdrawal or amendment of the admission.").

lawyer to find "reasonable ground" for refusing to admit a matter.[98] So, they each drafted and served limited requests for admissions and responded in kind to the requests they received.

D.   Expert Discovery

At the same time they were assembling the factual information needed to try their cases, Lane and Tweedy also proceeded along the second, parallel discovery path concerning experts. You will learn much more about experts in your Evidence class. For now, you should know that in civil litigation, an "expert" is someone who has "knowledge, skill, experience, training or education" such that he or she is able to assist the finder of fact (*i.e.*, the judge or the jury) understand some concept beyond their normal everyday experience.[99] Experts are in some sense hired guns. A lawyer will retain an expert to advise him or her about technical issues in the case and perhaps to testify at trial. It is often said that you can find an expert to testify about almost anything,[100] even though this may be an exaggeration and certainly is contrary to the intent of the Rules of Evidence to keep "junk science" and the like out of the courtroom.

Lane understood the importance of experts generally and particularly in employment discrimination litigation.[101] Early on she retained Dr. Robert Stevens, a faculty member in the statistics department at a major university. She wanted Dr. Stevens to analyze Full Moon's employment statistics and determine (1) whether there was a significant disparity between employees terminated who were protected under the ADEA versus those who were

---

[98]Rule 37(c) insulates a party from sanctions for refusing to admit a matter later proved at trial when, among other things, the party had "reasonable ground" to believe it would prevail on the disputed matter or other "good reason for the failure to admit."

[99]*See* Fed. R. Evid. 702. *See also* BLACK'S LAW DICTIONARY (Fifth Edition) at 519 (West 1979) (defining "expert testimony" as "[o]pinion evidence of some person who possesses special skill or knowledge in some science, profession or business which is not common to the average man [sic] and which is possessed by the expert by reason of his special study or experience.").

[100]*See, e.g.,* Jack B. Weinstein, *Improving Expert Testimony*, 20 U. RICH. L. REV. 473, 482 (1986) ("an expert can be found to testify to the truth of almost any factual theory, no matter how frivolous.").

[101]Of course, a lawyer should not retain an expert without consulting with her client and considering the needs of the particular case. For example, a given case might not warrant an expert due to the amount of money at issue. Similarly, there might not be issues that truly require an expert. Once again, the key lesson is to take each of your cases on their own terms and act appropriately.

not, and (2) whether any such disparity could be explained by controlling for other, lawful factors. Lane knew that such information, supported by expert testimony, was an important source of proof in ADEA cases.[102]

The Federal Discovery Rules recognize the pivotal importance of experts. As with factual discovery, the Federal Rules create a regime under which expert discovery proceeds in two phases. First, the parties must exchange certain information concerning experts "who may be used at trial."[103] The timing for this disclosure is usually set by the court based on the parties' recommendation.[104] The second phase of expert discovery occurs after the Rule 26(a)(2) disclosures have been made. In this phase, the parties are allowed to take additional expert discovery by way of interrogatories and depositions.[105]

---

[102]*See, e.g., Benson v. Tocco, Inc.*, 113 F.3d 1203, 1208-09 (11th Cir. 1997) (discussing importance of expert testimony in ADEA cases); *see also Culley v. Trak Microwave Corp.*, 117 F. Supp. 2d 1317, 1319–21 (M.D. Fla. 2000) (recognizing the importance of statistical evidence in ADEA cases but rejecting such evidence in the particular case due to fatal errors in the plaintiff's expert witness testimony).

[103]*See* Rule 26(a)(2).

[104]*See* Rule 26(a)(2)(C). If the parties do not agree on a time for disclosure, the default under the Rules requires that the disclosure essentially be made at least 90 days before trial.

[105]*See* Rule 26(b)(4).

Question 5.6

A.   What information would Lane need to disclose about Dr. Stevens and in what form would these disclosures have to be made? Be specific about the Rule governing her disclosure.

B.   Assume that in addition to Dr. Stevens, Lane retained and consulted Dr. Benjamin Todd, another statistician, about Full Moon's employment data. After reviewing the data, Dr. Todd concludes that they show no statistically significant correlation between employees' ADEA-protected status and Full Moon's reduction in force. Lane ultimately decides she will not call Dr. Todd as a witness at trial.

   (1)   What information must Lane disclose about Dr. Todd and his conclusions?

   (2)   Assume that Tweedy learns that Lane has consulted with Dr. Todd. Will Tweedy be permitted to depose the doctor?

After receiving Dr. Stevens' report, Tweedy studied it closely. He also shared it with his own, non-testifying expert statistician to get her input. Whenever cost allowed, Tweedy retained two experts on important subjects. One expert would be designated to testify at trial. The other expert would be Tweedy's sounding board. He could freely discuss his thoughts and conjectures with this second expert and he could receive an informal evaluation of the opinions of his testifying expert. In this way, Tweedy could ensure that the testifying expert remained "pure" for trial. That is, there would be no danger that the testifying expert might be exposed to information Tweedy did not want to disclose.[106] So, although Tweedy would definitely send Full Moon's report to his testifying

---

[106]*See, e.g., Amster v. River Capital International Group, LLC,* 2002 U.S. Dist. LEXIS 13669 at * 5–*6 (S.D.N.Y. July 26, 2002) (generally discussing requirement under Rule 26(b)(2)(B) that expert must disclose the "data and other information" upon which she bases her opinion and noting that this requirement has been held to include producing attorney client privileged or work product information disclosed to an expert).

expert, he would not take the chance of discussing that report with the testifying expert in any great detail, at least not at this point.

Now Tweedy needed to decide what to do with the Olmans' expert, Dr. Stevens.[107] Following his ususal practice, Tweedy decided to take a brief deposition of Stevens. Accordingly, he served the appropriate notice and prepared to take the deposition.

* * * * *

Having completed discovery, Lane and Tweedy now turned in earnest to resolving the parties' dispute. While they ruled nothing out, given the negotiations to date it did not appear likely that the Olmans and Full Moon would settle the lawsuit. Thus, the lawyers prepared to present their cases, first at summary judgment and then later at trial. We cover these litigation stages in Chapters 7 and 8. But before doing so we consider how the lawsuit was initially structured and how, even now, it could be restructured to reflect developments in the case. These matters concern the joinder of claims and the joinder of parties, which we address in Chapter 6.

---

[107]A lawyer needs to be careful that she does not give too much away in an expert deposition. A common tendency among lawyers is to charge into an expert deposition and aggressively question the expert about every error and deficiency in his or her report. There may be some cases where this is a good strategy, as when a lawyer believes this approach will foster serious settlement discussions. In most cases, however, this approach will actually be welcomed by opposing counsel. As soon as the deposition is concluded, opposing counsel will begin work correcting the errors and deficiencies brought to his or her attention. Imagine how much more effective it would be to raise these errors during the expert's trial testimony. As a result, many lawyers use the expert deposition for two rather limited purposes: (1) to clarify any ambiguities in the expert's report; and (2) to get a first hand look at the expert and assess how he will come across to the jury or judge.

CHAPTER SIX:
JOINDER & AMENDMENT

Rule References: 4, 7, 11, *13, 14, 15, 16, 18, 19, 20, 24,* 26

A.   Structuring a Lawsuit

From the outset Lane had been alert to the possibility of amending the complaint to change the claims and possibly the parties. A lawyer seldom has thorough knowledge of the facts when she files her initial pleadings. So long as the initial allegations have some "evidentiary support" under Rule 11, a lawyer can plead based on imperfect information. As a consequence, the initial complaint represents a lawyer's tentative judgment about which claims and parties to include. That judgment may change as more is learned about the case, and it may be necessary to amend the initial pleadings. Federal Rule 15(a) accommodates this need by endorsing a policy of "liberal" amendment.[1]

In this chapter we examine two issues: (1) how the rules of joinder permitted the parties in *Olman* to structure their initial pleadings, and (2) how these rules, used in conjunction with Rule 15, permitted the parties to amend that structure. We begin by examining joinder rules that permitted the Olmans to include the claims and parties found in their initial complaint. We then consider how joinder rules permitted Full Moon to add its own claims to the suit. Next, we follow Lane as she contemplates amending the complaint later in the suit, and we consider the procedural, strategic, and ethical issues she must address.

Joinder can be one of the more challenging topics addressed in Civil Procedure. To help you understand joinder issues in *Olman v. Full Moon*, we proceed step-by-step through the process of constructing the case pleadings. As each claim is added to the pleadings, we both *diagram* the claim and ask that you consider how its assertion is supported by a *particular* rule of civil procedure.[2]

---

[1]*See Foman v. Davis,* 371 U.S. 178 (1962).

[2]We recommend that you develop the habit of diagraming the structure of cases you study in Civil Procedure. This habit will prove invaluable as you try to understand joinder rules and apply them to more complex cases. Diagraming is also valuable when, for example, you need to access whether a court has subject matter jurisdiction over claims in a suit.

1.   Otis' Claims Against Full Moon and Belcher[3]

We begin with the lead plaintiff, Otis Olman. The heart of Otis' case was his charge that Full Moon discriminated and retaliated against him in violation of age discrimination statutes. For many reasons, Otis wanted to assert all these related claims against Full Moon in one complaint. These reasons included: litigating in the most efficient manner possible, presenting the strongest case against Full Moon, obtaining the widest variety of remedies, and ensuring that no claims were forfeited by failing to plead them.[4]

Consider the structure of Otis' claims against Full Moon:[5]

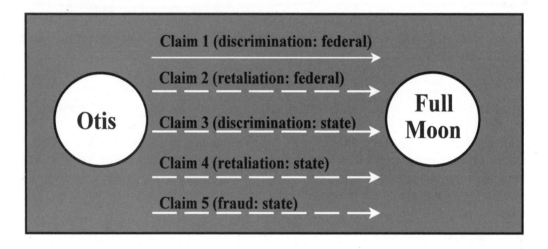

---

[3]We suggest you refresh your memory of the claims and parties identified in the initial complaint. A summary of these is found at p. 31. You might also want to refer to the actual complaint (pp. 37–44) and answer (pp. 77–82).

[4]This last point refers to the doctrine of claim preclusion, or res judicata. In federal court, this doctrine generally requires that all transactionally related claims be pled in a single suit; otherwise, they are forfeited.

[5]Note that, as an additional claim is added to the pleadings, we have designated that claim with a broken line (- - - -). In parentheses, we first provide the nature of the claim (*e.g.*, "discrimination") and then provide the source of applicable law (*e.g.*, "federal").

Now consider how Rule 18 authorized Otis' joinder of these claims against Full Moon.

Question 6.1

According to Rule 18, was there *any* limitation on Otis' right to join his five claims against Full Moon?[6] Does Rule 18 require that Otis' counts be factually related? Does Rule 18 require that they be based on the same law? Does Rule 18 itself require that Otis allege all his claims?

Recall that, in Count V of the complaint, Otis also asserted his claim for fraud against Belcher.[7] But Rule 18 addresses the joinder of claims not parties. Consequently, Otis had to identify a joinder rule authorizing the addition of another *defendant* in order to assert a claim against Belcher. The pertinent rule is Rule 20. After using Rule 20 to join Belcher as co-defendant to the fraud claim, the case might be diagramed as follows:

---

[6]Those of you who have studied jurisdiction will be aware that Otis had to satisfy other requirements before asserting his various claims in the suit. First, he had to verify that the federal court had *subject matter jurisdiction* over each claim. Subject matter jurisdiction is discussed in Appendix B. Second, Otis had to verify that the court had *personal jurisdiction* over both defendants with regard to all claims. Personal jurisdiction, also discussed in Appendix B, was not a problem.

[7]Although we have diagrammed the fraud claim against Belcher as a sixth claim, note that it is combined into a single "count" (count V) in the complaint. The diagrams distinguish each substantive legal *claim* because this is required when applying the rules of joinder.

[173]

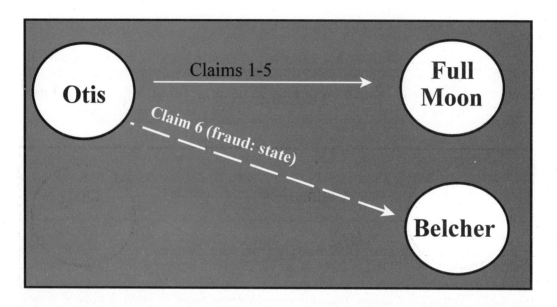

Notice that Rule 20 governing joinder of parties is more restrictive than Rule 18 governing joinder of claims by a single party. Rule 20 authorizes "permissive joinder" of additional defendants when a plaintiff seeks relief against the additional defendant (a) "arising out of the same transaction, occurrence, or series of transactions or occurrences" that is the subject of a claim against a co-defendant; and (b) there is "any question of law or fact" common to both defendants. Consider the following question related to the joinder of Belcher:

Question 6.2

According to Rule 20, why was Otis permitted to join Belcher as co-defendant? Specifically, what is the "common transaction or occurrence" that underlies Otis' fraud claim against Belcher and an existing claim against Full Moon? Does it matter that the fraud claim against Belcher does *not* appear to arise out of the same occurrence underlying Otis' discrimination and retaliation claims (claims 1–4) against Full Moon?

2.   Fiona's Claims Against Full Moon

Now that you understand how Otis was permitted to join all his claims against Full Moon and Belcher in one complaint, consider the claims of co-plaintiff Fiona. Fiona, you recall, wanted to assert her own claims for age discrimination under both federal and state law. After adding Fiona's claims, the structure of the case now looked like this:[8]

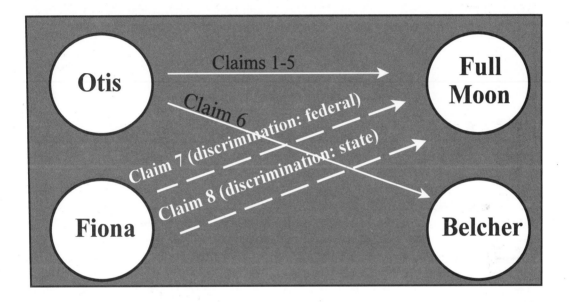

Now consider how Rules 18 and 20 permitted Fiona to join these claims in the complaint.

---

[8]Again, we have numbered and diagramed the parties' "claims" rather than the actual "counts" in the complaint. Claims 7 and 8 in the diagram appear as counts 6 and 7 in the complaint.

Question 6.3

A.   According to Rule 20, why was Fiona permitted to join Otis as co-plaintiff? Specifically, what is the "common transaction or occurrence" that underlies their claims?" What is the "question of law or fact" common to the claims asserted by Fiona and Otis? Can you think of any argument Full Moon might make that the Olmans' joinder as plaintiffs does *not* satisfy Rule 20?

B.   Once Fiona properly joined as co-plaintiff with Otis, did Rule 18 impose any limitation on her assertion of *additional* claims against Full Moon?

3.   Full Moon's Counterclaim Against Otis

Once a party has been placed on the defensive by having a claim asserted against it, that party is permitted to go on the counter-offensive. Rule 13 authorizes the assertion of counterclaims against an "opposing party," and classifies these counterclaims as either compulsory (Rule 13(a)) or permissive (Rule 13(b)). Unlike Rules 18 and 20, Rule 13(a) sometimes compels a party to assert a claim. The Olmans' suit following Full Moon's assertion of its counterclaim might look like the diagram below.

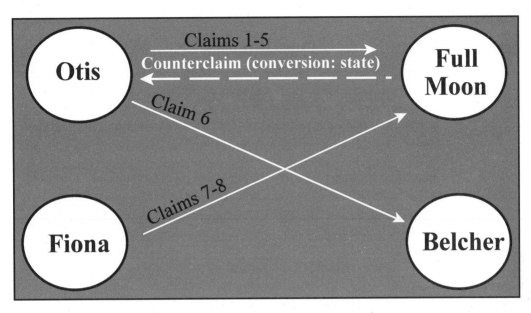

Now consider the following question concerning Full Moon's assertion of its counterclaim:

Question 6.4

A.   Review Rule 13 parts (a) and (b). Was Full Moon's counterclaim against Otis a compulsory or permissive counterclaim? Why?

B.   According to Rule 13, how does a party go about asserting a counterclaim, *i.e.,* in what pleading is it included? According to Rule 7(a), must the opposing party respond to a counterclaim? How?

Finally, you may recall that Full Moon considered asserting a cross-claim against co-defendant Belcher to seek "indemnification" if it was required to pay for Belcher's fraudulent acts. Rule 13(g) permits the assertion of cross-claims against "co-parties" arising out of the same transaction or occurrence that underlies an existing claim or counterclaim. Consider the following question concerning Full Moon's potential cross-claim against Belcher:

Question 6.5

A.   Is a cross-claim for indemnification authorized by Rule 13(g)? Why will a cross-claim for indemnification inevitably satisfy the requirement that it arise out of the same transaction or occurrence underlying an existing claim?

B.   According to Rule 13(g), how does a party go about asserting a cross-claim, *i.e.,* in what pleading is it included? According to Rule 7(a), must the opposing party respond to a cross-claim? How?

As you can see, the structure of the parties' initial pleadings was authorized by a handful of joinder rules. Next let's examine what happened when, as the suit progressed, Lane obtained more information and considered amending the complaint.

B.   Lane Considers Whether to Amend the Complaint

One of the most common reasons a party seeks to amend the pleadings during litigation is to add a *claim*. For example, information obtained during discovery may support a claim for which there was insufficient evidence at the outset of the suit. Although Lane remained alert to the possibility of asserting new claims against Full Moon, none was suggested by developments in the case. Lane's initial understanding of the law and the facts had largely been confirmed during discovery,[9] and she felt confident going forward against Full Moon based on the claims already alleged in the Olmans' complaint.

However, Lane now had reason to consider adding additional parties to the suit. As discussed below, the possibility of adding parties raised issues of procedure, litigation strategy, and ethics.

1.   Joining a New Defendant

Based on deposition testimony obtained during discovery, Lane believed she had grounds for adding Sid Shockley as a new *defendant*. Shockley, you will recall, had replaced Otis as manager of the Jacksonville store. Deposition testimony confirmed that

---

[9]*See generally supra* Chapter 5.

Shockley had continually disparaged Otis in the months leading up to Otis' replacement as manager. These disparaging comments may have contributed to Full Moon's decision to replace Otis, even they were largely unsubstantiated. Evidence of Shockley's conduct would be useful at trial to rebut Full Moon's claim that it had "good cause" to replace Otis. But Lane believed Shockley's conduct might justify adding him as a co-defendant.

Lane thought that Shockley had maliciously poisoned Otis' relationship with Full Moon.[10] Legal research suggested that Shockley's behavior might constitute "tortious interference with a business relationship." To establish this tort, Lane would need to prove four elements:

1. Existence of a business relationship between the plaintiff (Otis) and a third party (Full Moon);

2. Defendant's (Shockley's) knowledge of that relationship;

3. Defendant's intentional and unjustified interference with the relationship; and

4. Resulting damage to the plaintiff.[11]

Lane thought she had evidentiary support for each of these elements.

Now consider the procedural issues Lane had to address if she wanted to join Shockley as co-defendant.

---

[10]Lane was not persuaded that she had adequate evidence to allege a claim for libel against Shockley. *See supra* at pp. 29–30 (discussing the elements of libel). But a claim for tortious interference with a business relationship might succeed even if she lacked sufficient evidence to show that Shockley libeled Otis.

[11]*See, e.g., KMS Restaurant Corp. v. Wendy's Intern., Inc.,* 361 F.3d 1321 (11th Cir. 2004).

Question 6.6

A. Recall that all the required pleadings in the Olmans' case were served months ago. If Lane now seeks to add Shockley as a defendant in her complaint, what procedural steps must she take? Make sure you consider Lane's obligations under both Rule 4 and Rule 15.

B. Does Lane's attempt to add Shockley satisfy the requirements of Rule 20 governing joinder of defendants? Make sure you consider the likely arguments of both Lane and Tweedy.

In addition to considering whether procedural rules permitted joinder of Shockley, Lane also had to decide whether joinder made strategic sense.[12] The principal value in joining Shockley as co-defendant was to improve Otis' chances of recovering damages. If Shockley tortiously interfered with Otis' business relationship with Full Moon, he would be liable for resulting damages.

On reflection, Lane did not believe the possibility of obtaining damages from Shockley provided a compelling strategic reason to join him in the suit. First, the damages from Shockley's conduct essentially overlapped with those already recoverable from Full Moon. Second, Full Moon might seek to mitigate its own liability by *shifting* blame to Shockley. If Full Moon succeeded in shifting blame, Lane was unsure that Shockley had sufficient assets to satisfy Otis' judgment. All things considered, Lane was not convinced that the potential recovery of damages from Shockley outweighed the risks and additional procedural costs of joining him.[13] It was probably better to call Shockley as a witness at trial

---

[12]She would also need to consider whether there was subject matter jurisdiction over the claims she sought to add. If you have already addressed subject matter jurisdiction in your course, you might want to identify the possible jurisdictional bases for these new claims. Finally, she would need to verify that the court had personal jurisdiction over Shockley. Subject matter and personal jurisdiction are discussed in Appendix B.

[13]Discussion in the next section of this chapter reveals some of the problems Lane might encounter in seeking to amend the complaint at this point in the suit. These problems would apply equally to joinder of Shockley.

and let the jury impose liability on the sole defendant, Full Moon. After Lane conferred with the Olmans and shared her judgment, they agreed to leave Shockley out of the suit.

2.   Joining an Additional Plaintiff

Lane next considered the possibility of adding a new *plaintiff* to the suit. Several months after agreeing to represent the Olmans, Lane also agreed to represent Rubi Dubidoux, former manager of a Full Moon store in Savannah, Georgia. Dubidoux, like Otis, was over 40 years old and had been replaced by a younger manager. On advice of Lane, Dubidoux had previously filed a complaint with the EEOC alleging age discrimination. The administrative process had recently ended, and Dubidoux's claim was ripe for filing in court.

While investigating Dubidoux's case, Lane discovered that her client's complaint was not limited to one of age discrimination. In recent years Dubidoux had struggled with chronic illness and, as a result, had incurred substantial medical costs under Full Moon's health insurance plan. Lane suspected that Dubidoux's termination may have resulted, at least in part, from Full Moon's efforts to control its health care expenses by terminating employees with costly medical problems. Consequently, Dubidoux's complaint would need to allege two separate causes of action, reflecting the fact that her termination may have been the product of two unlawful motives.[14]

First consider the procedural issues Lane had to address in deciding whether, and how, to join Dubidoux as co-plaintiff.

---

[14]

See, e.g., Vaszlavik v. Storage Technology Corp., 183 F.R.D. 264 (D. Colo. 1998) (discussing the distinct cause of action available to older employees who have been terminated to reduce health-care costs).

Question 6.7

A.   What procedural steps must Lane take to join Dubidoux as co-plaintiff?

B.   Does Lane's attempt to add Dubidoux satisfy the requirements of Rule 20 governing joinder of plaintiffs? Make sure you consider the likely arguments of both Lane and Tweedy.

C.   If the court permits Dubidoux to join as co-plaintiff in the Olmans' suit for age discrimination, will Dubidoux also be permitted to assert the claim that her termination was motivated by her high health care costs? Or does Dubidoux's second claim fail because it does not satisfy Rule 20's requirement that a co-plaintiff's claim arise out of the same "transaction or occurrence" underlying the Olmans' claims of age discrimination?

Regardless of how Lane resolved the procedural issues posed by the possible joinder of Dubidoux, she had to consider the strategic advantages and disadvantages of joinder. Lane saw several potential advantages. Like Otis, Dubidoux had a long employment record with Full Moon and had contributed substantially to the success of the store she managed. And like Otis, Dubidoux had worked under regional manager, Bruce Belcher. As a result, the claims of Otis and Dubidoux were mutually reinforcing. Besides, Dubidoux was a person who would likely have a lot of jury appeal.

There were, however, several disadvantages to joining Dubidoux as co-plaintiff. Most important, Dubidoux's joinder would inject new issues in the case not directly pertinent to the Olmans' claims. As mentioned, Full Moon's termination of Dubidoux might be attributable, in whole or in part, to her medical history. The Olmans' claims had nothing to do with their medical history. A jury might find it difficult to sort out the varying claims. Second, because Dubidoux had been employed in a different city and state (Savannah, Georgia) than the Olmans, Lane anticipated that Full Moon would argue that Dubidoux's claims should be litigated in a federal court in Georgia rather than in Florida.[15] At a minimum, Full Moon's argument would delay Lane's prosecution of the Olmans' claims. Finally, joinder of Dubidoux at this point in the Olmans' suit would require that the trial court change the scheduling order that had governed the case so far.[16] For example, the parties would have to conduct new discovery pertinent to Dubidoux' claims, which would inevitably delay the scheduled trial date.

The possible addition of Dubidoux as co-plaintiff also raised an ethical consideration for Lane. Under rules of professional responsibility, Lane had to consider whether it was in *each* of her clients' best interests to join them as co-plaintiffs. According to Model Rule 1.7(a), a lawyer may not represent multiple clients if there is "a significant risk that the representation of one or more clients will be materially limited by the lawyer's responsibilities to another client." This rule required that Lane consider whether any of her clients would be disadvantaged by joining Dubidoux in the pending suit. It also required that Lane carefully confer with her clients and explain the potential risks, ethical and strategic, involved with joinder.

Lane and her clients eventually agreed that joining Dubidoux as co-plaintiff was inadvisable. There was simply too much divergence between the Olmans' situation and that of Dubidoux. Joining Dubidoux would complicate the jury's task and might detract from efficient proof of the Olmans' case. And her joinder would certainly disrupt the trial court's litigation plan—even assuming the judge would agree to revisit her plan. As a consequence, Lane told her clients she could likely provide more effective and more ethical representation by litigating their claims in separate suits. Her clients agreed.

Consequently, Lane decided that she would forego amending the complaint and allow the case to retain its original structure. However, in carefully considering her amendment options, Lane had complied with her ethical obligations to competently and zealously represent her clients.

---

[15]If you have already studied the materials in Appendix B, you should be able to articulate Full Moon's venue objection. How would you respond if you represented the Olmans and Dubidoux?

[16]*See supra* pp. 96–97.

3.   Amending the Pleadings: The Importance of Timing

a.   The Potential Impact of Rules 15 *and* 16

As mentioned above, any attempt to add new parties to the suit would undermine the case management plan already worked out by the existing parties and approved by the trial court. This raises an important issue regarding amendment of pleadings. How willing are courts to permit amendment of the pleadings when the parties have advanced far in the pre-trial process?

The Supreme Court has stated that permission to amend pleadings under Rule 15 should be "freely given."[17]   According to the Court, amendment should normally be permitted unless the *opposing* party can show either that it will be unduly prejudiced, or that the movant has acted in bad faith. "Prejudice" does not mean that the opposing party will risk greater liability if a new claim is added. Instead, prejudice refers to the adverse *procedural* consequences that result from the movant's failure to allege the new matter earlier in the suit. For example, the party opposing an amendment might show that amendment of the pleadings will now cause it to incur substantially greater expense in responding to the new allegations than it would have incurred at an earlier date. Or the opposing party might show that the movant's delay now prevents it from obtaining discovery that would have been available had it known of the amended allegations earlier in the suit.

Lane knew that, if she sought to amend the complaint to add a new plaintiff or defendant, Full Moon would argue "prejudice" within the meaning of Rule 15. The court would then decide whether Full Moon had met its burden of proving sufficient prejudice to overcome Rule 15's policy of liberal amendment. Lane recognized that Rule 15 sometimes conveys a misleading impression of courts' willingness to permit amendment of the pleadings. In particular, Rule 15 standing alone fails to take into account the *court*'s interest in seeing that the parties comply with the litigation plan issued at the outset of a suit.

As discussed in Chapter 4, Rule 26(f) requires that parties confer early in the suit and develop a plan and schedule for litigation. After the parties confer, the trial court is

---

[17]*See Foman v. Davis,* 371 U.S. 178 (1962) ("In the absence of any apparent or declared reason—such as undue delay, bad faith or dilatory motive on the part of the movant, repeated failure to cure deficiencies by amendments previously allowed, undue prejudice to the opposing party by virtue of allowance of the amendment, futility of amendment, etc.—the leave sought should, as the rules require, be 'freely given.'").

required by Rule 16(b) to issue a case management order. Rule 16(b) specifically provides that this order may "limit[] the time" to "file motions." Rule 16(b) also states that this order "*shall not be modified except upon a showing of good cause.*"[18]

In most cases, the case management order will contain a deadline for amending pleadings. Violation of this deadline provides an additional ground to object to a proposed amendment. If a party moves to amend after this deadline has passed, *he or she* bears the burden of showing "good cause" for deviating from the case management order. In other words, the case management order effectively *reverses* the burden typically imposed by Rule 15(a), which requires that the party *opposing* an amendment show he will be "prejudiced."

If you re-examine the case management order in *Olman v. Full Moon*, you will find it states that motions to amend are "distinctly disfavor[ed]" after the date of the order's *issuance*.[19] In other words, the order expresses the court's preference that all amendments be made *before* discovery. The order's restriction on amendment seems somewhat at odds with the "liberal" amendment policy of Rule 15(a). It also seems a bit unrealistic. Discovery—which often does not commence till after the order's issuance—may be necessary to determine which claims are factually supportable. To "disfavor" amendments made before discovery is conducted places greater emphasis on expedited litigation while undermining the goal of informed pleading.

Nonetheless, such deadlines are now commonly included in case management orders, and the majority of courts enforce them unless a party seeking to make an untimely amendment shows "good cause."[20] This emphasizes a point made earlier in this Guide:[21]

---

[18]Emphasis added.

[19]The case management order, we might note, is derived from a standard case management order used by several judges in the United States District Court for the Middle District of Florida.

[20]*See, e.g., O'Connell v. Hyatt Hotels of Puerto Rico*, 357 F.3d 152 (1st Cir. 2004) ("Rule 16(b)'s 'good cause' standard, rather than Rule 15(a)'s 'freely given' standard, governs motions to amend filed after scheduling order deadlines").

[21]*See A Concluding Note Concerning: The Sources of Procedural Law, supra* at 33–34.

Court orders are a source of procedural "law" that can be as important as the rules themselves.[22]

Consequently, the case management order would have created a serious impediment to Lane's efforts to amend the complaint at this point in the suit. This procedural impediment reaffirmed Lane's strategic and ethical decision to decline to bring new parties into the suit.

b. Beating the Statute of Limitations and Rule 15(c)

One final point regarding the timing of amendments merits attention. On occasion, delay in seeking an amendment may be fatal because the applicable statute of limitations has expired. As discussed earlier, each claim in a suit is subject to a particular statute of limitations. If a party seeks to amend his or her complaint and add a new claim *after* its limitations period has expired, the opposing party may challenge the amendment on the ground the claim must fail.[23]

Rule 15(c) provides a means of circumventing the statute of limitations defense in appropriate circumstances. If the new claim to be added arises out of the "conduct, transaction, or occurrence set forth or attempted to be set forth in the original pleading," it "relates back" to the date of the original pleading. That means any new claim the Olmans added to the suit through amendment would not run afoul of the governing statute of limitations if (a) it arose out of the factual allegations set forth in their original complaint, and (b) the *original* complaint was filed before the statute of limitations applicable to the new claim expired.

To affirm your understanding of the "relation back" doctrine, consider the hypothetical question below.

---

[22]It also is an important reminder of the power district courts have over pretrial matters under the Federal Rules.

[23]Rule 8(c) specifically identifies a "statute of limitations" defense as an affirmative defense that should be pled.

Question 6.8

A.   Assume that Lane moved to amend the complaint to add a new claim on behalf of Otis. This claim alleges that, upon Otis' termination, Full Moon failed to pay him for unused vacation time as required by his employment contract. Under the applicable statute of limitations, the period for filing this claim expired one month *after* Lane filed the original complaint. Is the claim untimely under Rule 15(c)?

B.   Assume that Lane moved to amend the complaint to add Shockley as a defendant and assert a claim for tortious interference with Otis' business relationship with Full Moon. If the statute of limitations for this claim had already expired at the time the motion to amend was filed, why does Rule 15(c) *fail* to provide Otis a means for circumventing this limit?

C.   Some Concluding Joinder Issues: What Might Have Been

Rarely does a single case require application of all rules of joinder. The dispute between the Olmans and Full Moon, for example, does not provide occasion for using several important joinder devices you will study in Civil Procedure. Before leaving the subject of joinder, however, we would like to provide a very brief introduction to a few other rules that *might* have applied if the facts in *Olman* were different. These include Rules 14 (impleader), 19 (necessary and indispensable parties), and 25 (intervention).

1.   Impleader

Rule 14 provides a procedural mechanism by which a defending party can "implead" non-parties who may be liable for all or part of the liability judgment the plaintiff obtains against the defending party. By authorizing the defending party to implead such a "third party," Rule 14 helps the defending party reduce the impact of a judgment. The defending party may be able to obtain its *own* judgment from the third party obligating it to reimburse damages paid to the plaintiff.

One common application of Rule 14 occurs when the defending party is being sued based on the principle of "respondeat superior." For example, employers are often held liable for the wrongdoing of their employees that occurs within the scope of employment. Rule 14 may permit an employer to implead the culprit-employee and obtain its own judgment requiring the employee to reimburse the employer for damages paid to the plaintiff. The key legal question in determining whether impleader is authorized is, under applicable law does the employer have a *right* to reimbursement?

If an employer has the right to reimbursement, it may assert that right in the pending suit in one of two ways.[24] First, if the employee is already a defendant in the suit (for example, the plaintiff has sued both the employer and the employee), the employer can simply cross-claim against the employee under Rule 13(g). In Chapter 3, we briefly mentioned Full Moon's possible use of Rule 13(g) for this purpose to assert a claim against Belcher. Second, if the employee has not been sued, Rule 14 permits the defendant-employer to serve a "third-party" complaint on the employee and add him to the suit as "third-party defendant."

Now let's consider Rule 14's potential relevance in the Olmans' suit.

In Chapter 1, we discussed how age discrimination statutes render an "employer" liable for age discrimination perpetrated by managers like Bruce Belcher. This raises a question: Since Full Moon is being sued by the Olmans for what might have been the wrongdoing of Belcher, could Full Moon seek reimbursement for any judgment it has to pay the Olmans? If Full Moon had the right to reimbursement, it could either (1) cross-claim against Belcher if he was already a co-defendant in the suit, or (2) implead Belcher if he was not a party to the suit.

Alas for Full Moon, it could use neither option. The reason is that, while Full Moon might be found liable for wrongful acts of Belcher, age discrimination statutes do *not* give it a substantive right to seek reimbursement. According to courts that have addressed this issue, because age discrimination law expressly creates "employer" liability, by implication it does not impose liability on employees or supervisors whose conduct renders their employer liable.[25] This form of employer-only liability is common in employment discrimination laws.

---

[24]The employer also has the right to seek reimbursement later in a separate suit.

[25]*See, e.g., Stults v. Conoco, Inc.*, 76 F.3d 651(5th Cir. 1996).

As a consequence, Full Moon would have to pay any judgment the Olmans obtained for age discrimination and could not seek any reimbursement from Belcher. Because Full Moon had no substantive right against Belcher, neither Rule 13(g) nor Rule 14 applied.

Recall that Otis Olman originally sued Full Moon for common law fraud as well. The alleged fraud was apparently committed by Belcher. According to applicable state tort law, if Full Moon was forced to pay a judgment based solely on Belcher's misconduct, Full Moon *would* have a right of reimbursement or "indemnification".[26] As a consequence, when Full Moon was served with the Olmans' complaint, it had the right to seek reimbursement from Belcher. If Belcher was also named as a defendant (the original facts), Full Moon could assert a cross-claim for reimbursement from Belcher under Rule 13(g). On the other hand, if only Full Moon had been named as defendant, it could have impleaded Belcher under Rule 14. Both strategies were ultimately mooted, you may recall, when the trial court dismissed Otis' fraud claim.

2.   Necessary and Indispensable Parties

Rule 20 gives the plaintiff the right to choose who will be parties to the suit. For example, Otis Olman could choose whether to include Fiona or Dubidoux as co-plaintiffs, and could choose whether to sue Full Moon, Belcher, Shockley, or some combination of these. Rule 20 permits joinder of multiple plaintiffs or defendants, but does not mandate joinder.

In some suits, however, joinder is not permissive. According to Rule 19, some parties may be "necessary" or even "indispensable" to a suit. Necessary parties are those who must be joined "if feasible." Indispensable parties are a sub-category of necessary parties; if their joinder is not feasible, the suit must be dismissed.[27]

Rule 19 does not prescribe a specific formula for determining whether someone is a "necessary" or "indispensable" party. To determine whether someone is a necessary party who should be joined, Rule 19(a) directs a court to consider several factors. Two of the more important ones are (1) whether failure to join an absentee will jeopardize his or her interests, and (2) whether failure to join an absentee will expose an existing party to a substantial risk of incurring multiple or inconsistent obligations. If the court concludes that an absentee is a necessary party, it should order his joinder unless joinder would create

---

[26]*See, e.g., Stuart v. Hertz Corp.*, 351 So.2d 703 (Fla. 1977).

[27]*See* Rule 19(b).

jurisdictional or venue problems.[28] If the absentee cannot be properly joined, the court is required to consider alternatives to dismissal that will protect the interests of both the absentee and existing parties.[29] If the court cannot develop measures to protect those interests, Rule 19(b) requires dismissal.

Recall that the Olmans sought monetary damages from Full Moon. They did not want their old jobs back. Given the limited relief sought by the Olmans, it is highly unlikely that Full Moon could have successfully argued that either it, or some absentee, would be prejudiced if the suit remained limited to existing parties. However, consider the possible consequences had Otis Olman sought non-monetary relief.

Assume that the original complaint demanded that Otis be reinstated as store manager. Upon receiving the complaint, Tweedy met with Full Moon personnel and considered the company's options. The company was now party to a three-year contract with Shockley permitting him to continue as store manager unless Full Moon had "good cause" to terminate him. When Full Moon informed Shockley about Otis' demand that he be reinstated as store manager, Shockley said that he would be "very unhappy" if he was forced to give up his position. Full Moon then explored with Shockley the possibility of reaching some sort of settlement with Otis that would "address both men's concerns." In particular, Full Moon raised the possibility of transferring Shockley back to his former position as manager of the store's extreme sporting goods department, but at his new salary level. Shockley was "cool" to the idea. Further, Shockley pointed out that Full Moon had just hired a new manager of the extreme sporting goods department. Although the new manager, Caliope Wacker, had no contract with Full Moon (she was an "employee at will" who had no legal right to continued employment), she would probably be very unhappy if she lost her position in the store.

---

[28]Specifically, Rule 19(a) requires joinder of necessary parties "subject to service of process and whose joinder will not deprive the court of jurisdiction over the subject matter," unless the necessary party makes a valid objection to the court's venue.

[29]See Rule 19(b). Specifically, Rule 19(b) directs the court to consider "to what extent a judgment rendered in the person's absence might be prejudicial to the person or those already parties; . . . the extent to which, by protective provisions in the judgment, by the shaping of relief, or other measures, the prejudice can be lessened or avoided; . . . whether a judgment rendered in the person's absence will be adequate; [and] whether the plaintiff will have an adequate remedy if the action is dismissed for nonjoinder."

Assume that, at present, the only parties to the suit are the Olmans and Full Moon. In light of these facts, consider the following question:

Question 6.9

A.   Does Full Moon have persuasive grounds for arguing that Shockley is a necessary party? That Caliope Wacker is a necessary party?

B.   If for some reason Shockley and Wacker cannot be made parties to the Olmans' suit, are they indispensable? Or can you think of any action the court might take to insure that neither their interests nor those of Full Moon are jeopardized if the suit proceeds in their absence?

C.   By the way, how does Full Moon go about asserting its contention that either Shockley or Wacker should be joined under Rule 19? (Hint: Consider Rule 12).

3.   Intervention

Another procedural mechanism for changing the cast of parties selected by the plaintiff is intervention under Rule 24. According to Rule 24, an absentee can move to intervene in a suit "upon timely application." Rule 24(a) addresses the situation where the prospective intervenor has a "right" to participate in the suit. To establish his right to intervene, an absentee must prove three things: (1) that he has an "interest" related to the transaction that is the subject of the suit, (2) that his absence from the suit "may as a practical matter impair or impede [his] ability to protect that interest"; and (3) the absentee's interest is not "adequately represented by existing parties." An absentee who cannot satisfy these criteria may nonetheless seek court permission to intervene under Rule 24(b). Permissive intervention may be granted if "an applicant's claim or defense and the main action have a question of law or fact in common."

Now consider how Rule 24 might apply in the hypothetical scenarios below.

Question 6.10

A.   Assume, again, that Shockley and Wacker find themselves in the circumstances described in the previous section. Do they have persuasive grounds for seeking to intervene in the Olmans' suit as a matter of right? Do they have grounds for seeking permissive intervention?

B.   Now consider the earlier discussion regarding Lane's decision not to join Ruby Dubidoux as co-plaintiff. *See supra* pp. 177–179. Assume that, in response to Lane's decision, Dubidoux retains other legal counsel. She now asks new counsel to file a motion to intervene in the Olmans' suit. Does she have persuasive grounds for seeking to intervene as a matter of right? For seeking permissive intervention?

C.   Finally, consider the situation of Bruce Belcher, whose alleged wrongdoing constitutes a critical part of the Olmans' claim that they were the victims of age discrimination. As explained earlier, Belcher is not liable for age discrimination under applicable law, only his former employer is. Assume that Belcher was never named as a party in the Olmans' suit. However, after learning more about the Olmans' allegations, Belcher decides it is important that he appear in the case "to defend his good name." Does Belcher have persuasive grounds for seeking intervention as a matter of right? For seeking permissive intervention?

CHAPTER SEVEN:
SUMMARY JUDGMENT

Rule References: 5, 7, 11, 52, *56*, 78

A.   Tweedy Moves for Summary Judgment

From the outset of the Olmans' suit, Tweedy anticipated he would file a motion for summary judgment. In fact, one of the reasons Tweedy often recommended that his clients choose federal court over state court was the improved prospect of obtaining summary judgment.[1]

Judge Goodenough's case management and scheduling order had set a deadline for filing "dispositive motions" of August 1, 2005, one month after discovery closed. Toward the end of discovery Tweedy began reviewing deposition transcripts, documents, and the like and began drafting a summary judgment motion. Tweedy was optimistic he could succeed in having several of the Olmans' claims resolved.

1.   The Standard for Summary Judgment

Rule 56 permits a party to seek full or "partial" summary judgment. In practice, a defending party like Full Moon usually seeks summary judgment on *specific claims* with the hope that the plaintiff's suit can be whittled down to a few counts if not fully resolved. Rule 56(c) is the heart of the rule. It states that summary judgment can be granted when there is "no genuine issue as to any material fact," and "the moving party is entitled to a judgment as a matter of law." Based on this standard, Full Moon could win some form of summary judgment by proving one of two things. First, Full Moon could show that one of its *defenses* to liability was *indisputably proven*. Second, Full Moon could show there was *no credible evidence* (*i.e.,* evidence a reasonable juror might believe) to support the required elements of the *Olmans' claims*.

---

[1] Since the Supreme Court announced the "*Celotex* trilogy" of decisions in 1986, federal courts have shown greater willingness to grant summary judgment. *See Matsushita Elec. Indus. Co. v. Zenith Radio Corp.*, 475 U.S. 574 (1986); *Anderson v. Liberty Lobby, Inc.*, 477 U.S. 242 (1986); *Celotex Corp. v. Catrett*, 477 U.S. 317 (1986). You will probably examine some of those cases during your study of Civil Procedure. The increased availability of summary judgment extends to suits like the Olmans' involving claims of age discrimination; federal courts now grant summary judgment in an appreciable number of ADEA actions. *See* Andrew Ruzicho & Louis Jacobs, LITIGATING AGE DISCRIMINATION CASES § 9.03.

Summary judgment did not address the question of who *would* win at trial. Rather, the issue was whether Otis and Fiona *could* win. If they could not win at trial on the facts and law, there was no need to have a trial at all. It was this reality that Rule 56 enforced.

The key insight of the Supreme Court's summary judgment decisions is that, if summary judgment is to test whether there should be a trial, the allocation of responsibility for presenting evidence should generally be the same at both stages. In other words, if Otis had a responsibility to present evidence at trial, he had the same responsibility at summary judgment. This responsibility is called the burden of production, or the burden of coming forward.[2] The party with this burden must present some admissible evidence from which the fact finder *could* find in its favor. Failure to meet this burden means he or she loses. Satisfaction of the burden means he or she survives summary judgment and can argue his or her case to the jury.

Tweedy knew that as the movant on summary judgment he would have the initial responsibility to show that the motion should be granted. How he met that responsibility depended on the assignment of the burden of production on the issue at stake. If Full Moon had the burden of production on the issue, it had the duty to submit affirmative evidence on the issue. At that point, Lane would need to submit evidence showing there was a material dispute of fact. On the other hand, if Otis had the burden of production, Tweedy could *either* submit affirmative evidence showing Full Moon was entitled to judgment *or* he could point to the absence of evidence supporting Otis' position. If Lane did not respond with affirmative evidence on the issue, summary judgment would be appropriate. After all, at trial she would have to present evidence and the Rules required that she do so at summary judgment as well.

In most cases, a party seeks summary judgment after the discovery process is completed. This timing reflects the fact that summary judgment tests whether an opponent has sufficient evidence to go forward with his case. If the opponent has failed to identify evidence to support his claims during discovery, a court can fairly dismiss those claims. However, there is no requirement that a party wait until discovery is completed to move for summary judgment. Consider the following questions that might have arisen if one of the parties had sought summary judgment early in the case.

---

[2]The burden of production should be distinguished from the burden of persuasion. We discuss the latter burden in Chapter 8.

Question 7.1

A.   According to Rule 56, could Tweedy have moved for summary judgment when he first received the Olmans' complaint?

B.   According to Rule 56, could Lane have simultaneously filed the complaint and moved for summary judgment?

C.   Assume Tweedy moved for summary judgment at the same time he filed Full Moon's answer. He argues that Lane currently has no admissible evidence showing that Full Moon acted with ageist motive. Lane recognizes that, at this point in litigation, Tweedy's contention is true. Is there anything Lane can do under Rule 56 to avoid summary judgment?

2.   Full Moon's Grounds for Summary Judgment

a.   Proving the Affirmative Defense of Waiver

All of Fiona Olman's claims would fail if the waiver she signed when she left Full Moon was enforceable. Tweedy had brought this waiver to Eleanor Lane's attention earlier in the suit when he sent a Rule 11 notice asking that she dismiss Fiona's claims.[3] At the time, Lane contended that the waiver was unenforceable because it failed to advise Fiona of her right to seek advice of a lawyer before signing the release. According to Lane, federal law required that the waiver specifically advise Fiona to consult an "attorney," rather than an "advisor" as stated in the waiver.

Tweedy doubted whether Lane's legal quibble, as he thought of it, would defeat the waiver. But he had deferred moving for a summary judgment earlier because he wanted to investigate the facts surrounding Fiona's signing of the waiver. Now that he had deposed both of the Olmans, he felt confident he could establish the waiver was enforceable. During their depositions, both Fiona and Otis admitted that Fiona considered consulting a lawyer

---

[3]We discussed this earlier in Chapter 3.

when originally asked to sign the waiver. However, she had made the conscious decision not to seek legal counsel after concluding she was "done with Full Moon."

Tweedy, therefore, would seek summary judgment and support his motion with the signed waiver and those portions of the Olmans' depositions discussing the waiver. He would argue (1) that the waiver's admonition to consult an "advisor" substantially satisfied federal law, and (2) that in any event Fiona had made an intelligent choice not to seek legal advice that rendered the specific language of the waiver moot.

Question 7.2

To re-affirm your understanding of the distinction between a Rule 56 motion for summary judgment and a Rule 12(b)(6) motion to dismiss for failure to state a claim, explain why a Rule 56 motion was the proper method for Tweedy to seek disposition of Fiona's claims.

---

b. Challenging Otis' Claims that Full Moon Acted with Ageist Motive

Otis had asserted claims of age discrimination under both federal and state law.[4] To succeed on these claims, he needed to prove that age-based animus had a "determinative influence" on Full Moon's decision to replace him as store manager.[5] Improper *motive* was critical to his claims.

Courts are often reluctant to resolve discrimination claims by summary judgment. An oft-cited opinion expressing this reluctance in age-discrimination suits is the Second Circuit's decision in *Carlton v. Mystic Transportation, Inc.*[6] In *Mystic Transportation* the court observed:

---

[4]Otis was required to prove the same elements to prevail under both federal and state law. *See* Appendix A. In the following discussion, we address only the federal claims although this discussion applies equally to the state law claims as well.

[5]*See Hazen Paper Co. v. Biggins*, 507 U.S. 604, 610 (1993).

[6]202 F.3d 129 (2d Cir. 2000).

> Because this is a discrimination case where intent and state of mind are in dispute, summary judgment is ordinarily inappropriate. . . . [A] trial court should exercise caution when granting summary judgment to an employer where . . . its intent is a genuine issue.[7]

As Tweedy knew, however, many employers have won summary judgment in age-discrimination suits, notwithstanding the courts' preference for letting juries decide issues of intent or motive.[8]

To win summary judgment Tweedy needed to show that Otis' allegations of ageist motive were factually unsupported. Tweedy had developed strong evidence showing that Full Moon had *economic* motives for replacing Otis as store manager through discovery. Otis' salary was exorbitant and his sales figures had slipped appreciably in the years preceding his replacement. By comparison, Shockley had dramatically increased sales for extreme sporting goods during this period and was well-suited to lead the Jacksonville store as it re-focused its marketing on extreme sports customers. Full Moon would argue that economic motives, rather than discriminatory intent, led to Otis' replacement.

A Note to Students:

Summary judgment law is often more complex in employment discrimination suits than in other forms of litigation. In particular, the Supreme Court has developed special procedures for resolving questions of motive when defendants seek summary judgment in employment discrimination cases. These special procedures are referred to as the "*McDonnell Douglas*"[9] standard, which would apply in assessing Full Moon's motion for summary judgment.

Our goal is to introduce you to summary judgment procedure rather than the complexities of employment discrimination law. For that reason, we recommend that you *not* concern yourself with the technical aspects of discrimination law, including the *McDonnell Douglas* standard, when you read the following materials. Instead, keep *two* things in mind: (1) When Full Moon identified evidence supporting its argument that it

---

[7]*Id.* at 134.

[8]*See, e.g., Slattery v. Swiss Reinsurance America Corp.*, 248 F.3d 87 (2d Cir. 2001); *Minton v. American Bankers Insur. Group*, 2003 WL 2130330 (11th Cir. 2003).

[9]*See McDonnell Douglas Corp. v. Green*, 411 U.S. 792 (1973).

replaced Otis because of economic motive, Otis had to respond to that evidence or suffer entry of summary judgment; and (2) to successfully respond to Full Moon's evidence of economic motive, Otis had to produce evidence showing that Full Moon's explanation was a "pretext."[10] If Otis presented enough evidence to support a jury finding that Full Moon's economic justification was a pretext, he would satisfy his burden of production and his ADEA claims would proceed to trial.[11] The key issue remained Full Moon's motive, and the existence of evidence to support Otis' claim that its motive was discriminatory.

> c. **Challenging Otis' Claim that Full Moon Terminated Otis in Retaliation**

Otis' second principal complaint was that his firing occurred in retaliation for his letter to Full Moon president, Bertie Lurch, in which he accused the company of age discrimination. Tweedy was less optimistic about Full Moon's chances of winning summary judgment on Otis' retaliation claims.

To prevail on his retaliation claims, Otis would have to show that he engaged in some form of "protected" activity in response to what he perceived was unlawful age discrimination. Clearly Otis' letter of protest to Lurch was a protected activity.[12] Otis would also have to show that his firing was causally connected to his sending of the letter. The fact that Lurch fired Otis on the heels of this letter provided circumstantial evidence of causation.

To rebut Otis' allegation of retaliatory motive, Full Moon would have to show that it already had lawful reasons to fire Otis when Lurch received the letter, and that Full Moon acted on those reasons. But no matter how strong this evidence, it probably was not so overwhelming as to preclude a reasonable jury from believing that retaliation had a "determinative influence" on Lurch's decision.

---

[10]*See, e.g., Machinchick v. PB Power, Inc.*, 398 F.3d 345, 350–51 (5th Cir. 2005) (discussing application of the *McDonnell Douglas* standard at summary judgment).

[11]The Supreme Court has concluded that, in most cases, proof that an employer has given a false reason (a "pretext") for taking action against an employee permits a jury to *infer* that the unlawful reason (discrimination) alleged by the employee is the true one. *See Reeves v. Sanderson Plumbing Products, Inc.*, 530 U.S. 133, 147 (2000) (it is "permissible for the trier of fact to infer the ultimate fact of discrimination from the falsity of the employer's explanation.")

[12]*See Paquin v. Federal Nat. Mortg. Ass'n*, 119 F.3d 23, 31 (D.C. Cir. 1997) (holding that an employee's letter protesting unlawful firing is protected activity under the ADEA).

Rule 56 did not require that Tweedy assert his weak argument for summary judgment on the retaliation claims. According to Rule 56(a) and (b), a party may move for summary judgment on "all or any part of" a case. This meant Tweedy could seek partial summary judgment on Otis' age discrimination claims, and leave the retaliation claims for resolution at trial. Yet Tweedy declined to use this option. Even though he anticipated the court would deny summary judgment on the retaliation claims, Tweedy believed his motion would force Otis to disclose the evidence and arguments he intended to present at trial. This would assist Tweedy in trial preparation.

Use of Rule 56 to "smoke out" an opponent's position is common in practice. But in Tweedy's case this tactic raised a possible ethical issue. Consider the following question:

Question 7.3

Rule 11 states that by presenting a "written motion" to the court, Tweedy was certifying that the his legal contentions are "warranted by existing law" and not "presented for any improper purpose." Can an argument be made that Tweedy would violate Rule 11 by including a challenge to the retaliation claims in his motion for summary judgment? What would Tweedy's response be? Which is the better argument?

3.   Preparing and Supporting the Summary Judgment Motion

Full Moon's motion for summary judgment was a simple document in itself. Below is the motion Tweedy filed. Notice the materials Tweedy refers to in support of his motion.

OTIS AND FIONA OLMAN,

     Plaintiffs,

vs.   Case No. 03-2222-CIV-M-46-B

FULL MOON SPORTS, INC.,
& BRUCE BELCHER

     Defendants.

DEFENDANT'S MOTION FOR SUMMARY JUDGMENT

Defendant Full Moon Sports, Inc., moves for an order entering summary judgment on all counts of the complaint. In support of its motion, Defendant submits the following materials: Defendant's Statement of Uncontested Facts; Defendant's Memorandum in Support of Its Motion for Summary Judgment; and Defendant's Appendix of Summary Judgment Materials.

                    Respectfully submitted,

                    _____

                    Harrison Ames, Esq.
                    Bart A. Tweedy, Esq.
                    Counsel for Full Moon Sports, Inc.
                    [Address, phone number, etc. omitted.]

Certificate of Service

[omitted]

As you have already learned, any motion filed in federal court must be supported by a memorandum explaining the relief sought and the grounds for that relief.[13] Unlike many other pre-trial motions, however, a summary judgment motion is often supported by extensive documentation. This supporting documentation reflects the fact that summary judgment is intended to provide a comprehensive overview of the key evidence in the case and show the court that there is no "genuine" issue of material fact and a trial is unnecessary.

Much of the evidence supporting Tweedy's motion would be the product of discovery, including deposition transcripts, answers to interrogatories, admissions, and documents. Yet discovery product is not automatically filed with the court when it is served on the parties (which would create quite a paper storage problem for the clerk of court)! According to Rule 5(a), discovery product "must not be filed until . . . used in the proceeding. . . ." Summary judgment often provides the first opportunity to file copies of discovery product with the court. Once "on file," Rule 56(c) states that the court may enter summary judgment based on this discovery product.

Rule 56 also permits the parties to file "affidavits" to support or resist summary judgment. Affidavits are sworn statements made by a person "competent to testify" that can be used to supplement evidence found in discovery product on file. Affidavits are often submitted by the parties, even though the parties' position on key issues in dispute may already be stated in their pleadings. Pleadings, you may recall, are usually signed by the parties' lawyers but not by the parties themselves.[14] Because most pleadings are not "verified or accompanied by an affidavit" of the parties,[15] testimonial evidence of the parties must be independently introduced through discovery product (*e.g.*, a deposition transcript) or affidavit. This is one reason parties may not "rest" on the allegations contained in their pleadings when responding to summary judgment.[16]

---

[13]*See, e.g.,* Rule 7(b).

[14]*See* Rule 11(a) (requiring that every pleading be signed by the attorney of record but not requiring signature of the represented client).

[15]*See id.*

[16]*See* Rule 56(e) ("an adverse party may not rest upon the mere allegations or denials of the adverse party's pleading").

The use of affidavits to support or resist summary judgment might, at first glance, seem dubious. Does this not enable a party to make any self-serving affidavit statement needed to support its position in summary judgment? To some extent this is a fair criticism. Affidavits are usually drafted by lawyers to provide testimony specifically tailored to support their clients' position. There is no opposing lawyer to cross-examine the affiant and expose doubts about his credibility (as there would be in an actual deposition). At the same time, the frequent use of affidavit testimony reflects the fact that summary judgment is *not* the occasion to resolve issues of credibility.[17] Provided an affiant is competent to testify about an issue in dispute, his credibility should not be assessed at the summary judgment phase.[18]

So, Full Moon's motion would be supported by discovery and any affidavits Tweedy thought necessary. This material is referred to in the motion as "Defendant's Appendix of Summary Judgment Materials." In addition, many federal courts require that the moving party file a "Statement of Uncontested Facts," also referenced in Full Moon's motion, succinctly stating the salient facts not in issue together with a citation to the supporting record evidence. As you might imagine, there is often dispute as to whether facts are "uncontested."

One option Tweedy had, although he did not exercise this option, was to request an oral argument. Rule 78 authorizes district courts to resolve motions based on written submissions without benefit of oral argument. Increasingly courts decide motions without conducting a hearing. To some extent this makes sense in the case of summary judgment motions, since courts are not permitted to assess witness credibility in ruling on these motions. Case precedent affirms that a party has no right to demand a hearing on motion for summary judgment.[19] However, as with many other topics we have discussed, much depends on the practice of a particular court or judge.

-----

[17]*See Anderson v. Liberty Lobby, Inc.*, 477 U.S. 242, 255 (1986).

[18]There is one important exception. A party is usually not permitted to defeat summary judgment by giving affidavit testimony that *contradicts* earlier sworn testimony, like that given at a deposition. Only if the party provides an explanation that explains the apparent discrepancy will the contradictory affidavit testimony be accepted. *See, e.g., Cleveland v. Policy Management Sys. Corp.*, 526 U.S. 795, 804 (1999).

[19]*See, e.g., Cruz v. Melecio*, 204 F.3d 14, 19 (1st Cir. 2000)(holding that it is not a denial of due process to deny a hearing before deciding a motion for summary judgment).

Set forth below are excerpts from Full Moon's "Memorandum in Support of Its Motion for Summary Judgment," together with an illustrative affidavit. We have included only those excerpts relevant to Full Moon's request for summary judgment on Otis' ADEA claim of age discrimination. We emphasize, again, that you need not be overly concerned with the discrete legal points raised by Full Moon's motion for summary judgment. Stay focused on one question: *Is there sufficient evidence to support a jury finding that Full Moon replaced Otis based on ageist rather than economic motive?*

IN THE UNITED STATES DISTRICT COURT
FOR THE MIDDLE DISTRICT OF FLORIDA
JACKSONVILLE DIVISION

OTIS AND FIONA OLMAN,

    Plaintiffs,

vs.   Case No. 03-2222-CIV-M-46-B

FULL MOON SPORTS, INC.,
& BRUCE BELCHER

    Defendants.

MEMORANDUM IN SUPPORT OF
DEFENDANT'S MOTION FOR SUMMARY JUDGMENT

. . . . .

II. Plaintiff Otis Olman's Claim of Age Discrimination Should be Dismissed Because There is No Credible Evidence He Was Replaced as Store Manager Because of his Age.

Summary judgment must be granted when, after discovery, it is evident the nonmoving party will not be able to establish the essential elements of his case. *Celotex Corp. v. Catrett*, 477 U.S. 317, 321-22 (1986). When a plaintiff like Otis Olman alleges he was the victim of disparate treatment, his case must fail "unless the employee's protected trait played a role in the [decisionmaking] process and had a <u>determinative influence</u> on the outcome." *Hazen Paper Co. v. Biggins*, 507 U.S. 604, 610 (1993)(emphasis added).

The decisionmaking process leading to Olman's replacement as store manager has been extensively probed by the parties during discovery. The factors influencing that process are undisputed, and they show that Olman was replaced so that the Jacksonville store might be more profitable. There is no record evidence supporting Olman's speculation that his age somehow influenced the decision to replace him as store manager.

Full Moon owns and operates a chain of retail sporting goods stores throughout the United States. (Ex. C-1).* In the summer of 2003, due to declining profits and losses in many of its stores, Full Moon felt compelled to implement a nationwide reorganization, reduction in force, and reduction in salaries and benefits. One of the factors contributing to the company's lackluster economic performance was the salary scale implemented by prior corporate management, which often resulted in salaries for store managers and assistants some 15-25% higher than those paid by competitor companies.

To implement economic change, Full Moon established the "Reorganization Committee" ("Committee") at its headquarters in Atlanta, Georgia. The Committee consisted of four corporate officers, whose ages ranged from 33 to 54 years. Three of the Committee members were over the age of 40. By resolution of Full Moon's Board of Directors, the Committee had final authority to implement change related to the company's reorganization and reduction in force. Company president, Bertie Lurch, was a member of the Committee. Lurch is 48 years old. The Committee's chairperson was Chloé Michaela, who was 45 years old.

One of the Committee's decisions was to close unprofitable or marginally profitable stores. The Jacksonville store managed by Olman was among those considered for closure. But the Committee eventually decided to keep the store open, while shifting emphasis to the sale of extreme sporting goods. The Committee hoped this marketing shift might begin generating adequate profits.

Another Committee decision was to cap the salaries of all store managers at $60,000, with the potential for some store profit-sharing. The Committee decided that current store managers making more than $65,000 should generally be replaced or re-assigned to a different store at a reduced salary where feasible. It was the Committee's considered judgment that it was undesirable to retain a manager at the same store while substantially reducing his salary. After implementation of the Committee's policy, only two stores nationwide retained managers earning over $60,000; both stores had exceptionally high profits in recent years and neither manager earned a salary greater than $70,000.

---

*Full Moon's legal argument would contain specific references to record evidence supporting its factual assertions. This record evidence is often attached to the summary judgment motion as an appendix. We have eliminated specific record references in the remainder of this memorandum and in Otis Olman's responsive memorandum.

All regional managers were informed of the Committee's decision and instructed to file a report with the Committee concerning implementation of the new policy at individual stores. Soon after a report was received from Bruce Belcher, southeast regional manager for stores including the Jacksonville store managed by plaintiff Otis Olman. Belcher informed the Committee that Olman was currently receiving a salary of $85,000 a year. Belcher also informed the Committee that sales in Olman's store had held steady during the past three years, but only because of a substantial increase in the sale of extreme sporting goods.

The Committee reviewed store sales figures, which indicated that in the past three years the sale of extreme sporting goods had gone from accounting for less than 5% of store profits to accounting for most store profits. Absent those profits attributable to extreme sporting goods, the Jacksonville store would probably have been closed.

Belcher advised the Committee that, pursuant to its policy, Olman did not qualify for renewal as store manager. Belcher recommended, however, that Olman be retained by Full Moon in some capacity. Belcher commended Olman for his long service to the company and his popularity among a certain niche of store customers. Because Olman had indicated to Belcher that he did not want to be considered for a position as manager of another Full Moon store, Belcher recommended that Olman be made department manager of the Jacksonville store's camping section at a reduced salary. Finally, Belcher recommended promotion of the store's current manager of the extreme sporting goods department, Sid Shockley, to the position of store manager, at a salary of $50,000 with profit-sharing incentives.

Three of the Committee's members were deposed by Olman during discovery. All testified that their decision to replace Olman as store manager was based on his high salary, as well as the Jacksonville store's mediocre sales record in recent years. All testified that their decision to replace Otis was unaffected by consideration of his age. In fact, no Committee member was even aware of the ages of Olman and Shockley. Committee members also testified that Otis' salary of $85,000 was simply unsustainable in the company's new salary scale for managers.

Regional statistics for Full Moon stores confirm that the Committee's decisions to replace store managers were based solely on economic considerations. Thirty-five (35) store managers in the southeast region (encompassing Jacksonville) were replaced in 2003–2004. All but two store managers earning a salary greater than $60,000 were replaced (14/35). Among the remaining 21 who were replaced, 18 had salaries exceeding $50,000.

In but one instance was a manager making more than $65,000 retained in the southeast region. That manager, whose Atlanta store had recently generated profits far in excess of rates of inflation, was retained at a salary of $70,000.

Consequently, the record evidence is undisputed: Full Moon, acting through its Reorganization Committee, made a series of personnel decisions that were intended to make its stores more profitable. In the case of the Jacksonville store managed by Olman, this entailed cutting back on Olman's unjustifiably-high salary and replacing him with a store manager with a proven record in marketing extreme sporting goods.

Case precedent makes one thing clear: an employer can make prudent personnel decisions based on economic considerations without violating the ADEA. For example, in *Hazen Paper Corp. v. Biggens*, 507 U.S. 604 (1993), the Supreme Court unanimously held that an employer does not violate the ADEA when it bases its personnel decisions on economic factors (pension level in *Hazen Paper*), even if those factors happen to correlate with employees' age. The Court observed, "there is no disparate treatment under the ADEA when the factor motivating the employer is some other feature other than the employee's age." *Id.* at 611. As the Court commented, the ADEA is concerned with "older workers . . . being deprived of employment on the basis of inaccurate and stigmatizing stereotypes." *Id.* However, "when the employer's decision is wholly motivated by factors other than age, the problem of inaccurate and stigmatizing stereotypes disappears. This is true even if the motivating factor is correlated with age, as pension status typically is." *Id.*

Hazen Paper thus affirms that the decision to replace Olman as store manager was based on legitimate, non-discriminatory factors. As a leading case on salary-based personnel decisions observes, the *Hazen Paper* rationale "applies with equal force to cases where workers are discharged because of salary considerations." *See Anderson v. Baxter Healthcare Corp.*, 13 F.3d 1120, 1125 (7th Cir. 1994). Although the older employee in *Anderson* was terminated (not offered alternative employment at reduced salary as was Olman), the Seventh Circuit nonetheless upheld his termination under the ADEA: "Anderson could not prove age discrimination even if he was fired simply because [the employer] desired to reduce its salary costs by discharging him." *Id.* at 1126. The Seventh Circuit's application of the ADEA has been followed by other courts. *See, e.g., Snow v. Ridgefield Medical Center*, 128 F.3d 1201, 1208 (8th Cir. 1997) (entering summary judgment on employee's ADEA claim that "she was terminated because she had been employed at RMC longer than the other then-current employees, and thus earned a comparatively higher salary"). As one court has aptly stated, "Employers do not violate the law by discriminating against overpaid, unnecessary employees." *See Hennessey v. Good Earth Tools, Inc.*, 126 F.3d 1107, 1109 (8th Cir. 1997).

Because the record evidence overwhelmingly demonstrates that the Committee's decision to replace Olman as store manager was motivated by economic concerns, Olman's claim of age discrimination must fail. Aware that the theory of his case is foreclosed by precedent, Olman has attempted throughout discovery to find a shred of evidence that would show the Committee's economic justification was "pretext." Olman's "pretext" argument ultimately comes down to several isolated statements allegedly made by his replacement, Sid Shockley. Olman argues that Shockley's occasional comments about Olman's age somehow tainted the Committee's decisionmaking process in Atlanta, Georgia, even though there is no record evidence the Committee ever knew of these comments.

During discovery, Olman came up with the following evidence of alleged ageism in the Jacksonville store he managed:

> 1. Olman testified that Shockley often referred to him as the "old man;" and referred to older customers as the "boomers."

> 2. Olman's wife, Fiona Olman, and another store employee who lost her job during Full Moon's downsizing, testified they heard Shockley refer to Olman repeatedly as the "old man."

> 3. Bruce Belcher, regional manager, testified that he had no recollection of Shockley's ever referring to Olman as the "old man." He did recall one specific conversation with Shockley, some six months before the decision to replace Olman as store manager was made, in which Shockley expressed the opinion that he could improve store sales if he were given greater authority to expand the store's marketing of extreme sporting goods. Shockley also told Belcher that Olman seemed to have a "problem" with the

culture of extreme sports enthusiasts, particularly their dress and speech.

4. Shockley testified that he did occasionally refer to Olman as the "old man," an expression he acquired when serving in the Navy and intended to signify that Olman was the "boss" or store "commander." Shockley testified that he was never told that Olman or anyone else thought "old man" was a disparaging, ageist term. Shockley also affirmed the conversation about which Belcher testified, in which Shockley expressed the belief that the store's sales would improve if Olman would give greater support to extreme sporting goods sales.

5. Finally, Olman testified that he could not recall a specific occasion on which he complained to Belcher about Shockley's ageist remarks, although he is sure he informally complained at some point. The record confirms that Otis first formally complained about Shockley's remarks *after* he received notice of his replacement as store manager. At that time, Full Moon sent a formal letter of reprimand to Shockley warning him that future words or actions reflecting ageist sentiments would result in his termination.

The fundamental flaw in Olman's "pretext" contention is there is no evidence (1) that any member of the Committee had or expressed ageist sentiments (not surprising since three of the four committee members were over 40); or (2) that any member of the Committee was ever aware of the ageist statements attributed to Shockley. The Supreme Court has recognized that an inference of ageist motivation can be drawn when the person "principally responsible" for the employment decision has expressed ageist sentiments. *See Reeves v. Sanderson Plumbing Products, Inc.*, 530 U.S. 133, 151 (2000). But there is no record evidence in this case that would support an inference that anyone responsible for Olman's replacement was motivated by ageism.

Courts also recognize that a non-decisionmaker may taint an employment decision if that person has "influence or leverage over the official decisionmaker." *See Russell v. McKinney Hospital Venture*, 235 F.3d 219, 226 (5th Cir. 2000). As expressed by another court, "If the [formal decisionmakers] acted as the conduit of [an employee's] prejudice—his cat's paw—the innocence of the [decisionmakers] would not spare the company from liability." *See Shager v. Upjohn Co.*, 913 F.2d

398, 405 (7th Cir. 1990). But in Olman's case there is no evidence that the Committee was the "cat's paw" of Shockley, the only person alleged to have expressed ageist sentiments. The uncontroverted record evidence shows that the Committee made a purely economic decision to replace Olman as store manager, who was being grossly overpaid and whose store was being sustained by the sales success of his replacement. This decision to replace Olman was <u>dictated</u> to regional manager Belcher, who had no choice but to implement the Committee's instruction.

This Circuit has repeatedly affirmed that ageist statements made by a person having no role in employment decisionmaking do not provide credible evidence to justify a trial by jury. *See, e.g., Standard v. A.B.E.L. Services, Inc.*, 161 F.3d 1318, 1329–30 (11th Cir. 1998) (affirming summary judgment for employer where brother of decisionmaker had stated that "older people have more go wrong"); *Mauter v. Hardy Corp.*, 825 F.2d 1554, 1558 (11th Cir. 1987) (holding that statement by vice-president of company uninvolved in decisionmaking that company "was going to weed out the old ones" failed to present a genuine issue of material fact). Indeed, even statements made by one actually involved in company decisionmaking are not adequate to support an inference of age discrimination when the statements are "isolated remarks" that do not relate "directly, in time and subject, to the company's decision to terminate older employees." *See Minton v. American Bankers Insur. Group, Inc.,* 2003 WL 2130330 (11th Cir. 2003) (disregarding decisionmaker's isolated remarks that company needed "fresh new blood," and that older workers should step aside so that younger employees could achieve a measure of wealth).

In sum, Full Moon has presented uncontroverted evidence that its decision to replace Olman as store manager was motivated by economic concerns. The isolated statements of an employee uninvolved in corporate decisionmaking are not sufficient to raise a genuine issue whether Full Moon's decision was a "pretext."

· · · · ·

IN THE UNITED STATES DISTRICT COURT
FOR THE MIDDLE DISTRICT OF FLORIDA
JACKSONVILLE DIVISION

OTIS AND FIONA OLMAN

    Plaintiffs,

vs.   Case No. 03-2222-CIV-M-46-B

FULL MOON SPORTS, INC.
& BRUCE BELCHER

Affidavit of Chloé Michaela

I, Chloé Michaela, being first duly sworn, deposes and says:

1. I am Chloé Michaela, and have personal knowledge of the facts set forth herein.

2. This affidavit is submitted in support of defendant, Full Moon Sports, Inc.'s motion for summary judgment for the purpose of showing that there is in this action no genuine as to any material fact, and that Full Moon Sports, Inc., is entitled to judgment as a matter of law.

3. I am Vice-President of Sales for Full Moon Sports, Inc., and have served in that capacity since 1999. I am 45 years old.

4. I was Chairperson of Full Moon's Reorganization Committee from 2003-2004, which committee made all final decisions concerning the transfer, termination, demotion, promotion, and compensation of all store managers in the Southeast region of the United States.

5. I participated in all above-referenced decisions, including the decision to replace plaintiff, Otis Olman, as manager of the Full Moon Sports Outdoor Center in Jacksonville, Florida, and to place in that position, Sidney Shockley.

6. At no time during the consideration and making the above-mentioned decisions was I aware of the ages of Otis Olman or Sid Shockley.

[211]

7. At no time during the consideration and making of the above-mentioned decisions were the ages of Otis Olman or Sid Shockley mentioned by committee members.

8. At no time during the consideration and making of the above-mentioned decisions was the committee informed of alleged age-discriminatory statements having been made by Sid Shockley, former regional manager, Bruce Belcher, or any other person connected with the Jacksonville store.

9. The decision to replace Otis Olman as store manager was necessitated by company-wide guidelines, including guidelines related to Olman's compensation level and store profits.

10. The decision to replace Otis Olman as store manager was not influenced by the recommendation of Bruce Belcher, even though Belcher conveyed favorable impressions of Olman to the committee.

11. Had the committee been informed of any alleged age-discriminatory comments or behavior by any company personnel, it would have taken immediate action to ensure that no committee decisions were affected by age-discriminatory beliefs, opinions, or motives.

12. At no time during committee deliberations did Full Moon president, Bertie Lurch, express any comments about the age of Otis Olman, his fitness to serve as manager of the Jacksonville store, or Olman's attitudes or opinions regarding Full Moon's corporate downsizing.

_____
Chloé Michaela

Signed and sworn to before me on this day, _____.

[Further Notary Public information omitted.]

Question 7.4

Recall that a court should not make determinations about witness credibility on a motion for summary judgment. Could a juror review the evidence cited by Full Moon and still have "reasonable" doubts about the company's actual motivation in replacing Otis? Does the fact that Full Moon cites substantial evidence of its economic motivation preclude a jury's believing that ageism had a "determinative influence" on the company's decision, which is the critical legal issue under the ADEA?

B.   The Olmans' Response to Summary Judgment

Before responding to Full Moon's summary judgment motion, Lane considered whether she might file her own motion on behalf of the Olmans. Nothing in the Rules prohibits both parties from seeking summary judgment. However, Lane did not believe she had good grounds for seeking summary judgment. First, Full Moon had already abandoned its counterclaim alleging that Otis converted store property. Discovery had made clear that this counterclaim was based on misinformed speculation. When Tweedy learned that Full Moon's counterclaim lacked factual support, he obtained Otis' permission to voluntarily dismiss it under Rule 41(a)(1).[20]

As for the Olmans' remaining claims, Lane believed they were well supported but did not think she had enough evidence to obtain summary judgment. She did not want to undermine her own credibility by filing a motion that the court would readily deny. Further,

---

[20]Rule 41(a) provides a means for the parties, or in some circumstances, the plaintiff alone, to voluntarily dismiss a claim. A plaintiff may voluntarily dismiss a claim on its own so long as no answer or motion for summary judgment has been filed. *See* Rule 41(a)(1)(i). Once either of these documents has been filed, a voluntary dismissal is permissible only if all parties agree. *See* Rule 41(a)(1)(ii). In this case, both Full Moon and Otis agreed to voluntarily dismiss the conversion counterclaim. The stipulation of dismissal they filed with the court specified that the dismissal was with prejudice. This meant that Full Moon could not later reassert the claim. If the stipulation had not so provided, the default presumption was that the dismissal would have been without prejudice. *See id.* The most common use of voluntary dismissals occurs when the parties agree to settle their dispute.

she saw no need to "smoke out" Full Moon's case at trial because it was now set forth in the company's own summary judgment motion.

Upon reviewing Full Moon's motion for summary judgment, Lane found little she had not already anticipated. Lane always thought it important to conduct discovery with summary judgment in mind. This meant that she continually referred to the elements of the claims asserted in the complaint and made sure to focus discovery on the development of evidence that would support those elements.

Lane took Full Moon's summary judgment motion very seriously. She believed summary judgment posed the greatest threat to her clients' chance of success in litigation. Provided the Olmans could survive summary judgment, they would present attractive figures to a jury. They were plain spoken, and jurors would probably relate to two middle-aged folks who lost their jobs because a large corporation wanted to maximize profits by cutting salaries of its long-term employees. It also would not hurt that the Olmans were local Floridians going up against an out-of-state corporation. Moreover, the two leading witnesses for Full Moon were Bertie Lurch and Bruce Belcher. Lurch had come across during his deposition as someone who always has to be right and tends to be condescending to those who disagree with him. Belcher seemed a bit slippery and the circumstances of his departure from Full Moon would undermine his credibility.

Lane *had* to get this case to a jury. Here is how she assessed her risks on summary judgment.

1.   Responding to the Liability Release

Fiona Olman presented the greatest problem. Her deposition testimony appeared to undermine Lane's argument that the liability release she signed was defective because it admonished her to consult an "advisor" rather than a lawyer. Regardless of the release language, Fiona had admitted that she and Otis discussed consulting a lawyer but decided not to do so.

Yet, Lane believed she had grounds for resisting summary judgment. She would file an affidavit from Fiona attempting to clarify her deposition testimony. Although Fiona could not renounce that testimony, she could explain that (1) she failed to appreciate the importance of seeking legal advice until after signing the release, and (2) nothing in the release ever communicated the importance of seeking legal advice. Fiona had not, in fact, remembered anything about the release's admonition when asked during deposition. While Full Moon had now construed her and Otis' deposition testimony to mean that she made an intelligent choice not to consult a lawyer, Lane would try to argue that the deposition testimony merely showed that Fiona never fully appreciated the importance of seeking a lawyer. Construed in this light, Fiona's deposition might actually demonstrate the potential value of clearer language in the release.

Lane's argued interpretation of the deposition might inject enough ambiguity to persuade the court to deny summary judgment and let Fiona's claims proceed to trial. Lane would attempt to bolster Fiona's position by arguing that the court should strictly construe federal language governing waivers to prevent future confusion among employees. It was worth a shot.

2.   Responding to Full Moon's Contention that It Acted with Legitimate, Non-discriminatory Motive in Replacing Otis

Full Moon's economic justification for Otis' replacement was worrisome. During deposition, every member of the Reorganization Committee had emphasized the centrality of economic reasons for replacing higher-paid store managers. The Committee had strong documentation of its assertion that the decision to replace higher-salaried managers like Otis preceded any input from Belcher—the best conduit for discriminatory motive Lane had identified. Further, Full Moon correctly argued that federal courts construe the ADEA to permit the disturbing practice of getting rid of higher-salaried employees. Lane thought this was a lousy interpretation of federal law, but she thought it futile to argue a different interpretation.

Still, Lane thought there was more discretion involved in the decision to replace Otis than Full Moon suggested, and she believed she had credible evidence that exercise of this discretion might have been tainted by ageism. The key thing was to show that Belcher had sufficient influence to prevent Otis' replacement. If she could persuade the court that Otis' replacement remained an open issue during Full Moon's downsizing, and that ageism may have influenced the decision to replace Otis, she might defeat summary judgment on Otis' age discrimination claims.

3.   Raising Doubt About Full Moon's Motive in Terminating Otis

Lane was confident she could defeat summary judgment on Otis' retaliation claim. This issue came down to credibility. Would a jury believe that Lurch fired Otis for the reasons mentioned in his letter? Or, would it believe that Lurch fired him because he accused the company of age discrimination? This issue was simply not susceptible to resolution by motion for summary judgment.

Below are excerpts from the Olmans' Memorandum in Opposition to Full Moon's Motion for Summary Judgment. We have included only those excerpts relevant to Otis' claim of age discrimination under the ADEA. Once again, do not get bogged down by substantive employment discrimination law. Focus on the evidentiary issue that is key to determining whether there needs to be a trial.

IN THE UNITED STATES DISTRICT COURT
FOR THE MIDDLE DISTRICT OF FLORIDA
JACKSONVILLE DIVISION

OTIS AND FIONA OLMAN,

    Plaintiffs,

vs.   Case No. 03-2222-CIV-M-46-B

FULL MOON SPORTS, INC.,
& BRUCE BELCHER

    Defendants.

MEMORANDUM IN OPPOSITION TO
DEFENDANT'S MOTION FOR SUMMARY JUDGMENT

. . . . .

In ruling on Full Moon's motion for summary judgment, the court "must draw all reasonable inferences in favor of the nonmoving party, and it may not make credibility determinations or weigh the evidence." *Reeves v. Sanderson Plumbing Products, Inc.*, 530 U.S. 133, 150 (2000). Application of this standard requires that the Court deny Full Moon's motion for summary judgment on Otis Olman's age discrimination claim.

Full Moon attempts to create a wall between its Reorganization Committee and the ageist sentiments of regional manager Belcher and his chosen replacement for Olman, Sid Shockley. According to Full Moon, Olman's replacement was a *fait accompli* by the time Belcher was asked to implement the Committee's decision. Legitimate economic concerns, Full Moon argues, fully explain the decision to replace Olman.

A careful review of the record evidence shows that (1) Olman's replacement was not the inevitable result of economic factors, and (2) the ageist sentiments of Belcher and Shockley might have influenced Olman's replacement. Here is the critical evidence that, if believed by a jury, would support a finding of liability:

1. Otis Olman worked for Full Moon for twenty years before being terminated. In 1990, he accepted Full Moon's offer to become manager of its Jacksonville store, which had enjoyed "mediocre" success under prior management. As Full Moon's own witnesses agree, Olman transformed the Jacksonville store into a model of success.

2. In 2000, Full Moon was acquired by another company and replaced both its president and southeast regional manager. The new president and regional manager were, respectively, Bertie Lurch and Bruce Belcher.

3. In 2000, Olman received an attractive business offer that would have required his leaving Full Moon's employment. However, Lurch and Belcher induced Olman to remain with the company by offering him a contract with a salary of $85,000 a year—an increase of $10,000 per year. Although Olman expressed concerns about his job security under Full Moon's new management, Belcher stated unequivocally to Olman that "a guy with your track record shouldn't worry about his future with Full Moon. Jacksonville is your store as long as you want it to be. You can retire here."

4. That same year Shockley was hired to manage the new extreme sporting goods department of the Jacksonville store. Shockley had no prior retail sales experience. From the inception of his hiring, Shockley required careful training by Olman. As Shockley acknowledged during his deposition, "He taught me everything I know about retail sales. I owe it all to him."

5. Although Shockley "owed it all" to Olman, he continually expressed his age prejudice against Olman. He constantly referred to Olman as the "old man" both within and outside Olman's presence. On several occasions, Shockley expressed the view that the Jacksonville store could improve its sales if it turned attention away from older customers—called "boomers" by Shockley—and marketed to the "younger" customer base interested in extreme sports.

6. Olman declined to formally complain about Shockley's ageist sentiments and hoped that he would "mature." On one occasion, however, he felt compelled to counsel Shockley about

his slovenly dress and excessively slang speech. Before doing so Olman informed Belcher of his intention of speaking with Shockley. As Olman testified, Belcher responded by saying, "Lighten up Otis. You're being an old fart."

7. In the months leading up to Olman's replacement, Shockley told several store employees that he could boost store sales if Olman would "do more advertising of extreme sports." In fact, Olman was already allocating almost half the store's advertising budget to extreme sporting goods.

8. In July of 2003, Belcher informed Olman of the company's reorganization plans and asked him to consider relocating to another store. Belcher also asked for Olman's recommendations concerning reduction in force of store employees. Belcher conveyed the distinct impression that management in Atlanta was receptive to advice and recommendations. Belcher never indicated that Olman's demotion was dictated by management, and promised Olman "I'll take care of you."

9. In response to Belcher's request, Olman informed him that he did not want to move to another store and "push out some other manager." Olman also advised Belcher that the company should retain more senior employees who had "demonstrated their loyalty."

10. Olman soon learned that he was being replaced as store manager by Shockley. At that time he contacted Rex Ornstein, an advertising agent for Full Moon and Olman's former regional manager, to seek advice. Ornstein told Olman that "The extreme generation is young. We're not. Maybe it's time to move on." Ornstein was, at that time, based at Full Moon's headquarters in Atlanta.

11. Olman subsequently wrote a letter to Full Moon's president complaining about what he perceived as a pattern of age discrimination in the company's reorganization and downsizing. In response to the letter, Lurch terminated Olman.

12. As a result of Full Moon's reorganization and downsizing in 2003–2004, a greater percentage of managers over

the age of 40 were replaced. In particular 55% of the managers affected by downsizing were over 40.

This evidence raises substantial issues of fact regarding whether Olman's replacement was tainted by age discrimination. First, there is evidence that Full Moon tolerated a "corporate atmosphere hostile to older employees." *See Madel v. FCI Marketing, Inc.*, 116 F.3d 1247, 1252 (8th Cir. 1997). Regional manager Belcher was obviously aware that Shockley openly disparaged Olman as an "old man" ill equipped to appeal to a "younger" generation of customers. There was a "pervasive use of age-based epithets" in the Jacksonville store. *See id.* Yet, Belcher not only failed to take action to curtail Shockley's expression, he eventually recommended that Shockley take over management of the Jacksonville store!

Further, the record evidence contradicts Full Moon's claim that the "decision to replace Olman was <u>dictated</u> to regional manager Belcher, who had no choice but to implement the Committee's instruction." *See* Memorandum in Support of Defendant's Motion for Summary Judgment at __. As Full Moon concedes, at least two store managers with salaries in excess of $60,000 were retained after the company's reorganization. *See id.* at __. Particularly given the fact that *new* management at Full Moon (including Lurch and Belcher) asked Olman to remain with the company in 1999 at an increased salary of $85,000, a jury might find that the company exercised more discretion in 2002 than it now avows.

Nor does the alleged fact that the Reorganization Committee made the final decision to replace Olman insulate Full Moon from liability. Liability would still attach if the Committee acted "as a rubber stamp ... for a subordinate employee's prejudice, even if the [Committee] lacked discriminatory intent." *See Russell v. McKinney Hosp. Venture,* 235 F.3d 219, 227 (5th Cir. 2000). As one court has commented, the "decisionmaker" rule for liability "was never intended to apply formalistically, and remarks by those who did not independently have the authority or did not directly exercise their authority to fire the plaintiff, but who nevertheless played a meaningful role in the decision to terminate the plaintiff, [are] relevant." *See Ercegovich v. Goodyear Tire & Rubber Co.,* 154 F.3d 344, 354–55 (6th Cir. 1998). In Olman's case, there is ample, credible evidence that Belcher had potential to influence the decision whether to retain Olman as store manager and that Belcher's influence was tainted with ageism.

[220]

This assumes, of course, that the Committee acted innocently in ratifying the age-based recommendations of Belcher. But there is evidence that the Committee may not have acted so innocently. First, company *president*, Bertie Lurch, was one of four members of the Committee and likely had considerable influence over its decisions. As Olman's suit demonstrates, Lurch was the decisionmaker who took retaliatory action against Olman for complaining of age discrimination. Evidence of his retaliatory action raises a genuine issue whether the Committee's decisionmaking was in fact neutral. Second, the comments of Full Moon executive, Rex Ornstein, evidence a corporate culture of ageism. As Ornstein said to Olman at the time of his demotion, Olman lacked the youth Full Moon sought in its personnel and so it was "time to move on." Third, the statistical evidence in this case, indicating that approximately 55% of terminated managers were over 40, combines with the evidence of ageist sentiments in the company to create a genuine issue of fact whether age discrimination played a role in Olman's replacement. *See Maddow v. Procter & Gamble Co., Inc.*, 107 F.3d 846, 852 (11th Cir. 1997) (statistical evidence of disparate reduction in force combined with evidence of ageist statements created genuine issue of material fact precluding summary judgment for employer).

The Supreme Court has emphasized that "credibility determinations, the weighing of the evidence, and the drawing of legitimate inferences from the facts are jury functions, not those of a judge." *See Reeves, supra* at 150. Under this standard, "the plaintiff need produce very little evidence of discriminatory motive to raise a genuine issue of fact." *See Lindahl v. Air France*, 930 F.2d 1434, 1438 (9th Cir. 1991) (applying *McDonnell Douglas* standard). Olman's evidence greatly exceeds the "very little" required under case precedent to survive summary judgment.

· · · · ·

Question 7.5

A.   As you can see, Lane portrayed the evidence and case law much differently than Tweedy. What are the principal disagreements between the parties about the facts?

B.   Lane's primary focus is to show that Belcher was a conduit for ageist prejudice in the Reorganization Committee's decision to replace Olman. What particular evidence does Lane cite to show that Belcher may have acted with ageist motive? Do you think this evidence sufficient to persuade a "reasonable" juror? Did it persuade you? Or is Lane asking the court to engage in pure speculation and go beyond the reasonable implications of the evidence?

C.   Lane also refers to Lurch's membership on the Committee and asks the court to infer that evidence of his retaliatory response to Otis' letter also supports an inference of ageist motive? Do you find this tack persuasive? Or is Lurch's alleged retaliatory motive irrelevant to his motive in affirming Otis' replacement?

D.   Lane cites statistical evidence that 55% of the managers replaced during Full Moon's reorganization were over the age of 40. If you were counsel for Full Moon and had the opportunity to respond to this statistical evidence, what might you argue? What other information would you seek in preparing your response?[21]

---

[21]Full Moon would have the option of requesting permission to file a reply to the Olmans' response. Such a reply might be desirable if Full Moon believed it important to respond to the Olmans' use of record evidence or their interpretation of law. However, the court might give the Olmans permission to file their own reply—called a surreply—if they requested this opportunity.

C.   Judge Goodenough's Ruling

Once the parties' summary judgment briefing was completed, Judge Goodenough was faced with the task of reviewing their submissions and supporting evidence. In many, perhaps most courts, this review is conducted by the judge's clerk, at least in the first instance. The clerk will carefully review the parties' legal arguments, their citations to record evidence, and their representations of case law. The clerk will often draft an opinion for the judge that will provide the basis for further discussion between them. Eventually, the judge will finalize her views and issue a decision.

Judges vary in the length and detail of their opinions. In fact, Rule 52(a) expressly *dispenses* with any requirement that trial courts actually write an opinion.[22] Rule 52(a) reflects the belief that in many cases a written opinion explaining the court's reason for granting or denying summary judgment is unnecessary and imposes an unjustified increase in the court's workload. Nonetheless, appellate courts sometimes ignore the command of Rule 52(a) and require that trial judges explain their decision on motion for summary judgment. An amusing example of the clash between Rule 52 and appellate court preferences is found in *Fairhead v. DeLeuw, Cather & Co.*, 817 F. Supp. 153 (D.D.C. 1993).

In *Fairhead*, the district court had entered summary judgment without expressing its rationale. When an appeal was taken, the circuit court found itself "unable" to review the trial court's decision and remanded the case with directions that the court file written "findings of fact and conclusions of law" within 30 days. On remand the trial court complied, but not without first expressing its dismay at the circuit court's flouting of Rule 52. The trial court's comments provide an unusually candid view of the differing perspectives of trial and appellate judges:

> [The circuit court's] Order was puzzling to the undersigned in several respects. First, if the undersigned, with the assistance of a clerk, was "able" to decide the case, it is unclear why three experienced appellate judges, with their extensive law clerk and Staff Counsel's Office support resources, were "unable" to decide it, having not only the complete record which had been before this Court but also the addition of three appellate briefs. Second, Rule 52(a) specifically provides, without exception, that "[f]indings of fact and conclusions of law are unnecessary on decisions of [summary judgment] motions. . . ." Third, given the undersigned's

---

[22]*See* Fed. R. Civ. P. 52(a) ("Findings of fact and conclusions of law are unnecessary on decisions of motions under Rule . . . 56.").

overwhelming caseload and the passage of time, one result of which was that the law clerk who originally had analyzed the entire case had long since completed her clerkship (requiring a new law clerk to repeat the same work), it was extraordinary that three Article III judges would order another Article III judge to produce "findings of fact and conclusions of law" within 30 days.[23]

The trial court's decision was ultimately affirmed when it returned to the circuit court. Somewhat remarkably, the circuit court did not explain the basis for its affirmance: "The court has determined that the issues presented occasion no need for an opinion"![24]

In any event, Judge Goodenough wrote a memorandum explaining her summary judgment order.[25] Below are excerpts from the order and memorandum,[26] which focus on Otis Olman's claim of age discrimination.

---

[23]*See id.* at 154.

[24]*See* 1 F.3d 45 (1993).

[25]Notwithstanding Rule 52, the judge could not help but be aware of her circuit's preference for opinions and the greater risk of reversal if she did not explain her ruling. *See, e.g., Hulsey v. Pride Restaurants LLC*, 367 F.3d 1238, 1240 (11th Cir. 2004) (reversing trial court's entry of summary judgment and noting the "cursory" nature of its order).

[26]As with the parties' memoranda, the court's order omits citations to the record.

IN THE UNITED STATES DISTRICT COURT
FOR THE MIDDLE DISTRICT OF FLORIDA
JACKSONVILLE DIVISION

OTIS AND FIONA OLMAN,

    Plaintiffs,

vs.   Case No. 03-2222-CIV-M-46-B

FULL MOON SPORTS, INC.,
& BRUCE BELCHER

    Defendants.

ORDER

This cause comes before the Court for consideration of Defendant's Motion for Summary Judgment. The Court hereby orders as follows:

1. Defendant's motion for summary judgment on all claims of plaintiff Fiona Olman (counts six and seven) is GRANTED;

2. Defendant's motion for summary judgment on plaintiff Otis Olman's claims of age discrimination under the Age Discrimination in Employment Act ("ADEA") and the Florida Civil Rights Act (counts one and three) is GRANTED; and

3. Defendant's motion for summary judgment on plaintiff Otis Olman's claims of retaliation under the ADEA and the Florida Civil Rights Act (counts two and four) is DENIED.

· · · · ·

MEMORANDUM

· · · · ·

Plaintiff Otis Olman next claims that Full Moon acted with discriminatory motive when it replaced him as manager of the Jacksonville store and promoted Shockley to his position. Olman has adduced credible

[225]

evidence that he was over the age of 40, that he was qualified to serve as manager of the Jacksonville store, and that he was replaced by a person under the age of 40. Full Moon, in turn, has responded with credible evidence that it replaced Olman and numerous other store managers in the southeast region to reduce salary costs and improve the economic performance of stores. Under the *McDonnell Douglas* standard governing this motion, Olman must produce credible evidence that Full Moon's economic explanation is a "pretext" to survive summary judgment.

Olman's evidence of pretext takes three forms. First, he cites evidence that (a) Shockley expressed ageist sentiments prior to becoming store manager, (b) Belcher took no action to discipline Shockley, (c) on one occasion Belcher expressed an ageist sentiment himself, and (d) Belcher had authority to recommend that Olman be retained as store manager but declined to, allegedly because of his discriminatory attitudes toward older employees like Olman. Second, Olman argues that the retaliatory action taken against him by company president Bertie Lurch evidences ageism on the part of Lurch, who participated in the decision to replace Olman. Third, Olman points to statistical evidence that 55% of the managers replaced during Full Moon's downsizing and reorganization in 2003-2004 were over 40.

This Court finds that the evidence of ageist remarks by Shockley and Belcher falls short of providing a reasonable basis for inferring that Belcher acted with ageist motive in failing to recommend Olman's retention as manager. Initially, it merits emphasis that the supervisor who is pivotal to Olman's argument—Bruce Belcher—is the same person who renewed Olman in 2000 at a substantial salary of $85,000. As other courts have observed, when the same person charged with discrimination has previously taken favorable job action regarding the plaintiff the inference of ageism is unlikely. *See, e.g., Hennessey v. Good Earth Tools, Inc.*, 126 F.3d 1107, 1109 (8th Cir. 1997); *Horwitz v. Board of Educ.*, 260 F.3d 602, 611 (7th Cir. 2001).

In addition, there is no appreciable evidence indicating that Belcher shared Shockley's ageist sentiments (assuming that interpretation is properly given to Shockley's comments). One isolated comment referring to Olman as an "old fart," particularly a comment made at least two years before Olman's replacement, does not provide credible evidence of ageism. The ADEA is not a code of workplace etiquette, and courts should be wary of construing a flip comment as evidence of dark motive. *See Hardin v. Hussmann Corp.,* 45 F.3d 262, 266 (8th Cir. 1995) (Arnold, J., dissenting) ("There is evidently nothing that a person can say that cannot be remade into something dark and actionable by a sufficiently suspicious imagination").

Nor does the Court agree that Lurch's possible retaliatory action—which will be examined later at trial—provides evidence that he acted with ageist motive in replacing Olman. Lurch, a 48-year-old man himself, may have acted rashly and even illegally in terminating Olman after receiving a letter complaining of age discrimination. But retaliation against an outspoken employee differs from age discrimination.

Finally, statistical evidence indicating that 55% of the managers terminated in the southeast region were over 40 does not, standing alone, provide evidence of age discrimination. As Full Moon pointed out in response to the plaintiffs' statistical contention, the majority of Full Moon's managers both before *and* after its reduction in force were over 40. The relatively minor impact of downsizing on the total percentage of older managers does not present credible evidence of age discrimination.* Equally important, the large majority of those managers replaced drew salaries in excess of $50,000. As Olman must concede, an employer may lawfully take job action based on economic concerns, including action against high-salaried employees. *Hazen Paper* affirms that employers do not violate the ADEA when they make decisions based on legitimate economic factors that happen to correlate with age.

In sum, Olman has failed to produce evidence rebutting Full Moon's defense that it replaced him based on lawful, non-discriminatory factors. While this Court (a member of the age group protected by the ADEA) sympathizes with Olman, and questions the wisdom of corporate policy that penalizes the very employees who have attained economic success, the ADEA provides no authority to second-guess that policy.

· · · · ·

*Plaintiffs have not attempted to make a "disparate impact" argument based on this statistical evidence, likely reflecting the fact that the statistical disparity between under-40 and over-40 managers in this case is so small.

DONE and ORDERED at Jacksonville, Florida, this 31st day

of August, 2005.

———————————————
SARAH GOODENOUGH
United States District Judge

Question 7.6

A.   Are you persuaded that Judge Goodenough has properly applied the summary judgment standard of Rule 56?

B.   To what extent does the judge's opinion appear to be influenced by her intuitive views of human motive and behavior? Should she act based on these views, or is that the reason we have trial by jury?

CHAPTER EIGHT:
TRIAL

Chapter Rule References: 16, 43, 45, 47, 48, 49, *50*, 51, 54, 58, *59*

A.   Preparing for Trial

It is paradoxical that while civil trials are relatively rare events,[1] in many respects they drive the entire litigation process. It is usually not possible to determine at the pleading stage which cases will go to trial. Thus, a good lawyer will treat each case as if it will go the distance. Both Lane and Tweedy had approached the Olmans' suit this way. If they had not, by the time it became clear a trial was necessary it would have been too late to use the various discovery tools to prepare adequately.

Judge Goodenough's decisions on the dispositive motions left only two claims for trial: Otis' retaliation claims under the ADEA and the Florida Civil Rights Act. It was on these claims that the lawyers focused their attention. The first thing they did was refresh themselves as to the elements of the claims. In order to win under either federal or state law, Otis needed to establish:

1.   He engaged in statutorily protected expression;

2.   He suffered adverse employment action; and

3.   The adverse action against him was causally related to his protected expression.[2]

Otis would have the burden of production and persuasion at trial on these claims. Although most commonly known, the burden of persuasion is rarely dispositive in a civil case. The reason is that the party with this burden must demonstrate that it should win by a preponderance of the evidence, or a tip in the scales of justice. Thus, the only time the assignment of the burden of persuasion comes into play to dictate the "winner" in a civil case is when those scales are evenly balanced. In other words, it matters only when the jury simply cannot decide between two versions of events. In that instance, and that instance

---

[1]*See* Chapter 1 at n. 7 (providing statistics on jury trial frequency in federal courts).

[2]*See* 29 U.S.C. § 623(d) (2004); Fla. Stat. § 760.10(7) (2004); *Weeks v. Harden Mftg. Co.*, 291 F.3d 1307, 1311 (11th Cir. 2002).

only, the assignment of the burden of persuasion would be dispositive, with the person assigned the burden losing.[3]

The burden of production is a different story because it is quite important at various stages of civil litigation. If a party has the burden of production on an issue it means he must produce evidence from which a rational factfinder could rule in his favor. A failure to produce such evidence is fatal. We have previously discussed the burden of production in connection with Full Moon's motion for summary judgment.[4]

While the entire litigation process to this point had been largely a preparation for trial, the period after summary judgment was a time of heightened activity. After ruling on Full Moon's motion, Judge Goodenough scheduled a final pretrial conference for Thursday, September 15, 2005.[5] The trial was set to commence the following week, on September 19, 2005.

Lane and Tweedy knew the final pretrial conference was an enormously significant event in the case. This conference would establish the specific rules of the trial. During the conference, Judge Goodenough would resolve most disputes between the parties on a range of issues, including the admissibility of evidence and the legal instructions she would give to the jury. In order to put her and the parties in the best position to consider issues that could arise at trial, Judge Goodenough issued a final pretrial order that required the parties to do a number of things before the conference. These requirements included:

- The parties were to inform the court how long each anticipated trial would take.

- Lane and Tweedy were to work together to prepare the instructions that Judge Goodenough would give to the jury.[6] To the extent possible, Judge Goodenough wanted instructions on which both parties agreed. If they

---

[3]Of course, the assignment of the burden of persuasion, while not often dispositive, can certainly be important when of developing trial strategy or deciding which motions to file.

[4]*See supra* Chapter 8.

[5]*See* Rule 16(d) (requiring district to court to hold a final pretrial conference "as close to the time of trial as reasonable under the circumstances").

[6]*See* Rule 51.

were unable to agree on a particular instruction, each party was to submit its own version for the court's consideration.

- Each party was to submit a list of witnesses it expected to call at trial. If either party objected to a witness listed by the other party, the objection needed to be stated and briefed. The party offering the witness would then need to respond.

- Each party was to submit a list of documents it expected to introduce into evidence at trial. If either party objected to a document listed by the other party, the objection needed to be stated and briefed.[7] The party offering the document would then need to respond.

- Each party was to identify those portions of deposition transcripts it wished to read into evidence at the trial.[8] As with documents and witnesses, all objections to such designations needed to be stated at this point.

- The parties were to agree on any stipulations of fact to be read to the jury. The jury would be required to accept such stipulations as true.

Both Lane and Tweedy worked diligently to prepare the materials Judge Goodenough requested. The upshot of this preparation was that both lawyers essentially had to map out their entire trial strategy. They did not see Judge Goodenough's requirements as mere make work, as the requirements were designed to make the trial as efficient as possible.[9]

---

[7]The objections to both documents and witnesses would most often be based on the Federal Rules of Evidence. They could, however, also be based on procedural defects such as a failure to disclose matters as part of the Rule 26(a) process. *See, e.g.,* Rule 37(c)(1).

[8]*See* Rule 32 (concerning the "use of depositions in court proceedings").

[9]Judges usually require that the lawyers who will actually try the case be present at the final pretrial conference. Thus, if Tweedy's superior Harrison Ames were to try the case, he would have had to appear. Ames had decided, however, that Tweedy should try the case. Tweedy was most familiar with the facts and Full Moon had confidence in him. Plus, Ames recognized that the retaliation case was one that could easily go against Full Moon if the jury disliked Bertie Lurch. Ames figured it was just as well to let Tweedy more directly bear that risk of loss.

Both Lane and Tweedy complied with Judge Goodenough's order. They then appeared at the final pretrial conference, at which the judge ruled on their various objections and confirmed the trial date.

After the conference, Lane and Tweedy each continued their intensive trial preparations. For example, each prepared a "trial notebook" that contained all the materials they would likely need during trial. These materials included notes for examining witnesses and making statements to the jury; documents to be introduced; the jury instructions; and the motions each expected to make during trial. Lane was old-fashioned and felt more comfortable with paper, so she used actual notebooks. Tweedy, on the other hand, opted to use a laptop computer to compile his "notebook."

In addition, Lane and Tweedy were also working closely with the witnesses they would call at trial. The lawyers knew that a case could be won or lost based on a witness' performance on the stand. Thus, each of them spent many hours with their witnesses going over the form of the questions the lawyers would ask and the substance of their answers. They wanted to make sure that the witnesses felt comfortable with the questions they would be asked at trial by both attorneys. They also made sure that the witnesses understood they had to tell the truth. Finally, they made sure that the witnesses knew how their testimony fit into the overall trial.

Tactical Tip ✍

The Importance of Preparation

Most cases are won or lost long before an attorney steps through the doors of a courtroom. The preparation done from the moment a lawsuit starts pays its dividends at trial. From pleading the proper claims, to using discovery devices effectively, to preparing witnesses to take the stand, the lawyer who has thought about trial before it takes place will be in a far better position than one who has not. Thus, keep your eyes on the ultimate trial from the beginning of the case and prepare throughly if you want to best serve your client.

The night before trial was to begin Lane and Tweedy were tired but excited. After all, they had waited a long time to reach this stage of the adversary process.

B.   The Trial

1.   Structure of a Trial and the Role of Procedure

A trial is a fascinating experience. However, you will only get a brief glimpse of it in the *Guide*. Much of your learning about trial will come in classes on evidence and trial advocacy. There you will learn about things such as what evidence a jury will be allowed to hear, on what bases lawyers may object to evidence, where the lawyers stand in a courtroom to ask witnesses questions, and how lawyers should phrase questions for use with a hostile witness.

In Civil Procedure, the study of "trial" emphasizes how the Rules are used to guard against improper or untrustworthy results. The Rules do this by ensuring that (1) the jurors are unbiased;[10] (2) the jury is accurately informed about the law; (3) the jury makes rational decisions; and (4) the trial process and the jury verdict are free of defects that would require a new trial. We will touch on how these concerns arise in the *Olman* trial, although we focus principally on the third and fourth concerns.

In order to appreciate how procedure works at trial, you need to understand the basic structure of the trial. The trial is the epitome of the adversarial process itself. A neutral decisionmaker—the jury in the *Olman* case—is presented with two competing stories. For each thing a plaintiff does, the defendant gets its turn as well. So, for example, the plaintiff is allowed to make an opening statement to the jury after which it is the defendant's turn. After the plaintiff puts a witness on the stand and asks questions, the defendant is allowed to ask that witness its own questions. And back and forth the process continues.

---

[10]The Olmans' case will be tried by a jury. It is also possible to have cases decided by judges in what are called "bench" trials. From time to time we make reference to certain Rules and practices concerning the bench trial.

The basic structure of a civil jury trial is listed below.[11]   Those steps in which procedure plays a significant role, and on which we will focus our discussion, are listed in **bold**.

The Structure of a Civil Trial

- **Jury Selection**
- Opening statements
- Plaintiff's case

  - Direct examination
  - Cross examination by defendant

- **Motions testing sufficiency of plaintiff's case**
- Defendant's case

  - Direct examination
  - Cross examination by plaintiff

- **Motions testing the sufficiency of the cases of all parties**
- Closing arguments
- **Jury instructions**
- Deliberations
- Jury verdict
- **Post verdict motions**
- Entry of final judgment

The trial in *Olman* would follow this basic form.

---

[11]The process is more streamlined in a bench trial. There would obviously be no need to have jury selection or a verdict. In addition, the motions testing the sufficiency of the parties' cases are not part of the bench trial. Moreover, some judges dispense with opening statements or closing arguments. Most judges, however, find these parts of a trial useful and so retain them. At the conclusion of a bench trial the judge will issue a written opinion. That opinion will include the judge's legal conclusions but must also set forth his or her findings of fact. *See* Rule 52(a). As we will see, there is no similar requirement that a jury state its factual findings.

2.   **Selecting a Jury and the Beginning of Trial**

The first step in a jury trial is to select the members of the community who will serve as the finders of fact at the trial.[12] Members of the trial jury are selected from a group called the venire, who are citizens called to the courthouse for "jury duty." The venire must be randomly drawn from a fair cross section of the relevant community.[13] In the Olmans' case, the relevant community consisted of several counties in the eastern part of the Middle District of Florida.

Stu's Views   © 2002 Stu All Rights Reserved www.stus.com

Miss, you can't just "sign up" to be
on the next celebrity murder jury.

Once a proper venire is assembled, the question becomes how to select the actual trial jury.[14] The problem in some sense stems from the reality that neither Lane nor Tweedy

---

[12]Otis was entitled to a jury trial of his retaliation claims as a matter of statutory law. *See* 29 U.S.C. § 626(c)(2) (ADEA retaliation); Fla. stat. ch. 760.11(5) (FCRA retaliation). In the absence of a statutory right, entitlement to jury trials in civil cases in federal courts is governed by the Seventh Amendment to the United States Constitution.

[13]*See* 28 U.S.C. § 1861. The detailed procedures by which the venire is assembled and may be challenged are set forth in the United States Code. *See, e.g.,* 28 U.S.C. §§ 1861–1867.

[14]The jury would consist of between six and twelve citizens. Rule 48. The jury would need to reach a unanimous verdict unless the parties stipulated otherwise. *Id.*

really wanted an unbiased jury. Rather, if truth be told, they preferred a jury biased in their own client's favor. Jury selection is designed in part to counteract these desires by giving the judge power to eliminate persons who are obviously biased ("cause" challenges) and by giving the lawyers power to unilaterally eliminate an additional number of persons they suspect are disinclined to favor their client ("peremptory" challenges). The result of this process—called voir dire—hopefully approximates a collection of citizens who enter the case without a preconceived opinion as to which party should prevail, and who are capable of fairly considering all the evidence. However, much of voir dire is essentially guesswork.

"Kick Juror #4."

Biased jurors are removed for "cause." Judges tend to construe cause challenges narrowly. Any jurors who know the parties, the witnesses, the lawyers, or sometimes the judge will be struck for cause. In addition, any jurors who have personal knowledge of the events at issue in the case will be struck. Beyond these more bright-line characteristics, Judge Goodenough would have broad discretion in determining whether a potential juror should be struck for cause. If a party believed that a particular person should be removed for cause, it needed to request that the court take such action.

Once all cause challenges have been decided, the parties can strike up to three jurors from the panel for almost any reason or, in fact, no reason at all.[15] These challenges are known as "peremptory challenges." Peremptory challenges permit a party to exclude jurors it suspects are not favorably inclined to its position, even though the jurors have not demonstrated "cause" for being struck by the judge. The problem in exercising peremptory challenges is that lawyers usually have precious little information on which to base this decision. The information they do have will generally come from one of three sources. First, the lawyer will have a preconception of juror characteristics or attitudes that predispose the juror to favor one party.[16] Second, the lawyer will have limited information found in a questionnaire each juror must complete, including a juror's residence, age, occupation, and history of criminal convictions. Finally, each lawyer will have the opportunity to obtain some information from jurors during voir dire.[17] The reality, however, is that many peremptory challenges are the product of nothing more than intuition.

---

[15]*See* 28 U.S.C. § 1870 (granting each party in a civil case three peremptory challenges). A party can not base a peremptory challenge on the race or gender of the juror. *See Edmonson v. Leesville Concrete Co.*, 500 U.S. 614 (1991) (race); *JEB v. Alabama*, 511 U.S. 127 (1994) (gender).

[16]In most cases, lawyers' preconceptions are based on stereotypes about how certain types of jurors might react to the parties and the evidence. However, in a growing number of high-stakes cases lawyers employ professional jury consultants to help them develop more accurate (at least they hope) predictors of which types of jurors are desirable or undesirable. There are differing views as to the effectiveness of jury consultants in selecting jurors. One limitation to the potential effectiveness of professional jury consultants is that lawyers may not be permitted in voir dire to obtain the information needed to determine whether a juror "fits" the profile developed by a consultant. *See generally*, Shari Diamond, *Scientific Jury Selection: What Social Scientists Know and Do Not Know*, 73 JUDICATURE 178 (1990).

[17]*See* Rule 47(a). The Rule allows the judge to permit the lawyers to question potential jurors or to do so herself. This practice varies by judge, but many federal judges are inclined to ask the questions themselves in order to make the voir dire process more efficient. In this case, the parties were allowed to submit questions to the court for the judge to consider asking.

Task 8.1

Jury Selection

A.   What characteristics and attitudes would you want in a juror if you represented Otis? Why? What if you represented Full Moon?

B.   What questions would you want Judge Goodenough to ask potential jurors if you represented Otis? Why? What if you represented Full Moon?

After the jury was selected and Judge Goodenough gave them preliminary instructions concerning the nature of the case and the trial process itself, the parties were finally ready to try the case. Judge Goodenough called on Lane to give an opening statement for the plaintiff. An opening statement is important because it is usually the first chance an attorney has to speak to the jury about the substance of the case. The opening statement is not an argument; instead, it is meant to be a roadmap for the jury to follow when listening to the evidence that will be presented at trial.

Lane had two overarching goals for her opening. First, she wanted the jury to know the theme of her case and, therefore, be able to fit the evidence they would hear into that theme. Second, she wanted to introduce Otis as a human being. Lane accomplished the latter goal by spending time in her opening describing Otis' background, family, and interests, as well as his contributions to the "Full Moon family."

As for her theme, Lane did not try to hide the ball. She told the jury that this case was about a corporate decision to get rid an employee for standing up for what he perceived to be unlawful activity. She told the jury they would hear from Otis and learn that he discovered what Full Moon was actually doing in "restructuring" its retail operation: implementing the now unlawful philosophy of "out with the old and in with the new." She explained that the evidence the jury would see and hear would demonstrate that, as soon as Full Moon learned Otis was going to make a claim that age discrimination was at work, it fired him. This retaliation, she explained, was unlawful even if Full Moon was not, in fact, engaged in age discrimination. Finally, Lane promised that when all the evidence was in she would address them again, during which she would review the evidence and describe the specific award she wanted the jury to make to Otis.

It was then Tweedy's turn to speak to the jury. He, too, knew it was critically important to have a theme. And he knew it was necessary to personify Full Moon. Thus, he began by introducing the jury to Full Moon's President, Bertie Lurch, who was sitting at counsel table and would be present for the entire trial. Tweedy knew that Lurch was going to be a crucial witness at trial. If the jury believed him, Full Moon would win. If it did not, Full Moon would lose. Thus, Tweedy wanted the jury to see him as a person and not merely the "face" of a large corporation.

For his theme, Tweedy started out by making it clear to the jury that the case was not about age discrimination. He explained that, as Judge Goodenough would instruct them at the conclusion of the trial, Full Moon had not discriminated against Otis based on his age when it terminated him. Instead, the case turned on whether Full Moon fired Otis because Otis complained about what he perceived to be ageist motivations in corporate decisions. On this point, Tweedy explained that the evidence would show Full Moon fired Otis for two reasons unrelated to "retaliation." First, the evidence would show that Otis was no longer able to work in a constructive manner in the restructured Jacksonville store. Second, at the time of its decision Full Moon believed, erroneously as it later turned out, that Otis had been involved in the theft of merchandise from the store. Thus, Tweedy would ask the jury to return a verdict in favor of Full Moon at the conclusion of the trial.

3.   Otis' Case-in-Chief

It was now time for Otis to put on his case. Lane's goal was to make the case as simple as possible for the jury. In essence, she wanted the jury to see the case as nothing more than an example of Newton's law that every action produces an equal and opposite reaction. In this case, the action was Otis' sending his letter to Full Moon complaining about its ageist motives during the reduction in force. The reaction was the letter from Bertie Lurch firing Otis.[18] Lane wanted the jury members to follow their common sense and conclude that there was a cause and effect relationship between Otis' complaints and his firing.

In order to keep the case simple, Lane called only a few witnesses. Otis was the first witness. Through Otis, Lane was able to convey all the important details of her case.[19] She had Otis describe for the jury his background with Full Moon including all of the positive reviews he had received over the years. She then took Otis through the events

---

[18]This letter is set forth in Chapter 1. *See supra* at p. 11.

[19]Our description of the witnesses' testimony is not meant to be exhaustive. Rather, we have tried to give you a flavor of what the jury heard.

leading up to his termination. In particular, Lane made sure to have Otis explain why he believed that Full Moon's actions at the Jacksonville store had been the result of unlawful ageism. Then, Lane had Otis lay out the time line concerning his communication with Full Moon about ageism and his receipt of Bertie Lurch's letter terminating his employment a few weeks later. For this last point she used a visual aid to underscore the temporal proximity between these critical events.

After Lane examined Otis, Tweedy had a turn to cross-exam him. Unlike what one often sees on television, Tweedy was not hostile toward Otis on the stand. Tweedy knew that a juror was much more likely to identify with a witness than with a lawyer. So, Tweedy treated Otis with respect at all times. In addition, Tweedy did not use cross-examination solely to try to undermine Otis' story, the popular view of cross-examination. He also used the examination as a means to build Full Moon's defenses. Of course, Otis was not going to try to be helpful, but to the extent he had helpful information Tweedy tried to bring that out. The main point Tweedy tried to make was that Otis had no actual knowledge about what went into Full Moon's decision to terminate him. In other words, Tweedy tried to underscore for the jury that Otis' claim amounted to speculation based solely on the timing of the termination letter.

After Otis testified, Lane called two former employees of Full Moon's Jacksonville store. The purpose of this testimony was to preemptively address the claims that Full Moon would make during its case about Otis' alleged inability to work within the new corporate structure. The direct testimony was brief, as was cross-examination. Similar to his goal in cross-examining Otis, Tweedy wanted to show that these witnesses had limited knowledge. This reinforced his contention that Otis' case was based on supposition.

"What do you mean, no questions?"

Lane's final witness was an expert to discuss Otis' damages.[20] As you will recall, in his retaliation claims Otis sought lost wages (both back and future pay), the doubling of back pay under the federal statute, punitive damages under the state statute, interest, costs and attorneys' fees.[21] Of these damage elements, the one on which the jury needed expert testimony was damages for lost wages. The expert provided the jury with calculations concerning Otis' back and future pay. Other calculations were either questions of law to be decided by the trial judge (*e.g.*, interest on the judgment) or questions requiring no expert assistance (*e.g.*, punitive damages.)

---

[20]It would have been possible for Judge Goodenough to bifurcate or divide the trial into phases, one concerning liability and the other damages. *See* Rule 42(b) ("The court, in furtherance of convenience or to avoid prejudice, or when separate trials will be conducive to expedition and economy, may order a separate trial . . . of any separate issue . . ."). Judge Goodenough had determined, and neither party had contested, that the better course was to proceed in a single trial.

[21]*See* Complaint, Counts 2 and 4, *supra* at pp. 41–42.

After the damages expert finished her testimony on both direct and cross, Lane rested Otis' case. By resting, Lane essentially communicated to the judge that she believed that she had done everything necessary for Otis to prevail in the trial.

The declaration that the plaintiff has rested his case often prompts action by the defendant—the filing of a motion for judgment as a matter of law under Rule 50(a).[22] Rule 50(a) provides a means by which a party can test whether its adversary has satisfied the burden of coming forward with sufficient evidence to prevail. In other words, the Rule asks whether the party *may* win if a rational jury considers the evidence presented in the case. It does not test whether the party *will* win. Thus, the motion for judgment as a matter of law operates in many respects like a summary judgment motion except for the fact that it is made during trial rather than before.

The next question addresses the Rule 50(a) motion made by Full Moon.

Question 8.1

Based on the summary of the evidence introduced thus far at trial and the language of Rule 50(a), answer the following questions:

A.   What provision in Rule 50(a) allows Full Moon to make a motion for judgment as a matter of law at the conclusion of Otis' case? Why would it be improper for Otis to make such a motion at this point in the trial?

B.   What would be Full Moon's argument that "there is no legally sufficient evidentiary basis for a reasonable jury to find for" Otis on his claims?

C.   What counter-argument would you make on behalf of Otis?

---

[22]The motion for judgment as a matter of law used to be called a "motion for a directed verdict," and still is in some state rules of civil procedure. Many lawyers and judges still use the older terminology even in federal court.

Judge Goodenough had excused the jury so she could address the motion she expected Full Moon to make. Full Moon submitted a brief written motion for judgment as a matter of law, but the majority of its reasoning was addressed through oral argument. Lane argued against the motion. As was common for judges, Judge Goodenough did not rule on the motion but rather "took it under advisement." In other words, she waited to rule on the motion until later. She then directed Tweedy to begin Full Moon's case.

Notes Concerning:
THE JURY

The jury has a long pedigree in Anglo-American law. For example, the Seventh Amendment to the United States Constitution guarantees citizens the right to a trial by jury in federal courts if they had such a right when the amendment was adopted and there is more than $20 at stake.

In recognition of the jury's important historical role, many facets of the system are designed to give the jury freedom to make its factual conclusions. At the same time, however, the legal system is also concerned with fundamental fairness. Thus, we are reluctant to allow decisions to be made by juries that are not rational.

How should the legal system balance the right to a jury trial with the right not to be the victim of an irrational verdict? We have struck a balance by monitoring closely the inputs to the jury (for example, by using rules of evidence and instructions as to the law) and by comparing that input with the output of a verdict. If the output could have rationally been reached based on the input, then we generally uphold the jury determination. Notice, however, that we will not look behind the reason for jury's decision-making absent extraordinary circumstances such as an external influence like bribery or intimidation. In other words, we treat the jury as a "black box" by not looking behind the jury room door.

There is currently a debate about the wisdom of adopting additional practices to increase the chance that jurors will act based upon the evidence. For example, some judges allow jurors to take notes during the trial. Other judges do not allow notetaking, based largely on the theory that notetaking will distract jurors from what is taking place in the trial. A similar debate exists concerning the wisdom of allowing jurors to pose questions to witnesses (via the judge). As these debates illustrate, courts are continuing to struggle with the long-running question of how to balance a commitment to rational judgment with the desire to have the jury bring the "sense of the community" into the courtroom.

4.   Full Moon's Case-in-Chief

Tweedy had given a great deal of thought to Full Moon's case. In many ways he had reached the same basic conclusion about trying the case as had Lane. Tweedy had concluded that a simple and direct case was in Full Moon's interest. It is not always the case that parties will reach the same conclusion about basic case presentation. Indeed, in many situations one party will conclude it is in its best interest to make matters seem complicated or even confusing. Here, however, Tweedy wanted to drive home forcefully the direct evidence he had of Full Moon's motivations for firing Otis and contrast that direct evidence with Otis' circumstantial case. Tweedy made the tactical judgment to present only two witnesses at trial.

The first witness Tweedy called was the most important: Bertie Lurch. Lurch was the lynchpin of Full Moon's case. Through him, Tweedy brought out Full Moon's version of the chronology of events leading to Otis' termination. He had Lurch describe Full Moon's corporate restructuring and the ill will that this business move seemed to cause between Otis and Shockley. He explained that he was sorry that things had not worked out with Otis. Otis had been a good employee and Lurch had hoped that Otis would fit into the new corporate structure, but that had not come to pass.

Tweedy then asked Lurch to explain to the jury why Lurch sent the termination letter to Otis. Lurch gave two reasons: (1) growing tension in the Jacksonville store; and (2) information Lurch had acquired about missing inventory and what appeared to be Otis' involvement in those losses. Tweedy asked specifically whether Otis' complaint of ageism had played any role in the decision to terminate his employment. Lurch said it had not. As to the timing of the termination letter, Lurch's said this was coincidental. The fact was, Lurch explained, at the same time Otis was complaining about age discrimination he was making it more and more difficult for store personnel to work together.

It was now Lane's turn to cross-examine. Lane did not spend long with Lurch on the stand. She had two main goals. First, she went over in detail Otis' employment history with Full Moon. Her point was to discredit Lurch's testimony about why he terminated Otis. To believe Lurch's explanation, the jury would need to believe that Otis acted in a manner never displayed before. Lane's second point was to use Lurch as a means to remind the jury about the temporal proximity of the termination letter and Otis' complaints. It really did not matter to Lane that Lurch reiterated his position that there was no causal relationship between the two events.

Full Moon's next witness was Sid Shockley. Tweedy had thought long and hard about putting Shockley on the stand. To be frank, Tweedy did not really care for him. In the end, however, Tweedy concluded that it might be a good thing if the jury found Shockley a bit hard to stomach. This reaction could actually be useful in corroborating Lurch's testimony that Otis was not getting along with Shockley in his role as new store manager.

Tweedy largely limited Shockley's testimony to his tension with Otis after he was promoted to manager. On cross-examination, Lane focused on the help Otis had been to Shockley when he first began working at the store and, once again, took the opportunity to remind the jury of the relevant sequence of events.

After Shockley testified, Tweedy rested his case. He made a strategic decision to rely on his cross-examination of Lane's damages expert rather than call his own expert. Although Tweedy had an expert prepared to testify, he concluded that Lane's expert had not been particularly strong. In addition, he did not want to send a message to the jury that the case was about *how much* to award Otis. Rather, Tweedy wanted the jury to focus on whether to give Otis anything. Tweedy explained his approach to Full Moon and the company agreed with his decision.

After Full Moon rested its case, Judge Goodenough again excused the jury. She knew that both parties would likely have motions for her to consider. Once again, the motions would be made pursuant to Rule 50(a) and would assert that no rational jury could rule in favor of the opposing party.

Question 8.2

A.   Why are both Otis *and* Full Moon now allowed to make motions under Rule 50(a)?

B.   How would it be possible for Judge Goodenough to deny *both* motions?

C.   Regardless of the merits of Rule 50(a) motions at the end of trial, why might a court be tempted to deny the motions?

After listening to arguments, Judge Goodenough denied both parties' motions. She concluded that Otis had made out a prima facie case (*i.e.*, he had met his burden of production) by submitting evidence that he opposed conduct of Full Moon with a reasonable belief that its conduct was unlawful. Moreover, she ruled that the circumstantial evidence of the timing of Full Moon's action was sufficient for the jury to conclude that Full Moon's firing was in retaliation for Otis' opposition.[23] At the same time, she ruled that Full Moon had presented sufficient evidence to support a jury verdict in its favor. She told the attorneys to be ready for closing arguments in the morning.

5.   The Jury Deliberates and Reaches Its Verdict

Both Lane and Tweedy spent the evening getting ready for their closing arguments. Each planned to return to the themes they had laid out in their openings and developed throughout trial. Both of these experienced attorneys knew that, like most civil cases that go to a jury, this case could go either way.

After Lane and Tweedy completed their closing arguments, Judge Goodenough instructed the jury.[24] These instructions were quite important for controlling the jury. Among other things the instructions (1) summarized the parties' claims and defenses; (2) summarized the applicable burdens of proof; (3) explained how various forms of evidence (*e.g.*, direct and circumstantial) were to be used; (4) explained the jurors' right to assess the credibility of witnesses and resolve contradictory testimony; and (5) explained how jurors were to assess damages in the event they found the defendant liable. As mentioned earlier, Lane and Tweedy had worked to develop joint instructions and Judge Goodenough resolved any remaining disagreements.[25]

---

[23]*See, e.g., Farley v. Nationwide Mutual Ins. Co.*, 197 F.3d 1322, 1337 (11th Cir. 1999) (plaintiff has produced sufficient evidence of retaliation if "the decision-maker became aware of the protected conduct, and . . . there was close temporal proximity between this awareness and the adverse employment action.").

[24]*See* Rule 51 (concerning court's instructions to the jury).

[25]In many cases the court's task is assisted by the development of "standard" or "pattern" jury instructions. These instructions are often developed by committees appointed by courts (*e.g.*, the federal circuit courts or state supreme courts), and officially approved for use. Pattern jury instructions are tailored to address specific issues (*e.g.*, the elements of a cause of action, the meaning of a particular burden of proof), although they must be modified to reflect the circumstances of a particular case. For example, the United States Court of Appeals for the Eleventh Circuit has adopted pattern jury instructions to be used for claims of employer retaliation, *see* www.ca11.us.courts.gov/documents/index.pdf (pattern jury instructions in pdf format).

The judge also told the jury about the questions they were to answer on the verdict form. She had the option of having the jury answer several specific questions about the factual issues in the case.[26] For example, Judge Goodenough could have submitted "special interrogatories" to the jury keyed to the specific elements of Otis' retaliation claims. The use of such special interrogatories is most common in complex or lengthy trials.

Judge Goodenough believed that special interrogatories were not needed in the Olmans' case given the relative simplicity of the issues in dispute. Instead, she used a general verdict form asking the jury to simply find for Olman or Full Moon on the two retaliation claims. She did, however, included a few interrogatories she thought necessary to properly decide damages.[27] Under applicable law, the jury needed to decide whether Full Moon had acted in willful or reckless disregard of Otis' legal rights. If it did, Otis would be awarded "double back pay" under the ADEA, and possibly additional punitive damages under state law.

The general verdict form given to the jury to complete as part of its deliberations is set forth below.

---

[26]*See* Rule 49 ("The court may require a jury to return only a special verdict in the form of a written finding upon each issue of fact.").

[27]*See* Rule 49(a) (authorizing use of a general verdict form with specific interrogatories).

IN THE UNITED STATES DISTRICT COURT
FOR THE MIDDLE DISTRICT OF FLORIDA
JACKSONVILLE DIVISION

OTIS AND FIONA OLMAN,

        Plaintiffs,

vs.   Case No. 03-2222-CIV-M-46-B

FULL MOON SPORTS, INC.,

        Defendant.

Verdict Form

We the Jury unanimously find as follows:

I.   **Retaliation under the Age Discrimination in Employment Act**

    1.   With respect to this claim, we the Jury unanimously find in favor of:

        The Plaintiff Otis Olman   _____

                        OR

        The Defendant Full Moon Sports, Inc.   _____

If your verdict is in favor of the Defendant, proceed to Part II below. If your verdict is in favor of the Plaintiff, proceed to Question 2 in Part I.

    2.   If your verdict is in favor of Plaintiff, to what total amount of damages for *back pay and benefits* is Plaintiff entitled?

                        _____

                        (Insert dollar amount)

3. If your verdict is in favor of Plaintiff, to what total amount of damages for *front pay and benefits* is Plaintiff entitled?

_____
(Insert dollar amount)

4. If your verdict is in favor of Plaintiff, do you find that Defendant knowingly violated Plaintiff's rights under the Age Discrimination in Employment Act or showed reckless disregard for those rights?

_____
(Yes)

_____
(No)

II. Retaliation under the Florida Civil Rights Act

1. With respect to this claim, we the Jury unanimously find in favor of:

The Plaintiff Otis Olman _____

OR

The Defendant Full Moon Sports, Inc. _____

If your verdict is in favor of the Defendant, STOP. If your verdict is in favor of the Plaintiff, proceed to Question 2 in Part II.

2. If your verdict is in favor of Plaintiff, to what total amount of *compensatory* damages is Plaintiff entitled?

_____
(Insert dollar amount)

[252]

3.   If your verdict is in favor of Plaintiff, to what total amount of *punitive damages* is Plaintiff entitled?

_____
(Insert dollar amount)

SO SAY WE ALL

_____
Jury Foreperson

Dated:

After being instructed the jury began its deliberations. Thus began a period of anxious waiting for the parties and their lawyers. While the jury is out there is not much for the parties to do. They usually stay at the courthouse so they will be present when the jury reaches a verdict. The Olmans, Lane, Lurch, and Tweedy were all waiting when the court clerk informed them that the jury had reached a verdict. The jury had deliberated only two hours.

Once the parties, lawyers, and Judge Goodenough were in place, the jury returned to the courtroom. Judge Goodenough confirmed with the jury foreperson that the jury had reached a verdict. The judge then asked the foreperson to read the jury's answers to the questions on the verdict form. As the parties watched and listened intently the jury foreperson stated that the jury ruled in favor of Otis on both retaliation counts. The jury also awarded significant damages to Otis. Otis received $300,000 in damages for front and back pay ($100,000 in back pay and $200,000 in front pay) for his retaliation claim under the ADEA. The jury also found that Full Moon had acted "willfully" in violating the ADEA, which meant the Court would double the back pay award. Consequently, Otis' total recovery under the ADEA claim was $400,000. The jury awarded Otis no additional damages under his state law claim, apparently based on its conclusion that damages under the ADEA fully compensated Otis and punished Full Moon. In this respect, the jury may have been following the court's instruction not to award Otis duplicative damages. In addition, the jury did not award punitive damages to Otis on his state-law claim.

C.   Post-Trial Matters Before Judge Goodenough

The jury had returned a verdict. The clerk of court would now convert this verdict to a "final judgment" and enter it on the court's docket.[28] Below is the judgment he drafted and filed the next day.[29]

---

[28]*See* Rule 58(a)(2)(A) (clerk must "promptly prepare, sign, and enter the judgment" upon return of a general verdict).

[29]A "Judgment on Jury Verdict" is set forth as Form 31 of the Federal Rules.

IN THE UNITED STATES DISTRICT COURT
FOR THE MIDDLE DISTRICT OF FLORIDA
JACKSONVILLE DIVISION

OTIS AND FIONA OLMAN,

       Plaintiffs,

vs.   Case No. 03-2222-CIV-M-46-B

FULL MOON SPORTS, INC.,

       Defendant.

JUDGMENT ON JURY VERDICT

This action came on for trial before the Court and a jury, the Honorable Sarah Goodenough, United States District Judge, presiding, and the issues having been duly tried and the jury having duly rendered its verdict,

IT IS ORDERED AND ADJUDGED:

That Plaintiff Otis Olman recover under his claims of retaliation under the Age Discrimination in Employment Act from the Defendant Full Moon Sports, Inc. the sum of $300,000 as damages for front and back pay, with interest thereon at the rate of ___% as provided by law;

That said amount of damages reflecting back pay of $100,000 under the Age Discrimination in Employment Act be doubled; and

That Plaintiff Otis Olman recover from Defendant Full Moon Sports, Inc. his costs of this action, including reasonable attorneys' fees.*

Dated at Jacksonville, Florida, this 23rd day of September, 2005.

                                 _____

                                 Robert Smith
                                 Clerk of Court

---

* The specific amount of costs and attorneys' fees would be set based on a motion Lane would need to file with the court. *See* Rule 54(d).

[255]

Entry of judgment is an important, albeit routine step in litigation. For one thing, ten days after entry Otis could begin taking steps to collect the judgment.[30] Almost always, however, judgment enforcement is stayed by the court until it resolves post-trial motions.[31] A party wanting to assert a post-trial motion must usually file it within 10 days of the entry of judgment.[32] Two post-trial motions typically filed in a civil suit are (1) the renewed motion for judgment as a matter of law under Rule 50(b), and (2) the motion for a new trial. Both motions can be used to "control" the jury even after a verdict has been rendered.

Tweedy first drafted a renewed motion for judgment as a matter of law.[33] Consider the following question:

Question 8.3

A.   What would Tweedy have to argue to prevail in his renewed motion for judgment as a matter of law? Would the standard governing this motion differ from that applied by Judge Gooodenough to resolve the motion for judgment as a matter of law Tweedy made at the close of all evidence?

B.   If Tweedy had not made a Rule 50(a) motion at the close of all evidence, would he now be permitted make a motion under Rule 50(b)?

---

[30]*See* Rule 62(a) ("no execution shall issue upon a judgment nor shall proceedings be taken for its enforcement until the expiration of 10 days after its entry").

[31]*See* Rule 62(b) (authorizing court to stay enforcement of a judgment while certain post-trial motions are pending).

[32]*See* Rule 50(b) and 59(b). Unless the court otherwise orders, a motion for attorney's fees must be filed within 14 days of the entry of final judgment. *See* Rule 54(d)(2)(B).

[33]What the Rules now refer to as the renewed motion for judgment as a matter of law was formerly known as the judgment notwithstanding the verdict or "JNOV." Once again, many lawyers and judges continue to use the older terminology.

MOTION FOR JUDGMENT
NOTWITHSTANDING VERDICT

Tweedy also filed a motion for new trial under Rule 59. The motion for new trial essentially addresses two situations, although one needs to study case law to figure this out.[34] First, the motion can be used to correct flaws in the procedures leading to the verdict. For example, if Judge Goodenough concluded that she had erroneously admitted or excluded a piece of evidence or had given an improper instruction to the jury, she could use the Rule 59 motion to fix the problem. As we discuss in Chapter 9, Tweedy's Rule 59 motion included a challenge to improper comments made by Lane during her closing argument, which the court had permitted over Tweedy's objection.

The second use of the new trial motion is to challenge a flawed verdict. Tweedy could argue that the jury's verdict was against the great weight of the evidence. The argument was different than the one Tweedy made in the renewed motion for judgment as a matter of law. In the latter motion Tweedy claimed that no rational jury could have reached the verdict the jury actually reached. If Judge Goodenough agreed, Full Moon would go from losing to winning. In contrast, in his motion for new trial Tweedy argued that, while a rationally functioning jury *could* reach the verdict delivered, it is so unlikely that the court should no longer have faith in the verdict. The result of granting this motion is to grant a new trial with a new jury. As Tweedy thought of the result, it was like calling a "do over."

---

[34]Rule 59 is not itself helpful in defining the grounds on which a new trial may properly be granted. *See* Rule 59(a) ("A new trial may be granted . . . for any of the reasons for which rehearings have heretofore been granted in suits in equity in the courts of the United States.").

Question 8.4

A.   Can Tweedy make motions under both Rule 50(b) and Rule 59 consistent with his obligations under Rule 11?

B.   If Judge Goodenough independently realizes she made an error during the trial can she unilaterally order a new trial? What is your authority?

C.   If Judge Goodenough decides to grant the renewed motion for judgment as a matter of law, can she ignore the motion for new trial as moot? Why not? What should Judge Goodenough do in this situation?

Judge Goodenough considered both of Full Moon's post-verdict motions, as well as Lane's opposition. She denied both motions.

The only remaining matter for consideration by the court was Lane's motion for attorney's fees. Under Rule 54, Lane was obligated to file her motion within 14 days of the entry of final judgment. She had, and the judge would later hear argument on the motion. But the pending fee motion did not affect the "finality" of the judgment.[35] Thus, argument on the merits in *Olman v. Full Moon* had come to an end in the trial court. As we discuss in the concluding chapter, however, still more litigation activity was to come.

---

[35]A judgment is deemed final even though attorneys' fees have not yet been determined. *See Budinich v. Becton Dickinson Co.*, 486 U.S. 196 (1988) (a judgment is final and appealable even though attorney's fees remain in dispute).

CHAPTER NINE:
FINAL RESOLUTION

Rule References: 61, 62

A.   Considering Appeal

1.   The Olmans' Perspective

Although the Olmans were pleased with Otis' victory at trial, they were still dissatisfied with Judge Goodenough's pretrial termination of most of their claims. The heart of their case against Full Moon—that they were the victims of age discrimination—had never been considered by the jury. As Otis remarked to Lane, "I feel like we won on a technicality." The Olmans asked Lane whether they could appeal the judge's decisions disposing of their discrimination claims.

Lane explained that the Olmans now had the right to appeal.[1] However, the Olmans would need to make a decision soon because appellate rules gave them only *30 days* to file their "notice of appeal" once final judgment was entered and post-trial motions resolved.[2]

Lane then discussed the pros and cons of appealing. Fiona, of course, might win the right to try her case of age discrimination and recover the damages resulting from her termination. But Lane was not enthusiastic about Fiona's chances of winning on appeal. Fiona's argument really did hinge on a legal "technicality"—whether Full Moon's failure to specifically advise her to consult a "lawyer" invalidated the waiver she signed. The

---

[1]As discussed earlier, the judge's pretrial decisions on Full Moon's motion to dismiss and motion for summary judgment were not "final judgments" and so were not immediately appealable. The court's entry of final judgment on the jury's verdict brought finality to these pretrial decisions. As also mentioned earlier, the finality of the judgment was not deferred by Otis' pending motion for attorney's fees.

[2]*See* Fed. R. App. P. 4(a)(1)(A). Filing the notice of appeal preserves the right to appeal. The notice of appeal itself contains no legal argument. The actual appellate briefs are usually filed months later, after the parties have reviewed the record and completed their legal research.

Eleventh Circuit is often viewed as a moderate to conservative court and, unless Fiona's case was randomly assigned to a more favorable panel, she faced an uphill battle.[3]

Lane believed Otis had stronger arguments to make on appeal. She thought Judge Goodenough had erred in granting summary judgment on Otis' age discrimination claims. Lane believed she could persuade the appellate court that Full Moon's motives in downsizing raised a question of fact for a jury to decide, particularly since the jury had apparently found Bertie Lurch to be untrustworthy. Yet, Lane was troubled by the weakness of Otis' remaining claim of damages. The jury had already compensated him for all lost income and benefits. He might still recover under state law for the psychic damages Full Moon caused him, and possibly receive extra punitive damages.[4] But these damages were far more speculative than his lost earnings.[5]

If Otis appealed, Lane explained, Full Moon would surely file its own cross-appeal and seek to have Otis' judgment reversed. If Full Moon prevailed in its cross-appeal, Otis would no longer be entitled to the $400,000 awarded by the jury, and Lane would no longer be entitled to recover her attorney's fee from Full Moon.

The prospect of forfeiting Otis' hard-won verdict was sobering to the Olmans. Given the weakness of Fiona's legal claim and the uncertainty of Otis' remaining damages claim, they decided not to *initiate* an appeal. On the other hand, if Full Moon filed its own appeal, they would cross-appeal. At a minimum, a cross-appeal would improve the Olmans' leverage in the post-judgment settlement negotiations that were sure to come.

---

[3]Circuit courts almost always hear cases as three-judge panels. Thus, a given panel's membership can often be decisive on appeal.

[4]The breakdown of damages recoverable under state law is found *supra* at pp. 26–28.

[5]Lane also considered appealing the court's pretrial dismissal of Otis' fraud claim against Full Moon and Bruce Belcher. However, Lane thought Otis would have great difficulty proving damages resulting from the alleged fraud. At the outset of the suit, Otis believed he had lost out on a lucrative business deal in Key Largo as a result of the defendants' fraud. But Otis subsequently learned that his potential business partner—Izzy Able—had a poor business record that included a recent bankruptcy. Consequently, it would be difficult to prove Otis was damaged by his failure to join with Able in a business venture.

2.   Full Moon's Perspective

Bertie Lurch took personally Full Moon's loss at trial. And although Tweedy didn't say it, he believed Lurch *should* take it personally. Had Lurch only paused and sought legal advice when he received Otis' letter complaining of age discrimination, Full Moon would not be facing a $400,000 judgment.[6]

Full Moon expressed interest in appealing Otis' judgment. Tweedy's firm was willing to handle the appeal, but Tweedy was not overly encouraging about the company's chances of success. Tweedy explained to Lurch that most appeals fail. Appellate judges are fond of saying that, if you want to win on appeal, make sure you win at trial.

Tweedy thought the prospects of having the jury's verdict reversed as irrational or against the great weight of the evidence were slim. Full Moon's best chance on appeal was to identify an error committed by Judge Goodenough. Tweedy found no error in the judge's instructions, which had accurately portrayed the law of retaliation. But Tweedy believed the judge had committed a potentially harmful error during trial, when she permitted Lane to make a very colorful and inflammatory closing argument to the jury. Lane had liberally referred to Full Moon and Lurch as "corporate predators" who had "preyed on their most senior employees to earn a buck," even though age discrimination was not an issue at trial. Lane had even told the jury that she was "personally revolted" by Lurch's "vengeful and mean-spirited" treatment of Otis, and that she had "never seen such shabby treatment of an older employee during my years of practice." Tweedy had repeatedly objected to these comments during Lane's closing argument.[7] Judge Goodenough had instructed the jury to "disregard" Lane's improper comments, but denied Tweedy's motion for a mistrial. The court also denied Tweedy's later request for a new trial.

---

[6]In reality, this figure would be much higher. Full Moon would also need to consider both the attorneys' fees to which Otis was now entitled as well as the addition of interest on the amount of the judgment. And these considerations do not take into account the money Full Moon would pay to Tweedy's firm.

[7]In order to raise an issue on appeal concerning trial misconduct, lawyers must usually have made a "contemporaneous objection" when the conduct occurs.

"The jury will disregard the witness's last statement."

Tweedy believed that, even though the jury's verdict was otherwise supported by record evidence, an appellate court might reverse the verdict if it concluded Lane's conduct unduly biased the jury against Full Moon.[8] This, Tweedy advised Full Moon, was its best argument in seeking to have the judgment reversed on appeal.

Tweedy explained to his client that an appeal might have substantial costs. Unless Full Moon prevailed on appeal it would have to pay the legal fees of both Tweedy and Lane.[9] Tweedy estimated his firm's fee for the appeal would be in the range of $100,000 to $150,000, and guessed Lane's fee would be at least half that amount. Throughout the appeal interest would be accumulating on the judgment. There was also the risk that an appeal would increase the adverse publicity Full Moon was receiving from its defeat.

Yet Tweedy was not surprised when Full Moon directed him to file a notice of appeal.[10] Nor was he surprised when the Olmans responded with their own cross-appeal. The parties' appellate counsel would now begin the painstaking process of assembling and reviewing the record evidence and drafting their initial appellate briefs.

---

[8]*See generally* Charles B. Gibbons, FEDERAL RULES OF EVIDENCE WITH TRIAL OBJECTIONS C3 (2003). Lane's comments might also have violated Model Rule of Professional Conduct 3.4(e), which prohibits, *inter alia*, argument not supported by evidence and argument expressing a lawyer's "personal opinion" about the justness of a client's position.

Tweedy would have to prove that Lane's comments might have affected the verdict. According to Rule 61, trial courts should not upset a verdict because of error at trial if it is "harmless error." The same rule applies in appellate proceedings.

[9]As discussed earlier, a prevailing plaintiff is entitled to recover his attorney's fees under the ADEA. This entitlement includes fees incurred on appeal.

[10]A notice of appeal is a simple, one page document indicating that a party is exercising its right to appeal. The quite lengthy brief and other supporting materials laying out the specific grounds for the appeal come later in the process. Thus, it takes little in the way of resources to file a notice of appeal, and a party can later dismiss its notice if it settles the case or changes its mind about the wisdom of appeal.

IN THE UNITED STATES DISTRICT COURT
FOR THE MIDDLE DISTRICT OF FLORIDA
JACKSONVILLE DIVISION

OTIS AND FIONA OLMAN,

    Plaintiffs,

vs.   Case No. 03-2222-CIV-M-46-B

FULL MOON SPORTS, INC.,
& BRUCE BELCHER

    Defendants.

NOTICE OF APPEAL

Notice is hereby given that Full Moon Sports Inc., defendant in the above-named case, hereby appeals to the United States Court of Appeals for the Eleventh Circuit from the Final Judgment entered on September 23, 2005. The Notice of Appeal is timely filed pursuant to Rule 4(b) of the Federal Rules of Appellate Procedure.

                        Respectfully submitted,

                        _____

                        Harrison Ames, Esq.
                        Bart A. Tweedy, Esq.
                        Counsel for Full Moon Sports, Inc.
                        [Address, phone number, etc. omitted.]

[Certificate of Service Omitted]

[264]

B.   Settlement Negotiations Continue

Tweedy and Lane knew there would be continuing settlement discussion now that proceedings in the trial court were completed.[11] You might ask, why? After all, Otis had a judgment requiring Full Moon to pay $400,000, plus attorneys' fees and interest.[12] Why would *he* want to discuss settlement?

There were several reasons. First, as long as appeal remained an option, the ultimate outcome remained uncertain. Otis was in a much better settlement position than before trial, and Full Moon was in a much worse one. But this fact affected *settlement values* (*i.e.*, how much the parties might pay to resolve the dispute) more than the parties' willingness to consider settlement.

Otis was also influenced by the desire to avoid further attorney's fees and related expenses.[13] As discussed in the previous section, an appeal costs both sides money. And a successful appeal by Full Moon could lead to further proceedings in the trial court. Those proceedings would cost still more money.

---

[11]Indeed, settlement negotiations had occurred in some form since the Olmans filed their complaint with the EEOC.

[12]When a party has won a monetary judgment, he is entitled to enforce that judgment once the trial court disposes of various post-trial motions. He is now a "judgment creditor" of the losing party, who is called a "judgment debtor." However, the judgment debtor may defer collection of the judgment while the case is on appeal by posting a "supersedeas bond" equal to the value of the judgment plus interest. *See* Rule 62(d). The supersedeas bond accomplishes two things. First, it assures the judgment creditor a source of payment for the judgment if it is upheld on appeal. Second, it assures the judgment debtor that, if it succeeds in having the judgment reversed, it can recover the bond monies it had deposited with the court.

If the judgment debtor is *not* able to afford the cost of a supersedeas bond, it may still prosecute its appeal. However, the judgment creditor can now seek to enforce the judgment while the appeal is pending—assuming he can discover sufficient assets to satisfy the judgment. If he cannot, he may be motivated to settle the case for less than the amount of the judgment. Otherwise, the judgment creditor runs the risk that, at the end of the appeal, he will be left holding a piece of paper called a judgment that has little or no cash value.

[13]For example, the appellant would likely have to pay the court reporter for a copy of the trial transcript. Transcripts can be quite costly especially for longer trials.

Third, Otis had non-monetary reasons for ending the dispute. By this point he and Fiona had been in litigation for years. The personal costs had been considerable. There was appreciable non-monetary value in accepting less money than they might recover after an appeal and putting the dispute behind them.

Finally, the appellate court would likely require the parties to participate in a formal settlement process anyway. Applicable court rules contemplated mediation of disputes on appeal.[14] The Eleventh Circuit, like many other courts, usually refers civil disputes such as the Olmans to mediation. Consequently, settlement negotiations are often inevitable.

These same factors also influenced Full Moon's willingness to discuss settlement. Therefore, once the parties' notices of appeal were filed, Tweedy spoke with Bertie Lurch and then called Lane. Tweedy asked if Lane would be available to sit down and discuss "where the case was going from here." He suggested meeting for lunch at a reasonably nice restaurant in Jacksonville. Tweedy hoped that his willingness to travel to Jacksonville from Atlanta showed he was serious about settlement. He was not concerned with being seen as "too eager." The trial was over. Lane held many important cards, and everyone knew it. Tweedy would do everything he could, within reason, to resolve the case without an appeal. If he was unsuccessful Full Moon had agreed to fund an appeal. As far as Tweedy was concerned, he had nothing to lose by sitting down with Lane.

In light of the risks for her own clients, Lane agreed to meet Tweedy for lunch. At their luncheon meeting, following some small talk, Tweedy broached the subject of avoiding an appeal. He did so by first casually mentioning how nice it was to have a client like Full Moon that paid its bills and was willing to take litigation to the end of the line. He then discussed the strengths and weaknesses of his case on appeal. Lane, of course, responded to these comments by acknowledging some of the weaknesses in Otis' appeal but reinforcing the reality that he had won at trial.

Discussion continued over lunch. Tweedy finally raised the prospect of settling the case for $100,000, the jury award for back pay. Lane told Tweedy that anything in that range was a non-starter. The bargaining went back and forth. By dessert, both Tweedy and Lane knew the case was going to settle; it was just a question of the details. Tweedy finally proposed the following to Lane. Within 15 days, Full Moon would pay Otis $300,000

---

[14]*See* Fed. R. App. P. 33 ("The court may direct the attorneys—and, when appropriate, the parties—to participate in one or more conferences to address any matter that may aid in disposing of the proceedings, including simplifying the issues and discussing settlement."); Eleventh Cir. R. 33-1 (implementing mediation proceedings as part of Rule 33's mandate).

representing the jury's award of back and future pay. Full Moon would also agree to pay Lane's reasonable attorney's fee, an amount only slightly less than the fee request Lane had filed with Judge Goodenough. Otis would drop his appeal, forego recovery of the penalty award of double back pay, and forego recovery of interest. Lane said she would take the proposal to Otis and Fiona and recommend they accept it.

Within 24 hours the case was settled on the terms laid out at Tweedy and Lane's lunch.[15] The terms of the settlement were embodied in a settlement agreement signed by the parties. After the agreement was signed, the parties also signed and filed with the trial and appellate courts a "notice of dismissal" formally ending the litigation. Among other things, the settlement agreement provided (1) that Full Moon was making no "admissions" by entering into the agreement; (2) that the Olmans fully released Full Moon for any liability relating to the events giving rise to the suit; (3) that all parties agreed to keep the terms of the settlement confidential; and (4) that the Olmans had been specifically advised by counsel prior to signing the agreement. Although Otis Olman initially chafed at the idea Full Moon admitted no liability and prohibited Otis from discussing the settlement, he ultimately yielded to Lane's advice that such settlement terms were customary.

---

[15]These terms would be memorialized in a written settlement agreement. This settlement agreement is a contract enforceable as any other contract.

IN THE UNITED STATES DISTRICT COURT
FOR THE MIDDLE DISTRICT OF FLORIDA
JACKSONVILLE DIVISION

OTIS AND FIONA OLMAN,

    Plaintiffs,

vs.   Case No. 03-2222-CIV-M-46-B

FULL MOON SPORTS, INC.,

    Defendant.

JOINT STIPULATION TO DISMISS WITH PREJUDICE

    Otis Olman, Fiona Olman, and Full Moon Sports, Inc., through their undersigned counsel, hereby jointly stipulate to the entry of an Order dismissing this action with prejudice.

                             _____

                             Eleanor Lane, Esq.
                             Lane & Quincy, P.A.
                             Counsel for Plaintiffs
                             [Address, phone number, etc. omitted]

                             _____

                             Harrison Ames, Esq.
                             Bart A. Tweedy, Esq.
                             Counsel for Full Moon Sports, Inc.
                             [Address, phone number, etc. omitted]

* * * * * * * * * *

What you have read about *Olman v. Full Moon* is a fairly typical story of a federal lawsuit. It reflects the importance of understanding the Rules, consulting with your client, thinking strategically, and acting ethically. It also reflects a fundamental reality of litigation that you, as aspiring lawyers, should recognize now. Almost by definition the results of civil litigation are second best substitutes. For example, even though he won, Otis Olman would have far preferred to return to a time when he and Fiona worked at the Jacksonville store without Shockley and extreme sports. But the litigation process could not make that happen.[16] The best it could do was give Otis dollars to compensate for what he had lost. A significant part of your job as a lawyer is to make clients see this reality of modern American litigation.

We hope that the *Guide* has been useful to you in understanding how litigation really works in the federal court system and how the Rules of Civil Procedure are important tools you can use to advance your clients' interests. Good luck, have fun and do well!

Postscript

There is, of course, life after litigation. We thought you might be interested in what happened to some of the people involved in *Olman v. Full Moon*.

Otis and Fiona Olman

After the case ended, Otis and Fiona realized that they had been filling up their lives fighting Full Moon in litigation. Now that the litigation had ended, and they had the money from the judgment, they needed to figure out what to do with their lives. One day over breakfast Fiona suggested that they consider going into business for themselves. After careful consideration, the Olmans moved to Marsh Harbor in the Bahamas and opened a sea kayaking business with the proceeds of the litigation with Full Moon. Otis and Fiona couldn't be happier working in their own business and living in paradise.

Bertie Lurch

Lurch's corporate restructuring at Full Moon caught the attention of people at the parent company, Mizar. Lurch was eventually promoted to Mizar and rose in the ranks. Unfortunately he was caught up in another wave of accounting scandals. He is currently

---

[16]A similar dissatisfaction often arises in defendants, who believe that even when they win in litigation they never should have been required to defend against the plaintiff's claims in the first place.

awaiting trial in federal court on criminal securities fraud. He has also been sued by disgruntled investors who demand $25 million in damages.

Sid Shockley

Shockley didn't last long in management. He quit Full Moon because management "wasn't his thing." When last seen, Shockley was heading to Hawaii to take up professional surfing.

Bruce Belcher

Belcher worked for several years in a Connecticut retail sporting goods company. He was laid off during a corporate downsizing last year. His claim of age discrimination is now pending before the EEOC.

Eleanor Lane

Soon after the *Olman* case ended, Lane saw that Magistrate Judge Malarkey was stepping down and that the local district judges were taking applications to fill his position. Lane applied, got the job, and was sworn in as a United States Magistrate Judge.

Bart Tweedy

After billing 2000-plus hours for many years, Tweedy finally decided that he should find a job that would let him explore life a bit more. Today he is teaching civil procedure at a small law school in the south. He couldn't be happier. After all, he has the best job in the world!

APPENDIX A

CHARACTERS:

Parties

Otis Olman:
The primary plaintiff and former manager of the Full Moon Sports Outdoor Center in Jacksonville, Florida. Otis is 53 years old.

Fiona Olman:
Otis Olman's co-plaintiff and wife. She is the former manager of the kayak department of the Jacksonville store. Fiona is 49 years old.

Full Moon Sports, Inc:
Full Moon is a nationwide sporting goods retailer. It employed Otis Olman as manager from 1985 to 2003. Full Moon's principal place of business is in Atlanta, Georgia. It is incorporated in Delaware.

Bruce Belcher:
Belcher is the former regional sales manager for the region in which the Jacksonville store is located.

Lawyers

Eleanor Lane:
Counsel for the Olmans; partner in Lane & Quincy (Jacksonville, Florida).

Bart Tweedy:
Principal counsel for Full Moon; senior associate in Lord, Amercey & Taylor (Atlanta, Georgia).

Trial Judge
Honorable Sarah Goodenough, United States District Court for the Middle District of Florida, Jacksonville Division.

Magistrate Judge
Honorable Matthew Malarkey, United States District Court for the Middle District of Florida, Jacksonville Division.

Other Characters

Izzy Able: Entrepreneur who offered Otis Olman a one-half partnership in a kayak business in Key Largo, Florida.

Kay Bailey: Chairperson of Full Moon's Corporate Board of Directors.

Samantha Brown: An employee in Full Moon's Human Resources Department and the author of an internal report concerning Full Moon's corporate restructuring.

Judy Kaufman: Associate in-house counsel at Full Moon.

Chloé Michaela: Chairperson of Full Moon's Reorganization Committee, which made the decision to replace the Olmans.

Mizar, Inc.: Mizar is a parent corporation that owns many subsidiaries. In 2000, it purchased Full Moon Sports, Inc., and instituted numerous changes in the company.

Rex Ornstein: Former regional manager for Full Moon stores in the southeast region.

Ruby Dubidoux: Former manager of Full Moon's Orlando store, who is also represented by Eleanor Lane.

Sid Shockley: Current store manager of the Jacksonville store; replaced Otis Olman.

Noah Stephen: Full Moon Vice President of Information Management.

Dr. Robert Stevens: Statistics professor and expert witness for Otis Olman.

Dr. Benjamin Todd: A statistician and an expert consulted, but not used, by Otis Olman.

KEY EVENTS:

1982:   Otis Olman begins working for Full Moon.

1985:   Otis Olman given first store manager position with Full Moon.

1990:   The Olman family moves to Jacksonville, Florida, where Otis becomes manager of Full Moon's local store.

1995:   Fiona Olman begins working at the Full Moon Jacksonville store.

1998:   Fiona Olman becomes manager of the kayak department in the Jacksonville store.

2000:   Mizar, Inc. purchases Full Moon.

                Belcher becomes regional sales director for Full Moon.

                Belcher allegedly promises Otis Olman lifetime security if he will remain as manager of the Jacksonville store.

                Otis Olman signs a three-year contract with Full Moon, and declines an invitation to become managing partner of a kayak business in Key Largo, Florida.

                Sid Shockley becomes manager of the extreme sports department of the Jacksonville store.

2003:   Full Moon implements corporate downsizing.

                Fiona Olman terminated; signs liability release.

                Otis Olman initially offered position as manager of outdoor department in Jacksonville store at reduced salary.

                Otis Olman protests alleged discriminatory downsizing decisions by Full Moon in a letter to the corporate president.

                Otis Olman terminated.

The Olmans retain Eleanor Lane as counsel.

The Olmans file charges of age discrimination with the EEOC and state agency.

2004:   EEOC conducts investigation; issues right-to-sue letter to Olmans.

The Olmans sue Full Moon and Belcher in the United States District Court for the Middle District of Florida. The suit is filed on May 1, 2004.

Lord Amercey, through Harrison Ames and Burt Tweedy, enter appearance as counsel for Full Moon.

Belcher's lawyer belatedly enters his appearance.

2005:   Trial and final judgment in *Olman v. Full Moon*. The Olmans and Full Moon settle their dispute.

SUMMARY OF LEGAL CLAIMS (WITH ELEMENTS)

Age Discrimination (federal and Florida statutes)

1. Plaintiff-employee is aged 40 or over;
2. Employer took adverse job action against employee;
3. Job action taken "because of" employee's age; and
4. Employee suffered damages.

Retaliation:

1. Plaintiff-employee engaged in statutorily protected expression;
2. Plaintiff suffered an adverse employment action; and
3. The adverse action against him was causally related to his protected expression.

Fraud:

1. Defendant (or agent) made false representation of fact;
2. Defendant knew representation was false when made;
3. Defendant made false representation to induce plaintiff to rely;
4. Plaintiff justifiably relied on false representation to his detriment.

Conversion:

1. Defendant wrongfully exercised control;
2. Of plaintiff's property;
3. In a manner inconsistent with the plaintiff's rights in the property.

Tortious Interference With a Business Relationship:

1. Plaintiff was party to a business:
2. Defendant knew of plaintiff's business relationship.
3. Defendant intentionally and unjustifiably interfered with plaintiff's business relationship.
4. Defendant's interference caused damage to plaintiff.

APPENDIX B:
SELECTING A COURT TO HEAR THE SUIT

Rule References: 3, *4*, 7, *8*, 45

Note: This appendix addresses issues in the Olmans' suit dealing with (a) personal jurisdiction, (b) venue, and (c) subject matter jurisdiction. It also briefly examines aspects of the "Erie" doctrine and choice of law principles relevant to their suit. This appendix complements the material found in Chapter 1. If you have not studied these subjects at this point in your procedure course, you should defer review of this appendix until later.

Our placement of this material in an appendix does <u>not</u> mean that it is less significant. To the contrary, the choice of a court or the choice of law to be applied can be dispositive. Our placement simply reflects an organizational decision. Because Civil Procedure teachers and texts differ in the order in which they address jurisdiction and related issues, we have located this material in an appendix so it can be introduced at any point in a course.

Finally, you should recognize that our treatment of this material is not meant to be exhaustive—far from it. A single dispute like the Olmans will never provide occasion to examine all the diverse issues that arise in the study of subjects like jurisdiction and choice of law. The discussion below illustrates the small number of issues generated by the particular facts of the Olmans' dispute.

In Chapter 1 we discussed Lane's preparation for filing suit. As we observed, once Lane completed her investigation of the facts and the law she had three final decisions to make before filing. First, she had to decide upon the best geographic locale for the suit. Second, she needed to figure out how to "serve process" on the defendants and bring them into the suit. Third, she had to decide whether to bring suit in federal or state court.

Lane had clear preferences in answering most of these questions. If possible, she wanted the Olmans' suit to take place near Jacksonville, Florida, and she wanted it to occur in federal rather than state court. As we discuss below, Lane believed that suit in federal court near Jacksonville had decided advantages for the Olmans.

A.   Personal Jurisdiction and Venue

The choice of the geographic locale for a suit turns on the separate but related issues of personal jurisdiction and venue. Lane hoped that her analyses of these issues would reveal that suit could be filed in Florida, and specifically a court in or near Jacksonville. The Olmans lived in Jacksonville, and this is where Lane's law offices were located. In addition, Lane was admitted to practice law solely in Florida.[1] Further, northern Florida was where many of the witnesses to the dispute resided and would likely be subject to a court's subpoena power.[2] Finally, because the alleged employment discrimination and fraud had occurred in Florida, Florida law would likely apply in the suit.[3]

When determining whether a court in Florida had personal jurisdiction over the defendants, Lane knew it did not matter whether suit was filed in federal or state court. In the great majority of cases, federal courts exercise the same personal jurisdiction as the courts of the state in which they are located.[4] Consequently, Lane's first consideration was whether Florida jurisdictional statutes provided a basis for asserting personal jurisdiction over Full Moon and Belcher.

---

[1] If suit were filed in a Georgia court (of whose bar Lane was not a member), Lane would probably have to seek admission *pro hac vice* to appear in that court. Such admission usually requires that the lawyer associate with co-counsel already admitted in the jurisdiction. Lane wanted to avoid sharing either the responsibility for the case or her fee.

[2] *See, e.g.,* Rule 45(b)(2) (subpoena may be issued to witness anywhere within a federal district or within 100 miles of the "place of trial").

[3] This issue is discussed more fully below. *See infra* Appendix B, Part D.

[4] *See, e.g.,* Rules 4(e), (h) (federal court may exercise personal jurisdiction over individuals and corporations in accordance with local state law) and (k)(1).

Question B.1

Lane's research revealed that Florida's long-arm statute, Florida Statutes section 48.193, contained the following excerpted language:

(1)   Any person . . . who personally or through an agent does any of the acts enumerated in this subsection thereby submits himself or herself . . . to the jurisdiction of the courts of this state for any cause of action arising from the doing of any of the following acts:

      (a)   Operating, conducting, engaging in, or carrying on a business or business venture in this state or having an office or agency in this state.

      (b)   Committing a tortious act within this state.

         . . .

      (g)   Breaching a contract in this state by failing to perform acts required to be performed in this state.

         . . .

(2)   A defendant who is engaged in substantial and not isolated activity within this state, whether such activity is wholly interstate, intrastate, or otherwise, is subject to the jurisdiction of the courts of this state, whether or not the claim arises from that activity.

Recall that Otis wants to sue Full Moon for employment discrimination, retaliation, and fraud, and wants to sue Belcher for fraud. Recall also that Fiona wants to sue Full Moon for employment discrimination. Briefly discuss whether a court in Florida will have personal jurisdiction under the long-arm statute over Full Moon and Belcher if Lane alleges all these claims in her complaint.

As you now know from your study of personal jurisdiction, in order for a court in Florida to exercise personal jurisdiction over the defendants Lane had to do more than show that jurisdiction was proper under Florida jurisdictional statutes. Lane also had to demonstrate that exercise of jurisdiction comported with the Due Process Clause of the United States Constitution. According to leading Supreme Court precedent like *Burger King Corp. v. Rudzewicz*, 471 U.S. 462 (1985), due process usually requires that (1) a defendant have certain minimum contacts with the forum state; and (2) exercise of jurisdiction not offend principles of "fair play and substantial justice." Consider the following question:

Question B.2

Do Full Moon and Belcher have sufficient minimum contacts with Florida to satisfy due process? In addition, would it offend principles of fair play and substantial justice if these defendants were sued in a court in Florida? What Supreme Court precedent best supports your conclusion?

Lane was confident that a court in Florida had the power to exercise personal jurisdiction over both Full Moon and Belcher. She next needed to consider which particular court *within* the state in Florida would be proper for purposes of venue. Rules governing choice of venue further "localize" the site for litigation once a particular state has been identified under rules of personal jurisdiction. Although choice of venue is an issue regardless of whether suit is filed in federal or state court, we will focus discussion on the principles of federal court venue addressed.

Federal venue is governed by statute. In selecting the venue for federal court suit, a lawyer must identify the proper "district" court within which to file suit.[5] Below is a map

---

[5]Choice of venue may also require that a lawyer select a particular "division" with a district as well. For example, the Olmans' complaint recites that it has been filed in the "Jacksonville Division" of the federal district. Present discussion ignores how Lane identified the proper division within the federal district she selected, although in actual practice selection of the proper division is also important.

of the federal court system which shows the breakdown of district courts,[6] as well as the breakdown of the federal circuits (numbered) that handle appeals from these districts. As you can see from this map, Jacksonville, Florida (located in the northeast corner of the state) is in the United States District Court for the *Middle* District of Florida.

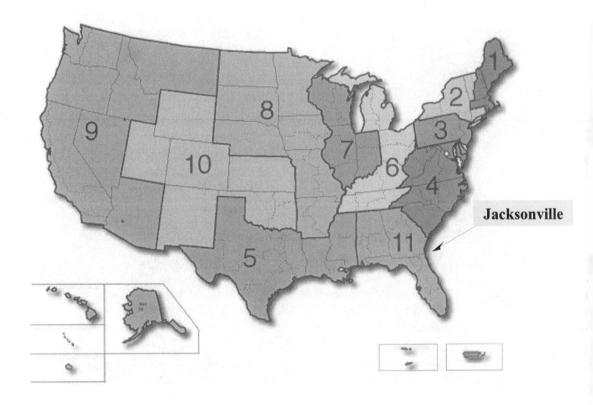

Jacksonville

---

[6]Because states with smaller populations have but one federal district (*e.g.*, Connecticut, Montana) the boundaries of the district are co-terminous with state borders. More populated states like New York, California, Texas, and Florida have several districts within their borders, and these are identified on the map with broken lines. For example, federal trial courts in Florida are broken down into the Northern, Middle, and Southern Districts.

Federal circuits, which serve as appellate courts, are distinguished by different shadings and are numbered one through eleven. Not shown on this map is the "United States Court of Appeals for the District of Columbia Circuit" and the United States Court of Appeal for the "Federal Circuit," which is also located in the District of Columbia and handles specialized appeals in such matters as those concerning tax and patents.

Federal venue in most private civil litigation is governed by 28 U.S.C. § 1391. Because jurisdiction in the Olmans' case was not based solely on diversity of citizenship, Lane would rely on sub-section 1391(b). Consider the following question in deciding whether venue was proper in the United States District Court for the Middle District of Florida encompassing Jacksonville.

Question B.3

A.   Section 1391(b)(1) authorizes venue in any district where "any defendant resides, if all defendants reside in the same state." As you will learn later in this appendix, defendant Belcher is now a resident of Connecticut. In the case of a corporation like Full Moon, section 1391(c) defines its "residence" as any district where the corporation is "subject to personal jurisdiction." Can the "residence" provisions of section 1391(b)(1) and (c) be used to obtain venue over Full Moon and Belcher in the Middle District? Why not?

B.   Section 1391(b) also authorizes venue in any district where (2) "substantial events or omissions giving rise to the claim occurred. . . ." Is venue in the Middle District proper under this provision? Would venue be proper in the Northern District of Georgia, which encompasses Full Moon's corporate headquarters?

B.   Formally Initiating the Lawsuit

Lane concluded that the United States District Court for the Middle District of Florida would have personal jurisdiction and venue in the Olmans' suit. But she still needed to take steps to formally *invoke* that jurisdictional power.[7] Although a federal suit

---

[7]As with the preceding discussion of venue, we assume that Lane can properly file suit in federal court.

"commences" when the plaintiff files with the court,[8] the defendants are not subject to the court's power until they are either served with "process" or consent to the court's exercise of jurisdiction.

Federal Rule 4 addresses service of process in federal court.[9] Rule 4 contains numerous provisions governing service, but we will focus on a few.

Question B.4

A.   Under Rule 4(e), how could Lane go about formally serving Belcher? Under Rule 4(h), how could she go about serving Full Moon?[10]

B.   According to Rule 4(m), how much time does Lane have to serve the defendants after she files the suit in federal court? What happens if Lane does not serve the defendants within this time?

C.   Assuming Lane timely serves the defendants, what must she do to inform the court that service of process has been accomplished?

The most common method of serving corporations is to serve the corporation's resident agent in the forum state. Most states require that, as a condition of doing business,

---

[8]*See* Rule 3.

[9]The "process" that is served to invoke personal jurisdiction consists of the summons and the complaint. *See* Rule 4(c)(1). You can examine a sample illustration of the summons in Form 1 of the appendices that accompany the Federal Rules of Civil Procedure. We provide an illustration of a complaint in Chapter 2.

[10]Lane had another important option for serving process on Full Moon and Belcher. According to Rule 4(e) and (h), Lane could use any method of service authorized by *state* law, including both the law of the state where suit was filed (Florida) or the law of the state where the defendant was to be served (the defendant's home state, for example).

businesses designate a "registered agent" in the state upon whom service can be made. The identity and address of these registered agents can easily be found on Internet sites maintained by the state. Full Moon, which was registered to do business in Florida, had such a registered agent in Tampa, Florida. For individuals, the most common way in which service is accomplished is by in-hand delivery of the summons and complaint.

There is, however, a less formal means by which a defendant can be brought into a suit. Under Rule 4(d), the plaintiff may ask a defendant to waive formal service requirements. Forms 1A and 1B in the appendices to the Federal Rules provide sample forms for accomplishing waiver of service. Consider the following question regarding waiver:

Question B.5

A.   What procedures must Lane follow to obtain a waiver of service from Full Moon?

B.   How should Lane transmit the request for waiver to a defendant? Can Lane send the request by email?

C.   Assume that Lane sends Belcher an appropriate request to waive service on May 1. Belcher responds on May 5 agreeing to waive service. By May 30, however, Belcher has still served no response to the complaint. Lane considers filing a motion for default based on Rule 12(a)(1) and Belcher's failure to serve a response to the complaint. Does Lane have good grounds for filing this motion.

Lane had already spoken with Full Moon's lawyer during pre-suit settlement negotiations and knew Full Moon would consent to waive service. Why would a defendant like Full Moon elect to "waive" service instead of forcing the plaintiffs to make formal service of process under Rule 4? The answer is that Rule 4(d) provides both a carrot and a stick designed to encourage Full Moon to cooperate with the Olmans. As for the carrot, by waiving service Full Moon receives 60 days from the date the request to waive service was sent to respond to the complaint, rather than the normal 20 days from the date of formal service.[11] The stick comes into play because, if Full Moon does not reasonably cooperate with a request to waive service, it may have to pay the Olmans' cost for formal service.[12]

If the rules are so stacked in favor of encouraging cooperation why would a defendant *not* agree to waive formal service? The most common reason would be that the defendant is ultimately not amenable to service.[13] If that is the case, neither the carrot nor the stick will be a useful means to encourage waiver. The defendant does not need additional time to respond to the complaint because the plaintiff will be unable to compel him to respond. For the same reason, the defendant who cannot be served will never be required to pay the cost of such service.

In the Olmans' case, Lane sent Full Moon's lawyer in Atlanta, Georgia, the appropriate request for waiver of service.[14] The waiver form was properly signed and returned to Lane. Lane then filed the waiver form with the court.[15]

Belcher presented more of a problem. Lane had recently learned from Full Moon's lawyer that Belcher no long worked for the company. He had taken a position with a sporting goods manufacturer in Stamford, Connecticut. Lane had mailed waiver-of-service forms to Belcher's new home address in Connecticut and had even placed a call to his home. She had heard nothing in response. Consequently, Lane was compelled to serve Belcher formally. To do so, she used Florida's "long-arm" service law, as authorized by Rule 4(e),

---

[11]*See* Rule 4(d)(3). In reality, the carrot is not worth as much as one might think. The potential defendant can get almost as much time, if not more, to respond to the complaint if it declines to waive formal service than if it agreed to the waiver. Can you see why?

[12]*See* Rule 4(d)(2),(5). Note that, by agreeing to waive formal service, Full Moon did not waive any objection to personal jurisdiction or venue. *See* Rule 4(d)(1).

[13]A person may not be amenable to service of process for any number of reasons. For example, she might reside in a foreign country in which service is not permitted by local law. Or the person's location or address might be unknown.

[14]Rule 4(d)(2) permits use of waiver of service on an individual, whether located in the United States or abroad, or a corporation or association.

[15]*See* Rule 4(d)(4).

and hired a professional process server to serve Belcher with a summons together with a copy of the complaint.[16]

C.   Subject Matter Jurisdiction

To this point we have assumed that Lane will file suit in federal court. It is now time to consider whether she in fact had that option and, if so, why she would exercise it.

The determination whether to file suit in federal or state court raises the issue of subject matter jurisdiction. Lane knew that state courts have *general jurisdiction* to hear cases based on either state law or federal law, unless the federal law claims are within the *exclusive jurisdiction* of federal courts. The Age Discrimination in Employment Act (ADEA), like most civil rights legislation, permits state courts to exercise *concurrent jurisdiction* over federal claims. So, Lane knew she could combine the Olmans' federal and state claims in a state court action.

Federal courts, on the other hand, are courts of *limited* jurisdiction. The plaintiff bears the burden of showing that a federal court has subject matter jurisdiction over all claims in the complaint. As you have learned by this point in your Civil Procedure course, the two principal bases for federal subject matter jurisdiction in private litigation are (a) "federal question" jurisdiction under 28 U.S.C. section 1331; and (b) diversity of citizenship jurisdiction under 28 U.S.C. section 1332. Now consider how these forms of jurisdiction might apply to the Olmans' suit, as well as the possible role of "supplemental" jurisdiction under 28 U.S.C. section 1367.

---

[16]The Complaint can be found in Chapter 2.

Question B.6

A.	Examine the claims Lane intends to assert, which are found at page 31. Which of these claims "arises under" federal law for purposes of section 1331? Why?

B.	Now consider those claims listed at page 31 that do not arise under federal law within the meaning of section 1331. Do these claims qualify for supplemental jurisdiction under 28 U.S.C. section 1367? Why? (Make sure you consider the specific factual basis for each of the claims.)

C.	Now consider the potential application of diversity of citizenship jurisdiction under section 1332. Assume that the Olmans are still citizens of Florida; that Full Moon is a Delaware corporation whose principal place of business is Georgia; and that Belcher was a citizen of Florida at the time of the incidents alleged in the complaint but has now become a citizen of Connecticut. Assume further that each of the Olmans seeks more than $100,000 from each of the defendants. Is there diversity of citizenship jurisdiction?

Lane felt confident there was federal subject matter jurisdiction over the Olmans' suit. She now explained to the Olmans the competing reasons for choosing federal or state court.[17]

First, the litigation process is often different in federal court. In federal court, a judge will "manage" the suit much more closely than will most state court judges. Shortly after the suit is filed, the lawyers meet to develop a plan for completing key matters like conducting discovery, filing dispositive motions, and holding the trial. The court usually

---

[17]State and federal court practice can vary *greatly* from jurisdiction to jurisdiction. The factors affecting Lane's decision were peculiar to her experience in the jurisdiction where she practiced.

confirms this plan in an order.[18]   This plan remains fairly firm throughout the pre-trial process and puts the parties on a timetable that results in trial in approximately one year. By comparison, in most state courts the trial judge largely leaves it up to the parties to schedule the litigation process and the trial date.   This can delay the date of trial substantially.

Second, there is a lot more "paper work" in federal court, consuming more of the lawyers' time.   Until trial, virtually every request the lawyers make of a federal court is made by written motion supported by a legal memorandum.[19]   These motions and supporting memoranda need to be well drafted and well researched, as they are scrutinized closely by the judge or the judge's clerks.   In many federal districts, motions are decided without an actual hearing before the judge.   In many state courts, by comparison, motions are orally argued in open court during a "motions session."   Further, written motions and memoranda in state court—if any—are usually brief.   As a consequence, a lawyer's skill in oral advocacy may play a greater role in the pretrial process in state court.

Lane, unlike some trial lawyers, was not intimidated by the more formal and time consuming legal writing required in federal court.   She was both a good researcher and a careful writer.   At the same time, she knew that her opponent might use the paper-intensive litigation process to her disadvantage.   Lane had observed that some defense lawyers file an excessive number of motions in federal litigation.   A few unscrupulous defense lawyers even boast of "papering the plaintiff to death," meaning they use motion practice to use up the plaintiff's time and money.   Even though Federal Rule 11(b)(1) prohibits filing a motion "for any improper purpose," it may be difficult to prove this rule has been violated.

A third difference between federal and state court concerns the judges and their supporting personnel.   In federal court, judges are appointed by the President of the United States and confirmed by the Senate, and thus are subject to more rigorous screening.   They also have lifetime tenure.   In contrast, some state trial judges (like those in Florida) are elected by the voters in campaigns that disclose very little about the judges' philosophy or competence, and have to stand for office every four years.

---

[18]This meeting and the resulting court action in the Olmans' suit are discussed in Chapter 4.

[19]*See* Rule 7(b) (applications for court orders, other than motions made during a hearing or at trial, "shall be made in writing, shall state with particularity the grounds therefor, and shall set forth the relief or order sought.").

Although Lane knew that federal judges are not necessarily more capable or fair-minded than state judges, they have certain advantages over the typical state judge. For one thing, federal judges are far more likely to have experience presiding over cases involving federal law. The judge assigned to the Olmans' case would probably have handled federal employment discrimination cases and, if she had not, would draw upon the research support of highly-credentialed judicial clerks to educate her about the law. Any particular state court judge, on the other hand, is less likely to have experience with federal employment discrimination laws. State judges frequently rotate among divisions, where they spend their time judging cases limited to particular subjects like probate and criminal law. And state judges often lack the support of a team of law clerks.

In addition, Lane recognized that the composition of the jury pool in federal court can differ from that in state court. If she filed the suit in Florida state court, the jury would be drawn from residents of the county where Jacksonville is located. If she filed in federal court, the jury would be drawn from a larger pool including several counties in the eastern part of the Middle District of Florida. The demographic composition of the jury might vary widely between state and federal court.

In the final analysis, however, Lane knew that the most important factor in choosing a court was unknown: to which *particular* federal or state judge would the Olmans' case be randomly assigned? This could prove a critical difference in the conduct of the litigation and the outcome, but it was beyond the parties' prediction or control. The Olmans' case would be assigned to a judge by the clerk when it was filed. In the past this random assignment was done by spinning a wheel or picking a name out of a box. Today, it is usually done by computer. No matter how the case was assigned mechanically, Lane would have to wait and see which judge would try the case.

Lane ultimately recommended filing in federal court. She had substantial experience litigating in the Middle District and had a solid reputation among its judges. In addition, she wanted to have a judge (and supporting staff) familiar with the substantive law of employment discrimination. Further, she suspected that even if she filed in state court, Full Moon's lawyers were likely to remove the case to federal court.[20] The Olmans approved her decision to file suit in federal court.

---

[20]28 U.S.C. section 1441 generally permits defendants to remove a case from state to federal court if the plaintiffs could have originally filed the suit in federal court. Many defendants believe it is in their best interests to litigate in federal court and will routinely remove a case that has been filed in state court.

D.   The Impact of Choice of Forum on the Law Governing the Suit

As explained in Chapter 1, Lane had to consider numerous sources of law (federal, state, local) and numerous types of law (constitutional, statutory, regulatory, common law, procedural rule) in formulating her clients' complaint. This leads to an important question: Did Lane's choice of a federal or state court have any effect on the *law* that would be applied in their suit? This question has two dimensions, as we discuss below.

1.   Choosing Between Different States' Laws

When suit is filed in state court, the court proceeds on the assumption that its own state's law governs issues in the suit.[21] This means that, had Lane filed suit in Florida state court, the trial judge would assume that Florida law governed all legal issues (like the issues of common law fraud) not otherwise governed by federal law. However, in appropriate circumstances the forum court has power to apply the law of some *other* state and will do so if a party meets its burden of showing that non-forum law should apply.

When asked to choose between applying forum law or the law of some other state, a trial court will consider the forum's *"choice of law"* principles. Choice of law principles are usually developed by the courts, although occasionally they are enacted legislatively. These choice of law principles guide a court when it is asked to determine which state's law applies to a dispute that involves several states. For example, the dispute between the Olmans and Full Moon clearly involved persons and events in the state of Florida; but it also involved corporate decisions made in Atlanta, Georgia, by a defendant whose principal offices are in Georgia.

If Full Moon wanted the trial court to apply Georgia law to govern the parties' rights and duties, Full Moon would have to argue that *Florida's* choice of law principles supported applying *Georgia* substantive law![22] For example, if Full Moon believed that Georgia's age discrimination laws, or its common law of fraud, should govern its liability, it would have to persuade the court that Florida's choice of law principles compelled application of

---

[21]As observed in Chapter 1, however, if *federal* law governs the rights and duties of the parties, it must be applied under the command of the "Supremacy Clause" of the United States Constitution. The present discussion focuses on issues that are properly governed by state law.

[22]Florida, like most states, has adopted some of the choice of law principles set forth in the Restatement (Second) of Conflict of Laws, which generally requires that the law of the state having the more "significant relationship" to the parties and the occurrence be applied.

Georgia's age discrimination and tort law. Because the Olmans had been employed in Florida and had suffered their legal injury in Florida, Lane thought it unlikely that Full Moon could persuasively argue that Georgia law should be applied. However, Full Moon had the option of making that argument.

Choice of law principles can be quite challenging. You will have the opportunity to study these principles later in law school if you take a course in "Choice of Law" or "Conflict of Laws." We will say no more about these principles in the present discussion. But two final points pertaining to Lane's choice of forum and the application of state law should be mentioned.

First, in *Erie Railroad v. Thompkins*,[23] the Supreme Court held that the federal courts usually lack constitutional authority to develop federal *common law* to govern the legal relationships between private parties. Thus, a federal court would be required to apply some state's common law of fraud in the Olmans' case instead of developing federal common law.

Second, as mentioned above a state court will determine which state's law governs a dispute by applying "local" choice of law principles. But what happens if suit is filed in federal court? Whose choice of law principles dictate which state's law applies? According to the Supreme Court in *Klaxon v. Stentor Electric Manufacturing Company*,[24] a federal court is usually required to apply the choice of law principles of the state where it is *located*. This meant that, if Lane filed suit in a federal district court in Florida, the district court would examine Florida choice-of-law principles to determine whether to apply Florida or Georgia substantive law. If Lane chose instead to file suit in a federal district court located in Georgia, the court would apply Georgia choice-of-law principles to determine whether to apply Florida or Georgia substantive law. As a consequence, Lane's choice of the geographic locale for suit might have effect on whose state law would be applied in the suit, but her choice of federal or state court would not.

2.   Choosing Between State Law and Federal Procedural Law

As already discussed, federal law governing the parties' substantive rights (*e.g.*, federal law prohibiting age discrimination or retaliation) had to be applied by both state and

---

[23]304 U.S. 64 (1938).

[24]313 U.S. 487 (1941).

federal courts under the command of the Constitution's Supremacy Clause.[25] But as you have learned during your study of the "*Erie*" doctrine, uncertainty may arise when federal *procedural* law is arguably inconsistent with state law and the inconsistency might have an impact on the outcome of litigation.

Lane knew that federal procedural rules and state procedural rules are often very similar, and she seldom found that the variations in procedure appreciably affected litigation. She also knew that, according to *Hanna v. Plumer*,[26] a federal court must apply the Federal Rules of Civil Procedure according to their letter and intent. But the Olmans' suit presented the atypical case where state and federal procedures vary and that variation might have bearing on the conduct, and possibly the outcome, of litigation.

Otis Olman was suing Full Moon and Belcher for fraud. According to Florida common law, he might recover punitive damages if he succeeded on the fraud count. Further, Lane knew that the potential threat of punitive damages provided her a certain amount of negotiating leverage.[27] So, it made sense for her to demand punitive damages under the fraud count she would assert on behalf of Otis.

But there was one potential problem. In response to a perceived exploitation of punitive damages claims by plaintiffs' attorneys, the Florida Legislature had enacted a law prohibiting a plaintiff from demanding punitive damages in his initial complaint. Instead, Florida Statutes section 768.72 first required that a plaintiff present "record evidence" to the trial court justifying a demand for punitive damages. This usually meant that a plaintiff could not demand punitive damages in his original complaint but had to seek court leave to amend the complaint at a later date when evidence supporting the demand became available. Lane anticipated that the defendants would use section 768.72 to have any demand for punitive damages contained in the Olmans' complaint stricken if she filed suit in state court.

---

[25]This result is also commanded by the Rules of Decision Act, 28 U.S.C. § 1652, which you study as part of the "*Erie*" doctrine.

[26]380 U.S. 460 (1965).

[27]Not only would the threat of recovering punitive damages provide Lane negotiation leverage, she might also have the right to conduct discovery concerning Full Moon's financial situation. For example, the state of Full Moon's finances would be relevant in determining how much of a penalty they should pay for their wrongdoing. And if Full Moon preferred to keep its financial information private, it might be willing to "pay" for its privacy by negotiating a settlement more favorable to the Olmans.

The *"Erie"* question for Lane was this: If she sued in federal court, would the court apply Florida's prohibition and prevent her from alleging punitive damages at the outset of litigation? Or would the federal court find that, under applicable Federal Rules of Civil Procedure, the Olmans had the right to demand punitive damages in their initial complaint? Particularly given the increased bargaining leverage she might have if the initial complaint demanded punitive damages, she did not want to be hobbled by Florida law on this point. If she could circumvent Florida's restriction on pleading punitive damages by filing suit in federal court, she had an additional reason to choose a federal forum.

As Lane read the Federal Rules of Civil Procedure, Rule 8(a) gave her the right to include in the initial pleading "a short and plain statement" alleging Otis Olman had been defrauded and demanding "the relief" he sought.[28] Nothing in the Federal Rules required her to receive the court's approval before demanding punitive damages. On the other hand, Full Moon would likely argue that the Federal Rules were simply silent on the issue and did not impliedly displace Florida law.

Based on your study of the *"Erie"* doctrine, consider the following question:

Question B.7

A.   Does Federal Rule 8(a) conflict with Florida law concerning the pleading of punitive damages? Is there any way a conflict can be avoided? If there is a conflict, must the federal court apply Rule 8(a)?

B.   Assume for purposes of this question that a federal court finds that the Federal Rules do not conflict with Florida law? Must the federal court now apply Florida law restricting the pleading of punitive damages? According to the *"Erie"* doctrine, what question must the court answer in deciding whether to require application of Florida law?

---

[28]Of course, Lane would also have had to comply with Rule 9(b)'s heightened pleading requirement concerning the allegation of fraud.

This "*Erie*" issue produced numerous, conflicting opinions in the federal district courts asked to reconcile the Federal Rules and Florida law. For the Eleventh Circuit's ultimate resolution of the issue, read *Cohen v. Office Depot*, 184 F.3d 1292 (11th Cir. 1999).

INDEX

Adding parties, 178–183. *See also* Joinder and amendment
ADEA, 21
ADEA remedies, 25–26
Administrative agencies, 15
Admissions, 165–166
Admit, deny, or DKI, 75
Adverse inference instruction, 117n
Affirmative defenses, 75
Age discrimination claim, 23–24, A-5
Age Discrimination in Employment Act (ADEA), 21
Alternative dispute resolution mechanism, 14n
Amendment of pleadings, 91–92, 184–186
Ancillary relief, 14
Answer, 73–83
Apex corporate officials, 153, 154
Appeal, 93–95, 259–264
Assigned to judge, B-13
Attorney-client privilege, 110–111, 143n
Attorney's fees, 17, 258

Bench trial, 235n, 236n. *See also* Trial process
Biased jurors, 238
Bifurcation of trial, 243
Brevity, 3
Burden of coming forward, 194
Burden of persuasion, 231–232
Burden of production, 194, 232

Case-in-chief, 241–244, 247–248
Case management, 92–98
Cause challenge, 238–239
Celotex trilogy, 193n
Choice of law. *See* Selecting a court
Circuit courts, B-5

Civil cover sheet, 54n
Civil trial. *See* Trial process
Claim preclusion, 50, 172
Clerk of court, 61n
Closing argument, 249
Closing the pleadings, 90–91
Common law, 21–22
Compensatory damages, 13
Complaint, 35–54
Concurrent jurisdiction, B-10
Confidentiality, 16
Contemporaneous objection, 261
Contingent fee, 17
Conversion, 89, A-5
Corporation, discovery of, 153, 154
Counterclaim, 75, 76, 78–83, 176–177
Cross-appeal, 260
Cross-claim, 75, 177, 178
Cross-examination, 242, 247–248

Damages, 13–14
Deposition, 150–165
Deposition upon oral examination, 150n
Deposition upon written questions, 150n
Direct examination, 241–244, 247–248
Disclosure, 100
Disclosure statement, 60n, 106–109
Discovery, 99–169
    admissions, 165–166
    corporation, of, 153, 154
    crafting your own rules, 101
    defined, 100
    deposition, 150–165
    disclosure statement, 106–109
    disputes, 140–149
    email, 141

errata sheet, 165
experts, 166–169
interrogatories, 125–129
mental/physical examination, 116n
motion to compel production, 143–149
privilege, 110–114
production of documents, 118–125
prohibition on filing, 109
protective order, 154–156
relevance, 110
responses, 130–140
tools of discovery, 114–116
withholding information, 140–141
Discovery disputes, 140–149
Discovery plan, 92, 93, 100
District courts, B-4 to B-5
DKI, 75
Doctor-patient privilege, 112
Document preservation, 116–118
Documentary discovery, 118–125
Documents
Answer and Counterclaim, 78–83
Answers and Objections to Interrogatories, 136–139
Case Management and Scheduling Order, 97–98
Complaint and Demand for Jury Trial, 37–44
Disclosure Statement, 106–108
Interrogatories, 128–129
Joint Stipulation to Dismiss with Prejudice, 268
Judgment on Jury Verdict, 255
Memorandum (and affidavit) in Support of Summary Judgment Motion, 204–212
Memorandum in Opposition to Summary Judgment Motion, 217–221
Motion for Summary Judgment, 200
Motion to Dismiss for Failure to State a Claim (and accompanying affidavit), 68–71
Notice of Appeal, 259–264

Order (summary judgment motion), 225–228
Request for Production of Documents, 121–123
Responses and Objections to Requests for Production of
Documents, 132–135
Verdict Form, 251–253
Drafting, 2–3
Due process, B-4
Duty to preserve evidence, 116–118

EEOC, 15
Elements of claim under ADEA, 23–24
Email, 141
Employment-at-will, 27
Enlargement of time, 73
Entry of judgment, 256
Equal Employment Opportunity Commission (EEOC), 15
Erie doctrine, B-15 to B-18
Errata sheet, 165
Ethical obligations, 16, 52–53
Ethical rules, 4
Example pleadings. *See* Documents
Exclusive jurisdiction, B-10
Expert
    deposition, 169
    discovery, 166–169
    testimony, 243–244
Expert deposition, 169n
Extension of time, 58n, 73

Fact situation, 5–12. *See also* Hypothetical case
FCRA, 26
Federal districts/circuits, B-4 to B-5
Federal *vs.* state courts, B-11 to B-13
Fee motion, 258
Fifth Amendment privilege, 112
Filing and serving complaint, 54–55

Final judgment, 254
Final judgment rule, 95
Final pretrial conference, 232–233
Finality of judgment, 258
Florida Civil Rights Act (FCRA), 26
Form books, 46
Fraud claim, 28, A-5
Freedom of information acts, 20

General jurisdiction, B-10
General verdict form, 250–253

Harmless error, 262
Hypothetical case, 1–12
    characters, A-1 to A-2
    key events, A-3 to A-4
    plaintiff's story, 5–12
    summary of legal claims, A-5

Impleader, 187–189
Injunction, 14
Interlocutory appeal, 93, 95
Interrogatories, 125–129
Intervention, 191

JNOV, 256
Joinder and amendment, 171–192
    adding a defendant, 178–181
    adding a plaintiff, 181–183
    amending the pleadings, 184–186
    impleader, 187–189
    intervention, 191
    joinder of claims, 173
    joinder of parties (rule), 173–174
    necessary and indispensable parties, 189–191
    Rule 20, 174

statute of limitations, 186
Joint instructions, 249
Judge, which one, B-13
Judge shopping, 74n
Judgment, 254–256
Judgment creditor, 265n
Judgment debtor, 265n
Judgment notwithstanding the verdict (JNOV), 256
Judicial clerk, 61n
Jurisdiction
    personal, B-1 to B-4
    subject matter, B-10 to B-13
Jury, 246
Jury consultants, 239n
Jury deliberations, 250–254
Jury duty, 237
Jury instructions, 249–250
Jury selection, 237–240
Jury trial. *See* Trial process

Lawyer, ethical obligations, 16, 52–53
Libel, 29–30, 76n
Limited jurisdiction, B-10
Litigation costs, 17
Litigation hold, 117
Local rules of civil procedure, 33

Magistrate judge, 147–149
Marital privilege, 112
McDonnell Douglas standard, 197
Mediation, 96
Mental/physical examination, 116n
Minimalist approach to pleading, 45
Model pleadings, 46
Model rules of professional conduct, 4, 16
Motion. *See* Motions

Motion for attorney's fees, 258
Motion for directed verdict, 244n
Motion for new trial, 257
Motion to compel production, 143–149
Motion to dismiss for failure to state claim, 66–71
Motions
    attorney's fees, 258
    compel production, 143–149
    judgment, for, 244–245, 256
    new trial, 257
    pleading, 64–71
    post-trial, 256–258
    power, 63
    pre-answer, 61–73
    protective order, 154–156
    substantive, 62
    summary judgment. *See* Summary judgment

Necessary and indispensable parties, 189–191
New trial motion, 257
Non-party production of documents, 124–125
Notice of appeal, 259, 263n, 264
Notice of deposition, 152, 153
Notice of dismissal, 267, 268
Notice pleading, 35

Opening statement, 240–241
Order (summary judgment motion), 225–228

Panel of judges, 260n
Partial judgment, 95
Partial summary judgment, 193, 199
Pattern jury instructions, 249n
Peremptory challenge, 239
Personal jurisdiction, B-1 to B-4
Physical examination, 116n

Physician-patient privilege, 112
Plaintiff's story, 5–12
Pleading motions, 62, 64–71
Pleadings. *See also* Documents
    amendment, 91–92, 184–186
    answer, 73–83
    closing, 90–91
    complaint, 35–54
    form books (model pleadings), 46
    minimalist approach, 45
    reply, 89–90
    specificity, 53–54
Post-trial motions, 256
Power motions, 62, 63
Pre-answer motions, 61–73
Pre-suit filing requirements, 14n
Preemption, 21n
Prejudice (rule 15), 184
Preparation, 234
Preparing to file suit
    determining applicable law, 20–31
    investigating the facts, 19–20
Preservation of error requirement, 87
Preservation of evidence, 116–118
Pretext, 198
Privilege, 110–114
Pro hac vice admission, 57, B-2
Procedural law, 4
Production of documents, 118–125
Prohibition on filing, 109
Protective order, 154–156
Public records, 20
Punitive damages, 14

Question of law, 243

Relation back doctrine, 186
Release, 88
Relevance, 110
Religious advisor-penitent privilege, 112
Remedies, 13–14
Removal of case to federal court, B-13
Renewed motion for judgment as matter of law, 256
Reply, 89–90
Request for admissions, 165–166
Request for production of documents, 121–123
Res judicata, 172
Respondeat superior, 188
Resting the case, 244, 248
Retaliation claim, 24, 198, A-5
Right to appeal, 259
Right to sue letter, 33
Rule 12 defenses, 61n
Rule 12(6)(b) motion to dismiss for failure to state claim, 66–71
Rule 26(f) conference, 92–93
Rule 30(b)(6) deposition notice, 152, 153
Rule 45 subpoena, 124–125
Rule 50(a) motion for judgment, 244–245, 248–249
Rule of Decision Act, B-16n
Rule references, 3
Rules of professionalism, 4

Sample pleadings. *See* Documents
Scheduling conference, 93–96
Scheduling order, 96–98
Selecting a court, B-1 to B-18
    choice of law principles, B-14 to B-15
    Erie doctrine, B-15 to B-18
    federal *vs.* state courts, B-11 to B-13
    personal jurisdiction, B-1 to B-4
    service of process, B-7 to B-10
    subject matter jurisdiction, B-10 to B-13

venue, B-4 to B-6
Service of process, 73n, B-7 to B-10
Setting aside default judgment, 84–85
Settlement agreement, 267
Settlement negotiations, 264–268
Simplicity, 3
Sources of law, 20–21, B-14
Sources of procedural law, 33–34
Special damages, 53n
Special interrogatories (jury), 250
Specificity in pleading, 53–54
Spoliation of evidence, 117
Standard (pattern) jury instructions, 249n
State *vs.* federal courts, B-11 to B-13
Statute of limitations, 32–33, 186
Subject matter jurisdiction, B-10 to B-13
Subpoenaing non-parties, 124–125
Substantive law, 4
Substantive motions, 62
Summary judgment, 193–229
    burden on movant, 193–194
    form of motion, 200
    grounds for motion, 195–199
    judge's ruling, 223–224
    McDonnell Douglas standard, 197
    order, 225–228
    partial judgment, 193, 199
    response/opposition to motion, 219–222
    supporting affidavits, 201–212
    timing of motion, 194
Supersedeas bond, 265n
Supporting affidavits (summary judgment), 201–212
Supremacy Clause, B-14n
Surreply, 222

Tactical tips
    alleging elements of cause of action, 48
    checklist of elements of claim, 23
    courts and discovering disputes, 143
    deposition, 157–158
    form books, 46
    model pleadings, 46
    party autonomy is discovery, 101
    preparation, 234
    subpoenaing non-parties, 124
Tort law remedies, 27
Tortious interference with business relationship, A-5
Trial notebook, 234
Trial preparation material, 113–114, 146, 149
Trial process, 231–258
    closing argument, 249
    cross-examination of defendant, 247–248
    cross-examination of plaintiff, 241–244
    defendant rests its case, 248
    defendant's case-in-chief, 247–248
    entry of judgment, 256
    expert testimony, 243–244
    final pretrial conference, 232–233
    judgment, 254–256
    jury deliberations, 250–254
    jury instructions, 249–250
    jury selection, 237–240
    motion for attorney's fees, 258
    motion for new trial, 257
    opening statement, 240–241
    overview, 236
    plaintiff rests its case, 244
    plaintiff's case-in-chief, 241–244
    preparation, 231
    renewed motion for judgment as matter of law, 256
    trial notebook, 234

verdict, 254
Types of law, 21

Unopposed motion to set aside entry of default, 85
Utility, 3

Venire, 237
Venue, B-4 to B-6
Verdict, 254
Verdict form, 250–253
Voir dire, 238, 239
Voluntary dismissal, 213, 267–268

Waiver of service, B-8, B-9
What's happening. *See* Hypothetical case
Withholding information (discovery), 140–141
Work product doctrine, 113–114, 146, 149